this signed edition of

Trump and the American Future:
Solving the Great Problems of Our Time

NEWT GINGRICH

on behalf of the
National Republican Congressional Committeee

NRCC

TRUMP
AND THE
AMERICAN
FUTURE

★ ═══════════════════ ★

TRUMP
AND THE
AMERICAN FUTURE

SOLVING THE GREAT
PROBLEMS OF OUR TIME

NEWT GINGRICH
and LOUIE BROGDON

CENTER
STREET®

NEW YORK   NASHVILLE

This book is dedicated to my wife,
Ambassador Callista Gingrich; Ambassador Lewis
Eisenberg; Ambassador Kip Tom; and the entire
Tri-Mission Italy community who served America
in Rome through the COVID-19 pandemic.
They are courageous patriots.

CONTENTS

CONTENTS

CONTENTS

TRUMP
AND THE
AMERICAN
FUTURE

★ ═══════════════════════ ★

Introduction

★ ▬▬▬▬▬▬▬▬▬▬▬▬▬▬▬▬▬▬▬▬▬▬▬▬▬ ★

UNDERSTANDING THE AMERICA THAT WILL EMERGE

When I began writing this book, the world seemed stable and definable. There was a clear split: The radical Democratic Left was on one side, and President Donald Trump and the Republicans were on the other. Trump was winning on seating judges, deregulation, and economic growth. The hatred and unending attacks of the Left, and especially of their media allies, were mostly bouncing off a successful Trump administration. The two sides were tied to a draw in national polling, but the radical Democratic Left could not hurt President Trump with his base.

In the four and a half years since he and Melania came down the big escalator at Trump Tower to announce for the presidency, Donald J. Trump had remade the Republican Party into a Trump Party. No Republican president, not even Ronald Reagan, had acquired the depth of loyalty and the capacity to anoint primary candidates that President Trump has exhibited.

The great divides between the traditional American system (the rule of law, free enterprise, work ethic, and individual achievement) on the Trump side, and the socialist-collectivist radical agenda on the other seemed predictable.

That was the world in which I began writing this book.

Then everything on the surface changed. The underlying struggle over America's future is still there—and it will resurface over time. The need for reforms to make America productive and safe is still there. If anything, they have been highlighted by problems in coping with the public health crisis and the shortages in domestic production of key items that had moved to China.

Beginning in January 2020, it became obvious that the novel coronavirus was gaining strength in China. By late February that pandemic was moving well beyond China.

The worldwide coronavirus pandemic, the depth of change being driven by the disease, and the increasingly stringent public health measures represent the largest change in our collective experience since World War II.

By the time this pandemic (and the government actions in response to it) have come to a halt, the individual and collective understanding of government, individualism, the economy, which institutions work, and so forth, will have changed significantly.

The Civil War was such a crucible that it forged two different Americas in the North and South. The North was more nationalist, patriotic, triumphal, optimistic, profitable, and confident than it had been before the war. The South was defeated, embittered, and impoverished. In response, it developed a sense of identity that rejected the North and maintained a segregated society with a Democratic political monopoly that lasted almost ninety years. Trying to understand American politics from 1865 to 1968 without accounting for the effect of the Civil War would be hopeless.

People are deeply frightened by the coronavirus. Many Americans are closer to panic than at any time in their lifetimes. The threat from the virus is both general and personal. It can wreck the country, and it can kill me and my family. The scale of the threat worldwide is confusing and unnerving. The breadth of the Chinese and Russian intervention in Europe and elsewhere is an enormous threat and challenge.

In this environment, every level of government—federal, state, and local—is going to acquire vast power comparable to that of an all-out war. If sheriffs want to close gun stores and keep open marijuana stores, they will. If governors want to outlaw church services with more than ten people attending, they will. If Twitter wants to redefine free speech to be only that which is acceptable to the public health experts, it can.

There was also a brief blame-minimization period, but as the crisis continued, a lot of fingers started pointing: The failure of the Centers for Disease Control and Prevention (CDC) with testing cost us three weeks of effort and made it impossible to go to a Korea-Taiwan-Singapore style of massive testing and isolating only the people who have the virus. In the absence of thorough testing, it is also impossible to discern the real mortality rate. It would probably be much lower than people think, but the full number of infected people cannot currently be tabulated. With widespread testing, those who have shown no symptoms or have had such minor symptoms they never paid attention to it would surface. The increased number of cases would lower the death rate dramatically. That would lower the sense of fear.

There will also be a hard look at how badly the Chinese dictatorship handled the virus—and how much blame they must bear for it spreading around the world. A lot of people died because the Chinese dictatorship tried to hide the virus and pretend it was not a problem.

As we live through several months of turmoil, our thinking about ourselves, and our families, communities, government, and country will evolve and shift as different events occur and as we talk with each other about what is happening and what we are experiencing.

With all this happening, we have to develop an in-depth approach to a dialogue with the American people to get some sense of how different people are reacting.

Americans will have gone through four extraordinary changes in just a few months:

1. They will have been frightened individually and collectively by a pandemic that stressed both the public health system and the medical delivery system.
2. They will have lived through enormous government intervention in their lives and their jobs, with an outpouring of money on a scale we have never seen in such a short time, and with a premium on understanding how to get money out of bureaucracies.
3. They will have experienced the largest growth in government power in American history. With the exception of rare, localized impositions of martial law, there has never been this kind of expression of government power—capable of telling you to stay home, fining you for being on the streets, and exercising decisive power to define if you can have any kind of gathering of any number. These impositions of government power will have been experienced by virtually everyone.
4. Every individual will have to think through how these three experiences change their understanding of life, American history, and core values—and then create a new sense of the future built around a changed America.

Understanding these changes requires thinking of, and interacting with, a wide variety of Americans, across all ages, ethnic backgrounds, income levels, educational experience, and so forth. Each will have a different story to tell.

What does it mean to the student and his family to have been sent home from school? What does it mean to have worked from home for weeks at a time? Do you miss the office and your friends, or do you like the convenience of not commuting? Did the government checks work? Do you want to get back to work, or do you want politicians to send you more money? Has your local government been helpful in surviving the pandemic, or has it been incompetent or overly intrusive? Are you more optimistic about the future, or are you shaken by the idea that something else we never thought of could happen to ruin your life?

Thinking through and designing the research to help understand how Americans are changing under the collective weight of what they are experiencing is enormously important. We need to identify the things we don't know. Then we need to create the questions we need answered to fill in the things we don't know. Here are some examples of what might happen as the immediate crisis is solved.

The Democrats decided to open House investigations into how the administration handled the pandemic. They are seeking to blame the president for every shortfall in the process. What if, in response, the Republicans emphasize the decisions of the Obama-Biden administration to cut funding for the CDC and to allow the supply of masks to remain virtually empty after the Asian flu epidemic used up 100 million of them? What if the Democrats decide to campaign on promises of a second and third check to American families? What if the Democrats decide to campaign on a pro-hospital plank of rebuilding and restoring every health facility in the country in a massive capital investment "to be ready for the next virus?" What if the anti-gun strategy of closing gun stores becomes a nationwide effort by Democrats? What if Democrats fight for radical immigration and voting reforms as the price of the next economic package in April or May?

We need to imagine the issues that might emerge in this new world by September. This may define the debate in October and the election in November (which actually begins weeks before Election Day).

This book is an introduction to the long-term struggles that will define America. While some of it may be altered by the immediate crises, in the long run these basic choices between traditional America and the radical Democratic Left will be the dominant struggle of our lifetime.

1.

★ ▬▬▬▬▬▬▬▬▬▬▬▬▬▬▬▬▬▬▬▬▬▬▬▬ ★

2020 IS VITAL

If President Donald Trump is reelected, and especially if he can help elect a Republican majority in Congress, he will be able to consolidate the dramatic gains he has made and create a remarkable future for all Americans.

Further, if he is successful, he will cement his place in history among the great disruptive presidents who have shaped America. Victory in 2020 will put President Trump in the same league as Thomas Jefferson, Andrew Jackson, Abraham Lincoln, and Franklin Delano Roosevelt. His opponents will be infuriated at this suggestion, but his record of achievements is already astonishing.

However, Trump's supporters should not kid themselves. The 2016 election was remarkable, but not decisive. It was a beginning. The decisive election is in 2020. If the combined weight of the radical Democratic Left—including the news media, billionaires, and unions—can defeat him, then President Trump will be recorded in history as a temporary detour on the march to a radical, government-controlled, socialist-leaning America.

To understand the importance of winning both the White House and Congress, consider this simple contrast: Speaker Nancy Pelosi or Speaker Kevin McCarthy. Imagine how limited the range of options will be for President Trump and his administration if they are still fighting with Speaker Pelosi instead of working with Speaker McCarthy. Similarly, if Republicans keep and grow our strength in the Senate, and Majority Leader Mitch McConnell remains in his post, steady progress toward a constitutional judiciary will continue. If President Trump has to confront Chuck Schumer as Senate majority leader, the real transformation of the judiciary will be virtually halted.

Of course, in reaction to Trump, the radical Democratic Left has become even more aggressive, and the deep state has become even more willing to resist him—even if it means bending or breaking the law.

One effect of the 2016 election and President Trump's bold policy changes has been to polarize America more clearly than any time since the election of 1860. As a result of this polarization, the election of 2020 will force the American people to choose between two radically different futures.

The Trump team will be advocating dynamic new proposals to fix the nation's problems, help relaunch the American economy after the coronavirus outbreak, strengthen the rule of law, and promote the culture of patriotism, which has historically defined American exceptionalism.

Former Vice President Joe Biden and the radical Democratic Left will be advocating extraordinary, deep changes in virtually every aspect of American life. These changes will be designed to centralize power in Washington bureaucracies, increase the influence of public employee unions, favor criminals over the police, impose radical societal values, and submerge America in globalism and multilateralism.

The Trump Phenomenon Behind
the Trump Presidency

The radical Democratic Left (including most of the news media, Hollywood, and the academic world) has such contempt for President Trump that its members can't examine facts and explore how we have gotten to this point. This lack of honest analysis distorts all their thinking and their reactions to the president.

To understand the Trump presidency, you first must look honestly at the man who creates it. As I wrote in my number one *New York Times* best-seller *Understanding Trump*, President Trump's unique style developed from his upbringing. But you can understand a great deal about him as a leader and politician by looking at his candidacy in 2015 and 2016. Candidate Trump had been remarkably successful in understanding customers through his golf courses, hotels, books, beauty pageants, and his hit television show *The Apprentice*. He brought to politics and government the key understanding that voters are customers.

When he came down the long escalator with his wife, Melania, at Trump Tower on June 16, 2015, to announce his campaign, he knew exactly what he was doing. He knew that he had a built-in support network of the millions of people who had sustained *The Apprentice* for fifteen seasons. He knew that he had a good implementation team, which had successfully sustained a worldwide empire of properties. He knew he had an airplane that, as he liked to say, was better than Vice President Biden's Air Force Two. He had been cheerfully fighting with the New York media for thirty years. He knew he didn't need a handler or a spokesperson.

It was from this position of strength in American business and culture that Donald Trump surveyed the political field. He knew that there would be a lot of candidates. In the traditional world of professional politicians, they would be formidable. However, he

knew that in the larger world of American consumers, these candidates and their consultants did not even exist. He was sure the
competition would hire boring, narrowly experienced Washington
professionals, who would put together boring, carefully calculated
campaigns. Then, they would bore most people.

Candidate Trump knew three big things about reaching large
numbers of people. In a sense this was the first building block of
the Trump phenomenon. These were lessons he had learned mar-
keting all his different enterprises:

Noise wins. Normal candidates would run around the country raising money to buy an occasional TV ad. Candidate Trump
would get up in the morning and tweet to a growing following,
including much of the news media. Then he would have a friendly
call with *Fox & Friends*. Then he would do some radio and TV
in local areas before the local primaries. Then he would have a
rally with tens of thousands of people (all of whom brought their
smartphones, took pictures and connected him to thousands more
electronically). Then he would go on Sean Hannity's show during
prime time. It was impossible for traditional candidates with traditional consultants to match the sheer volume of noise Trump generated every day. Notice: He has never stopped doing this.

Politics is combat. Candidate Trump had learned in the 1980s
that fighting with Page Six (the most widely read gossip column
in New York) simply worked. His constant back and forth with
the editorial board made him a persona in Manhattan—rather
than an interloper from Queens. This public fighting made his
first book, *The Art of the Deal*, a huge and continuing best-seller.
When he entered the presidential race, he knew it was an enormous advantage to have the courage to fight—and to keep the
audience's attention. You could argue that he was such a good
entertainer (and still is if you attend his rallies) that he totally
dominated the stage through a combination of personality and
skills. The other candidates were simply bewildered. In fact, even

after watching the Trump campaign gather momentum for fifteen months, the normal, boring professionals advising Hillary Clinton could not find any way to cope with him.

Social media beats national media. In the fall of 2015, the Trump team began to really develop its Internet capabilities, which put Trump in a different league from everyone else. Because candidate Trump was interesting and advocating bold policies, which about half the country really wanted, he rapidly developed a massive Twitter and Facebook following. This following on social media allowed for free, instantaneous communication with the American public. It enabled the growth of self-recruited local advocates, who would take the messages to their friends and loved ones at work, the diner, the bar, or the family gathering. Furthermore, it was the growth of the massive online following that made possible the enormous rallies. As with all things Trump, these are not traditional rallies. They are massive focus groups, which inform the candidate (and now the president) what policies, arguments, and lines work or fall flat. No one else has anything like this capacity to interact with tens of thousands of people with such enthusiasm.

The other great advantage candidate Trump had was that he really believed in his own policies. He had been thinking about the presidency for at least thirty years. In 1988, after Oprah Winfrey had talked to him about his ideas about trade—that America was getting ripped off by countries that do not pay their fair share— she asked him if he would run for president someday. At the time he said, "probably not," unless "things got really bad." But if he did run, "he wouldn't go in to lose."[1] In fact, on several occasions he had seriously considered running.

In political elections, many people love an outsider. Outsiders break up the current power structure and bring government closer to "we the people." Candidate Trump could campaign as an outsider because he really was an outsider. He did not need think tank analysts, the Washington policy establishment, or retired bureaucrats to tell him what to say. He had reflected long and hard on the changes America would need to make if it was going to continue to be the greatest country on the planet. When he took on illegal immigration, he knew he was speaking for many Americans who were tired of a broken system that allowed cheating. When he said there were too many regulations and bureaucrats—that the swamp needed to be drained—he knew it resonated in small-town America. When he said that trade had been one-sided and made other countries richer while killing American jobs, he knew there would be a huge chorus of blue-collar voters who felt their government had sold them out. When he said America's Middle East policies had become a trap, and young Americans were dying and being wounded with no ability to achieve victory, more and more Americans approved. When he said lower taxes, fewer regulations, and better trade deals would create jobs, he really believed it. As the only businessman running, Trump was confident he understood how to unleash the economy better than the politicians standing onstage with him.

Candidate Trump's personal and policy certainty, when combined with his ability to entertain and brand, gave him an unstoppable advantage. No one else could have coined "Low-Energy Jeb" and made it stick. Yet, with every candidate, including "Crooked Hillary," he was able to operate outside all accepted boundaries of traditional politics.

So when Trump became president, he continued these patterns to the delight of millions, the astonishment of many, and the hatred of some. One of the things that most upset the Republican establishment and the Left was the degree to which President Trump had been shaped by his career in business. Anyone who's read Trump's two best-sellers, *The Art of the Deal* and *The Art of the Comeback*, would have recognized that this was a very thoughtful, calculating, and daring businessman. He had made billions in the world of business. Furthermore, Trump was not a

Harvard Business School manager who calmly ran a traditional, orderly system with experts. While Trump had gone to the Wharton School of the University of Pennsylvania (a superb business school), his real education had come from negotiating, construction, and customer satisfaction. He has a relentless, energetic, entrepreneurial mind and is the antithesis of the orderly leader of a traditional corporation (or government bureaucracy).

The result was a style of abrasiveness, abruptness, and determination to rely on himself. He used the language of the construction worker rather than the smooth talk of an Ivy League professional. All of it drove the Republican establishment to despair and the Left to desperation.

So, Trump was interesting enough to win the nomination against competent but boring opponents. Then he proved tough and confrontational enough to defeat the Clinton machine. As her campaign grew more negative and nastier (attacking the "deplorables" and smearing Trump), the Trump campaign matched her punch for punch.

I can't imagine any other candidate having the nerve and toughness Trump had when the *Access Hollywood* story broke. This would have doomed any other campaign. Clinton thought she could take advantage of it. Trump simply brought the women who had accused President Bill Clinton of sexually predatory behavior to the debate. Instantly, it was Trump on offense and the Clintons on defense. Of course, the aggressive, rapid counterpunch is an integral part of the Trump system and goes back to his Page Six fights. I have never seen him accept an attack without immediately and aggressively counterpunching harder than his opponent. This is not a function of personality. It is a deliberate habit he acquired through long years of practice in New York.

Election night 2016 was a nightmare for those on the left— unlike any they had experienced in modern history. At eight p.m., they were sure Hillary Clinton was going to be president. The next

Supreme Court justice would be a liberal. The march of imposing radical Democratic values on the American people would continue. Many of them would have prestigious jobs in the Clinton
administration.

Yet by ten p.m., it was beginning to be obvious Clinton would
lose—and that meant Trump would become president. This was
unthinkable. This outcome was so shattering that many on the left
went into catatonic shock. Others suffered the political equivalent
of post-traumatic stress disorder (PTSD). This condition became
known as Trump Derangement Syndrome.

Many in the national news media, especially in Washington,
don't just cover the Left; they are active allies and personal friends
of the left. They are totally intermingled by career, marriage, or
education. They were as shocked and terrified by Trump winning
as any left-wing activist. They had suffered George W. Bush winning the presidency in the Electoral College, despite having the
minority of the popular vote. They had grown to deeply dislike
Bush, but he had not gone out of his way to enrage them.

After Bush, their patience paid off, and they had what they saw
as the golden days of the Barack Obama presidency: left-wing policies, left-wing appointees, left-wing bureaucracies. They enjoyed
a left-wing foreign policy of apologizing for America, submerg-
ing America in global and multilateral institutions, and appeasing
and paying our enemies. They saw enormous advances for new
sexual-gender-ethnic rules as the law of the land. It was a happy
time for leftists. Then, on election night 2016, this was all crashing
and burning.

Even before Trump won the Republican nomination, there
were some articles saying he would have to be impeached. The day
after the election there were already anti-Trump meetings in cities
across the United States. On Inauguration Day, the *Washington
Post* published an article proclaiming, "the campaign to impeach
President Trump has begun."[2] The day after the inauguration,

there was a massive left-wing women's rally on the Washington Mall attacking the new president.

President Trump's Miscalculation

The biggest miscalculation President Trump and his team made early on was the failure to think through how bitter and deep the counterattack would be. Citizen Trump had spent a lot of time with Washington and state-level politicians. They had come to his office asking for money. He had golfed with them. A number had come to Mar-a-Largo to see him. He had gone to innumerable dinners for politicians. He had actively helped Mitt Romney in 2012 (I know because I was with him helping Romney in Las Vegas during the general election). In the traditional world of American politics, you run hard. Someone wins, and someone loses. Everyone accepts the result as if it were a sporting event. Then there is a period of working together before the next election cycle ramps up.

What President Trump and his team did not understand was how deeply they had challenged the very survival of the Left and the traditional establishment. The Trump victory was not a partisan victory within the playing field that had been created by President Franklin Delano Roosevelt in 1933. Historically, Republicans had represented the conservative wing of the FDR consensus. Except for Senator Barry Goldwater, they had not broken out of that consensus. Even President Ronald Reagan (who had been a New Deal Democrat, supported President Harry Truman in 1948, and made commercials to help Hubert Humphrey win his first Senate race) was ultimately operating within the consensus except for his focus on defeating the Soviet Union.

If either Jeb Bush or John Kasich had won, those on the left would have been unhappy, but they would not have been alienated, threatened, and enraged. In fact, the insider style of Bush and Kasich probably would have guaranteed that they would have lost to Clinton—but they would have done so graciously, as Romney did in his loss to Obama in 2012.

The challenge for President Trump and his team during the transition was that they did not appreciate how deeply and profoundly they were challenging every aspect of the system. They were busy focusing on the personnel and policies of the new administration. Transitions are an enormous project, and for a couple of months absorb an immense amount of time and energy. So, the team focused on transition issues. Its members assumed the Left's hostility was a temporary irritation that would go away as Americans reverted to the normal behavior of accepting that the winner was the Trump administration. This meant Trump's team did not develop a strategy and system large and thorough enough to get ahead of the various assaults that would come from the Left. Yet the new administration's policies and speeches virtually guaranteed a radical opposition campaign would turn into a war.

President Trump's policies were a decisive, historic break with the Democratic-Republican establishment's system, which is why there were Republican Never-Trumpers joining in the hostility. The Republican Never-Trumpers were further irritated by Trump's style. Many of them were elegant Ivy Leaguers who could never appeal to the blue-collar workers who'd given Trump the margin of victory. They despised his blue-collar style, use of coarse language, and self-confidence.

The fact that Trump said the establishment was wrong on trade, the economy, military affairs, the Middle East, and a host of other issues simply infuriated them. He was equally infuriated by their efforts to supposedly educate him to their way of thinking. A good part of the first three years of the Trump administration was spent sorting out who wanted to educate President Trump (they virtually all left in frustration or were forced out) and those who wanted to implement the president's ideas (they seem to be flourishing).

The Never-Trumpers were a symptom of how radically different President Trump was. But some of them were mostly useful to the Left as validators who could be put on TV: what Lenin would have called "useful idiots." So the real problem for President Trump was the initial failure to recognize that he had declared war on the system, and the radical Left was going to declare war back.

A good case in point was the list of potential US Supreme Court nominees Trump had proposed. Candidate Trump turned to the Federalist Society and the Heritage Foundation to develop a list of highly qualified conservative nominees for the high court. Liberals had gradually taken over the American Bar Association (ABA) (and as far as they are concerned, it should be the only standard-setter for judges). The Federalist Society had been growing in stature. In a Trump administration, it became clear the Federalist Society would play a major role, and the ABA would be ignored. This was a pointed but significant revolution in the power to define American values by defining who was fit to serve on the federal bench. It was a switch from the increasingly radical Democratic Left to a firm commitment to constitution-minded conservative judges.

Ever since Earl Warren became a US Supreme Court justice in 1953 (which President Dwight Eisenhower looked back on as one of his biggest mistakes)[3] the court system had been moving to the left. It was the courts that had been the engine imposing radical rules on abortion, sexual behavior, immigration, crime, and more. Now, with the release of his list of ten conservative potential US Supreme Court justices, candidate Trump was threatening the heart of the radical-liberal system. None of us who supported candidate Trump fully appreciated that his success, like President Lincoln's in 1860, would create a crisis of survival for his opponents. As Allen Guelzo, a Civil War historian, has written, the viciousness and intensity of language smearing Trump after the election closely parallels the language of South Carolina newspapers in

1860 and 1861, which saw Lincoln's election as the death knell for their way of life.

The great challenge of wars of identity is that they become life-or-death. The election of President Trump, and his persistence in disrupting the old order, has created a backlash that is a matter of survival for the Left and for part of the establishment. This is why the intensity and the viciousness are so deep—and why the news media is so thoroughly dishonest. It isn't just fake news. it is maliciously and deliberately fake news.

2020 Is about Survival

Similarly, the 2020 election is not a normal election. We can now understand it is not a contest between two teams operating within a common overall framework. Unlike any election in modern times, this is an election about which set of values will survive and be fully implemented. To President Trump's credit, he really is as big a threat to the institutions and values of the Left as they think.

In his first three years, he has teamed with McConnell to fill a quarter of the federal judgeships, including placing two US Supreme Court justices. It is a truly historic pace. If President Trump is reelected and Republicans keep control of the Senate, it is possible that the Trump court system will have essentially replaced the liberal court system. Since the Trump team has cleverly insisted that new federal judges be under fifty, this change could easily last two generations. For the Left, this is a nightmare.

In his first three years, Trump's administration has repealed seven regulations for each one it has written. It is the largest deregulation effort in American history, and it is building momentum. By the end of a second term, so much power may have been moved from Washington back to states, local governments, businesses, voluntary organizations (including religious organizations), and individuals, the influence of Washington on our everyday lives will be back to a pre–Lyndon Johnson level.

It might even be approaching the level of the 1930s. For the elitist Left, which totally distrusts the American people, this undoes eighty years of work.

President Trump has broken two generations of bipartisan, international, elitist efforts that submerged American interests in global interests and structures. President Trump withdrew from the Paris climate accord on behalf of American jobs. He demanded revision of trade agreements that hurt American workers. He insisted that North Atlantic Treaty Organization (NATO) nations pay their fair shares for their own defense (something both Bush and Obama asked for but did nothing about). And he has described Western civilization as something worth defending. President Trump has again and again infuriated those in the foreign policy and national security establishment who see their decades of work going down the drain.

To a lot of people's surprise, President Trump is the most pro-life president in our history. His willingness to go to the March for Life and give a full-blown defense of protecting innocent life is a real breakthrough. Former pro-life presidents were always cautious about being too closely and publicly identified with the pro-life movement. In some ways, past presidents would treat it as if its members were so-called deplorables, speaking to them by telephone even when the march was right outside the White House. Trump has been willing to be seen with his allies even if (and especially when) it drives his opponents crazy. At a time when a former Democratic presidential candidate said flatly there was no room in the Democratic Party for anyone with pro-life views, the contrast could hardly be clearer.

The list goes on, but consider one last example: President Trump has been profoundly and consistently committed to fighting for religious liberty. He has argued that religious beliefs are as legitimate as sexual orientations. In all these steps, he angers the secular Left—including many in newsrooms across the country. It is just one more example of the clash of two worlds we are living in and the threat to the Left's world that President Trump represents.

When you look at the totality of the Trump agenda, you can see why the Left thinks its survival is at stake. However, in the transition period, and for at least a year afterward, the Trump team could not bring itself to believe that this war from the Left was as big, angry, and vicious as it has turned out to be. The Trump team's responses were too small and fragmented to meet the scale of the assault.

A key part of the reelection campaign—and the second term—will be adapting to and getting ahead of these attacks.

2.

★ ▬▬▬▬▬▬▬▬▬▬▬▬▬▬▬▬▬▬▬▬▬▬▬ ★

FRENZY, CORRUPTION, AND CONFORMITY

Aside from being interested in beating President Trump for its own survival, the radical Democratic Left is also dealing with someone who is antithetical to its views.

The American left has a tradition of self-righteous certainty, which has metastasized into a totalitarian belief that any other view is not only wrong, but it cannot be tolerated. The uniformity of views on college campuses are enforced by who gets tenure. The uniformity of views in the news media are enforced by who gets hired and promoted. In Hollywood, if you do not parrot the Left's line, you will be ostracized and unemployed (unless you are a big box-office star). It was this drive for conformity that ultimately forced Speaker Pelosi to proceed with an impeachment she had resisted for months.

Because there is such uniformity, when the Left gets together it has no reality check. People explain to each other how supposedly evil President Trump is. Then they convince themselves that if he is that evil, then anything they say or do against him is legitimate.

Then they begin moving toward hysteria and clearly crazed comments: *We will all die in the next twelve years if we don't act now on climate change; Immigration and Customs Enforcement resembles the Gestapo; American immigration centers with recreation facilities and medical care are concentration camps.* Now, since everyone on the left nods and chants the same emotional-but-crazy things, there is no check on what they can legitimately do to stop the evil they have identified.

This vehement passion is what leads to support of sanctuary cities, no cash bail systems for criminals in New York, abortion after a birth, blanket support for health care for illegal immigrants, and district attorneys who refuse to work with the police or prosecute criminals. At each step, the Left gets a little crazier. Since only the true believers are allowed in the room, there is no one to ask if these ideas really make sense or are good for Americans.

Theodore H. White described the radical shift on the left in his book *The Making of the President 1972* as transitioning from the liberal ideology to the liberal theology. White argued that it was the harsh inflexibility of the emerging liberal theology that doomed the George McGovern campaign to a catastrophic defeat.

Ideologies can be argued about, but theologies are religious systems. To challenge them is to commit heresy. The theological Left now lives in a world of good and evil. In this world, they are the good and the conservative nonbelievers are evil. Virtually anything you do or say in support of the good is forgiven, no matter how dumb. You submit to the system, or you are ostracized and driven out of acceptable society.

The radical Democratic Left's craziness and viciousness are protected by the news media, which shares most of the Left's more radical values. Recall that the *New York Times* wants to recenter all American history on slavery with its 1619 Project (which, as the *National Review*'s Rich Lowry has written, many legitimate scholars have debunked).[1] In fact, the news media is a major engine driving the radical Democratic Left to more extreme positions. It is the news media that made Greta Thunberg, a sixteen-year-old, a world spokesman for the climate, even though her positions are scientifically false, and her passion provides no reasonable solutions.[2] It is the news media that made Alexandria Ocasio-Cortez (AOC) a symbol of the younger House Democrats (to the extreme discomfort of most of her fellow freshmen, who know they will not survive if they become identified with her).

The Hostile Bureaucracy

Maybe the biggest surprise in the rebellion against the Trump victory was the aggressiveness of some elements of the deep state bureaucracy to try to destroy him. One thing that has surfaced from all the erroneous investigations throughout Trump's first term have been the amount of deeply disturbing, concerted efforts to destroy him. The joint efforts of the Clinton campaign, senior elements of the Federal Bureau of Investigation, rogue elements at the top of the intelligence community, and the news media is the stuff of novels and movies. It is astoundingly clear that there was a steady, deliberate effort that broke the law and used the power of the federal government to try to destroy Trump, both as a candidate and president. Much of the news media were participants, coconspirators, and enablers.

Apparently, the contempt for the law among senior intelligence officials and FBI leadership was an outgrowth of their commitment to Clinton's election. They apparently reasoned that if Clinton won the election, their various aggressive, dishonest, and illegal actions against Trump and his campaign would simply be ignored. After all, the FBI had ignored all the corrupt practices of the Clinton Foundation, all the foreign money going to that foundation, the Uranium One Deal, which enriched Russians who were donating to the Clinton Foundation—and the list goes on.

In fact, it is clear that senior FBI and intelligence officials were breaking the law in 2016 to stop Trump in the belief that a Clinton administration would overlook their criminal behavior. Then, when Clinton lost, in desperation, the same officials felt they had to go after the new president, because it was now clear they had put themselves in danger of going to jail.

This pro-Clinton bias was pervasive in the federal bureaucracy. In the Department of Justice, 97 percent of those who made political donations in 2016 donated to Clinton. In the State Department, the figure was 99 percent. At the Department of Education, it was 99.7 percent.[3] In a climate where 99 out of 100 of your colleagues is for one side, there becomes a presumption that anything you do to ensure victory is OK.

If we had not lived through it, and if we had not had continuing investigations into the depth of corruption, I would have thought the whole idea was an example of conservative paranoia. However, it is now clear that people such as Representative Devin Nunes and others, who warned that profoundly wrong and illegal acts were being committed, were right.

In many ways the House Democratic impeachment effort was just a continuation of the lawless and dishonest efforts that the deep state had been using to neutralize President Trump all along. The number of times Congressman Adam Schiff, using the prestige of his position as chairman of the House Intelligence Committee, just flat-out lied is staggering. The entire dishonest handling of the so-called whistleblower (who was an anonymous excuse for impeaching a president who had already been exonerated after a massive and lengthy investigation and report by Robert Mueller) is just astonishing.

The so-called whistleblower in the impeachment scam is the parallel to the Steele dossier in the Russian collusion investigation. Both were lies. Both were used to set up legal processes that should never have occurred. In both cases, the officials on the left in the

FBI and House of Representatives knew that they were using a lie to try to take down President Trump.

I'm writing this in late March 2020. Over the next few months, more will come out, and the system may end up sicker and more criminally dishonest than we thought possible. It is important to remember when discussing the hostility of the deep state that it involves far more resistance than these investigations.

The Washington bureaucracy and its lobbying and activist group allies are trying to slow-walk President Trump's reforms at virtually every front. If Trump wants transparency in health care costs, he will be opposed by hospitals, doctors, medical technology companies, and their lobbyists and allies. If Trump wants to move toward much less expensive and more innovative private companies in space, there will be elements of the NASA bureaucracy and the old, established big firms that will fight every inch of the way to keep the slow, expensive systems they are comfortable with. If Trump wants to create a new, modern Space Force, parts of the Department of Defense and the US Air Force will slow-walk the proposal and try to minimize the change. For them, it's better to be behind China than to shake up existing comfortable bureaucratic habits. Speaking of China, if Trump wants to defeat Huawei and ensure that the new 5G Internet is based on free-world principles instead of totalitarianism, he will find the Pentagon bureaucracy, the Federal Communications Commission (FCC), and the lobbyists for big telecom companies doing everything they can to stop him.

Yet, despite all this deep state, interest group, and bureaucratic resistance, there is hope for dramatic change. If President Trump gets reelected, there will be a substantial collapse of the resistance in the deep state.

First, the president and his team now have a lot better sense of how the system works, where the resistance is, and who they need to overcome to impose bold changes.

Second, the president's team has been able to identify the key centers of resistance and the various outside allies on which those centers rely.

Third, whatever question there was about President Trump's legitimacy will be wiped away by the reelection. If the American people choose Trump to be their president again—after having had four years to get to know him through unending attacks from the Left—it will be impossible to establish a moral center of resistance. The authority the American people confers on a president can lead to dramatic changes at a speed that seems impossible when the president's authority is still being contested.

A Movement, Not an Organization

One of the things which really confuses Republicans is the radical difference in both the psychology and organization of the radical Democratic Left.

Republicans like to be organized. As a party with a strong business background, they also like to be orderly and efficient. While Republicans like entrepreneurship in theory, in their politics they really want to follow the leader. Republicans in a sense are always looking for a quarterback to call the plays, and they want to be on the team.

The radical Democratic Left is a movement that also has a party. However, the Left is genuinely entrepreneurial. Anyone can emerge at any time and try to create a following or build a cause. When Will Rogers said, "I am not a member of any organized political party. I am a Democrat,"[4] he was hitting at something real. The absurdity of the collapse of the Iowa Caucus system sort of proved Rogers's point. The radical Democratic Left is a tumultuous, constantly evolving, impossible-to-control, and stunningly disorganized pattern of beliefs and activities. It doesn't have planning sessions. Because of its long, symbiotic relationship with its allies in the news media, it simply communicates by diffusion.

Watch how rapidly a term or meme can start and then be parroted by politicians, analysts, and the news media. (The overwhelming agreement on the defense of the so-called whistleblower's legal right to anonymity, which was baloney, is a good case study.) In 2016, all over the country, leftists gravitated toward an understanding that Trump had to be an illegitimate president, and the election had to be rigged. Within a few hours after the results were in, the legend had begun. Since Clinton could not have lost fair and square, there had to be something wrong. Some analysts believe the heart of the Russian collusion myth came out of election night. To the radical Democratic Left and its allies, it simply was not possible for someone as unacceptable as candidate Trump to have won. Therefore, the victory had to have an alternative explanation.

The speed of mass validation and commitment can also be seen in the rise of AOC. In both cases, people who had remarkably limited claims to being prophetic figures suddenly were chosen by the media to represent the future. These patterns of mass enthusiasm followed by gradual decay and disappearance are a major part of the energy of the Left—and the way the news media frames the news and the political dialogue to ensure the right is always on defense.

The charges against Justice Clarence Thomas and Justice Brett Kavanaugh reveal this kind of mass, rapid unity of message. In these cases, you have personal viciousness, media bias against questioning the integrity of the witnesses, broad acceptance of accusations as truth, and universal understanding that the accused should withdraw regardless of facts. In both cases, each member of the Left knew how to read the pattern, expand it, and drive it home. So, the Left has a speed of attack which conservatives and Republicans have not yet learned to match.

Part of what drives the Left crazy about President Trump is his ability to be a one-person war room communicator. The president's ability to spot a fight, analyze it, and tweet a response or make a comment on the way to Marine One gives us the first American leader capable of keeping the Left off balance, in real time, every day.

If the Republican Party is going to capture Congress and win state and local governments, it must learn to acquire more of the Trump speed and aggressiveness. We also need to recognize when the Left is on a new strategic communications effort. We must learn, in the tradition of British prime minister Margaret Thatcher, to win the argument and then win the vote. This means we must identify the argument early. Ideally, we might even decide that we will launch our own arguments and let the Left be on defense.

One of the keys to the Trump offense is his willingness to create new arguments, to stay on offense, and to relentlessly attack the Left in direct language every American can understand. It is a set of skills every Republican should acquire.

They Simply Have More Resources

All Republican planning must start with an assumption that our communications plans assume endless, unfair hostility from the news media, and be designed to reach the American people despite this bias. Of course, the better we get at reaching the American people without the media the more angry, bitter, and nasty the news media will become as it grows desperate.

When I see glowing reports of how much more Republicans are raising than the Democrats, I get worried. This is because I know it is only a small part of the resources available to the Democrats. Because Republicans are so much more orderly and organized—and because Republicans spend a great deal of effort gathering resources for the official party committees—they consistently raise more than the Democrats.

The Democrats' inefficiencies, and indeed incompetence, can be seen in just looking at the Democratic National Committee

(DNC) in 2016, and again in 2020. Compared with the Republican National Committee (RNC), the Democratic National Committee is disorganized, underfunded, and indeed a little pathetic. Comparing Reince Priebus and Ronna McDaniel (RNC chairs in 2016 and 2020) with Debbie Wasserman Schultz and Tom Perez (DNC chairs for the same years, respectively) gives you some insight into the difference of professionalism, management strength, and seriousness of the two national party organizations. As of this writing, according to Ballotpedia, the RNC has raised $294,533,798, while the DNC has raised $113,985,451.[5]

However, focusing on the two national committees overstates the relative resources of the Republicans and greatly understates the resources of the Democrats. The Democrats' great power centers are not their party committees. Their real power comes from the media, activist groups, unions, and dedicated billionaires—in that order.

First, when Harvard finds that CNN and NBC's coverage of President Trump is 93 percent negative, any serious Republican campaign plan must include offsetting the media bias.[6] Republicans must spend a lot of time and resources simply fighting their way back to even from the consistently negative and biased coverage they receive from the media. If we quantified the value of the constantly anti-Republican, anti-Trump news media, we would be shocked at how much they are worth to the radical Democratic Left's movement. It isn't just that they cover issues negatively or from a left-wing bias. The herd mentality of the news media enables the Left to define stories as important and appropriate (if they help the cause) or as irrelevant (if they help Trump).

Again, there was a huge, intense news media consensus that the so-called whistleblower at the center of the Democrat's impeachment plan could not be named. Reporters and hosts of news shows would cut off Republicans and try to shame them if they insisted on trying to name this person. So the news media created an entirely new rule that (without evidence) you could accuse the president of the United States of a crime, spur an impeachment effort, and remain anonymous. This violated Trump's basic right to face his accuser. It violated every principle of common sense. Something as serious as an impeachment should require basic evidence.

There was an equally strong news media consensus that former Vice President Joe Biden could not be investigated for having admitted on video to the Council of Foreign Relations to doing exactly what President Trump was accused of doing. Biden bragged that he threatened to withhold $1 billion of financial aid from Ukraine if the Ukrainian president did not fire the prosecutor investigating a business paying Biden's son $50,000 a month.[7] Ironically, Biden claimed he wanted the prosecutor gone because the prosecutor *wasn't* investigating corruption. Somehow, the media decided that the filmed admission by the former vice president's quid pro quo wasn't a big issue.

So, there's one thing every Republican needs to understand in 2020: The unending media hostility is not a problem. It is a fact. What we do about it is the problem.

Once again, Trump's philosophy can be the answer. It has, so far, been devastating in meeting the challenge of the Left head-on—and counterattacking intensely, consistently, and with enormous impact. Trump's knack for branding things was driven home to me when Callista and I were in Turin, Italy, at the second-largest Egyptian museum in Europe. Our guide was enthusiastically showing us around and pointed out a statue.

"The story they used to tell about that statue was fake news," he told us.

I stood there amazed that Trump's language was beginning to permeate to such a degree that an Italian tour guide could use it to describe a three-thousand-year-old event in Egyptian history.

It is this power of relentless branding, his enthusiasm for the fight, and the speed with which he counterpunches that has made

President Trump the most successful Republican in stopping the media in our lifetime.

However, the media is not the only hurdle. The left-wing activist groups are far bigger, more ideological, combative, and politically savvy than their conservative counterparts (if indeed they have conservative counterparts). Whether it is the Sierra Club or the National Education Association, the Left has allies and supporters that dwarf comparable systems on the right. This is especially true because most Republican-leaning business groups are deeply unwilling to be partisan. The left-wing groups use a sledgehammer, while the so-called conservative allies tend to pull their punches and seek to avoid controversy.

The same disparity of resources occurs when looking at activist billionaires. The 2018 election was made more anti-Republican by Mike Bloomberg dropping as much as $5 million in individual congressional races during the last two weeks before the election. George Soros has invested massively to elect left-wing, pro-crime, and anti-police district attorneys. There is nothing comparable on the right. Republicans must wage campaigns of such clarity and frame the choice with such power that it overcomes the quantitative advantage of the Left's system. Republicans must reach voters at levels that lead them to shrug off the Left's bigger system and campaign. In fact, this need to communicate so intensely and effectively is why I wrote this book.

Why This Book Matters

I decided I had to write this book because the stakes in 2020 are so critical.

Back in the 1980s, when we were trying to break decades of Democratic control of the House of Representatives, we developed a program called GOPAC. It helped our candidates, incumbents, and their campaign and legislative staffs develop new language and new solutions. We worked very hard to answer every

Democratic attack and develop clear ways to explain our positions and our answers.

Ultimately, this educational effort led to the 1994 Contract with America and a Republican Party that was sufficiently prepared to win the argument. As a result, for the first time in forty years, America elected a majority.

In 2020, we have five great goals, which call for a serious educational effort to win arguments—and then votes:

1. Reelect President Trump and Vice President Pence and prove that 2016 was not a detour but a profoundly historic turning point away from the Left and the deep state.
2. Elect a majority in the House, so McCarthy can replace Pelosi as speaker, Nunes can replace Schiff, and solid conservative reform legislation can be passed in collaboration with the Trump White House.
3. Gain Senate seats, so Majority Leader McConnell has a bigger margin to work with and has a solid future of retaining control of the Senate in 2022 and beyond.
4. Develop a powerful, consistent argument, which demolishes the lies of the Left and the fantasies of the radicals. There are campaigns in American history that profoundly reshaped the dominant ideology and vision of America. Jefferson in 1800, Jackson in 1828, Lincoln in 1860, McKinley in 1896, and Roosevelt in 1932 all shattered the opposition and, in Lincoln's words "put forward a new proposition." As the Democrats move toward the radical left, they create the opportunity for 2020 to be a decisive debate about the nature of America and the difference between rules that work and fantasies that fail. This is the most important reason for this book as a first step toward making this argument.
5. Republicans have an opportunity and an obligation to carry the argument into every neighborhood, every ethnic group,

and every age group. The gap between the positive world of opportunity and progress we will create and the nightmare of unemployment, big bureaucracy, government domination, and imposed radical values that the Left represents is a case we must make to every American. If we do this, we will win record support from Latino Americans, African Americans, Asian Americans, the young, and virtually everyone except the radical hard Left.

This book is focused on giving the arguments and facts to help every American who favors a more prosperous, safer, and American-based future make the 2020 election one of the great turning points in American life. Once the coronavirus pandemic is contained and defeated, the mission will be to rebuild our economy and prosperity. If we have President Trump leading the country, we will succeed. If the radical democratic left wins, we will face years of big government, slower growth, and crippling regulations.

3.

★ ▬▬▬▬▬▬▬▬▬▬▬▬▬▬▬▬▬▬▬▬▬▬▬▬▬▬▬ ★

THE FAILED COUP ATTEMPTS

As I am writing this in March 2020, roughly a month has passed since the radical Democratic Left, the deep state, and the national media wrapped up their latest attempted coup d'état against President Trump. Right now, it appears the failed impeachment circus will be the last effort to unseat the duly elected president of the United States before the 2020 election—although I will not be surprised if another scheme is hatched before then.

After the US Senate acquitted President Trump of the Democratic House's phony impeachment allegations in February, Speaker Nancy Pelosi—in what I expect was a frustration-fueled moment of carelessness—said that she had been personally working on President Trump's impeachment effort for two and a half years. Keep in mind, the impeachment inquiry had been announced only in September 2019.

I was surprised to hear Pelosi's statement. I don't mean I was surprised that she was involved in a multiyear effort to impeach President Trump for whatever she could find. I was surprised she said it out loud. Her comment illustrated the contempt and hatred the radical Democratic Left and the establishment have for President Trump and the people who elected him. That Pelosi freely admitted working on this effort for nearly his entire presidency was eye-opening.

Despite her admission, the total impeachment effort started long before Pelosi got involved. The truth is the radical Democratic Left's media allies started publicly seeking ways to overthrow a potential President Trump shortly after he descended the escalator at Trump Tower in New York to announce his candidacy on June 16, 2015.

The Impeachment Narrative

The media has played a key role in the Trump opposition by making impeachment—something which is historically rare—a part of everyday conversation. Remember, only two other presidents in history have been impeached: Andrew Johnson and Bill Clinton (Nixon resigned before the House voted on impeaching him). None have been convicted by the Senate. Like President Trump, Johnson and Clinton were acquitted.

One of the first major news stories which explored the possibility of a Trump impeachment was published by *Politico* on April 17, 2016—less than a year after he became a candidate and three months before he was the official Republican nominee for president.[1] The piece starts off disguised as a fairly straight report that some people in the Washington, DC, establishment were talking about impeaching Trump before he even became the Republican Party nominee. The author, Darren Samuelsohn, quickly acknowledges that such a move is highly unlikely to happen.

But then, after explaining that he spoke with "a dozen members of Congress, former Capitol Hill administration and presidential campaign aides and legal experts," the writer embarks on an absurd Washington elite daydream set in the summer of 2017 (a year into the future and mere months into President Trump's term). The *Politico* piece is useful because it is a perfect portrait of everything the so-called experts were wrong about when President Trump was still a candidate—and what those same experts continue to be wrong about today. It further shows the coziness between the elites and the national press—and the media's willingness to spread propaganda to protect this symbiotic relationship.

The *Politico* anti-Trump fantasy kicks off by asserting that in the first six months of his administration, President Trump will have deployed the National Guard to "round up" Muslim Americans in Detroit, Chicago, New York, and other cities. These Americans would be illegally held at secretly reestablished World War II–era detention camps, and at a reopened Alcatraz Island. This alone should give you some sense of the depth of the anti-Trump delirium on the left.

In this fiction, the United Nations would be calling for President Trump to be tried for war crimes over massive military airstrikes on civilians throughout the Middle East. (For perspective, as I'm writing now, the Trump administration has effectively defeated ISIS in Iraq, is near to signing a peace agreement with the Taliban, and has pulled a majority of American forces out of the conflict in Syria.)

Amusingly, in this fantasy, the Never-Trumpers have won and been elevated. The entire Republican Party would be working against President Trump, including Rush Limbaugh. (I find this particularly ironic, since Limbaugh was awarded the Presidential Medal of Freedom—the highest civilian honor the president can bestow—at the State of the Union address in February 2020.)

The story gets more and more detached from reality. In this delusion, South Carolina Senator Lindsey Graham would be leading the charge on impeachment from the Senate (where Republicans would be in the minority). Graham has of course become a stalwart ally of President Trump—largely because of the Trump administration's foreign policy and economic success. House

Republicans (who would be the majority) would be the ones to begin the impeachment investigation—and the House Democrats would nobly, soberly acquiesce. How ridiculous does this sound now?

In this fairy tale, Trump's poll numbers will have steadily declined to the point where Congress's job approval overshoots his own. (In reality, as I'm writing this, Trump's approval is at 46.9 percent, and Congress's is at 24.2 percent, according to the Real-Clear Politics average.)[2][3]

In short, the entire piece is complete baloney. It is a make-believe ideal future deeply hoped for by everyone in Washington, DC, who hates President Trump. It is no surprise that the writer came to these ridiculous conclusions, because the named sources in the piece included several Washington, DC, attorneys and consultants—along with current and former staff of Harry Reid, John McCain, and George W. Bush. Not a single Trump supporter is quoted.

But this was only the beginning of the effort to normalize and promote an impeachment narrative. On December 15, 2016, a month before Trump was inaugurated, *Vanity Fair* published a piece explaining how President Trump could be impeached on his first day in office if he did not entirely divest himself from his business dealings—specifically in the way that congressional Democrats prescribed. This claim was based on no legal foundation. The story was simply written to champion Democratic legislation touted by Senator Elizabeth Warren that would invent a path designed to impeach President Trump. The story ended by declaring that the president's plans to cede control of his businesses to his sons—who were not involved in the administration—created conflicts of interest that were "immensely harmful to the sanctity of the office he will soon hold."

In fact, President Trump did cut ties with his business, on *his* terms and with the advice of *his* attorneys. As he said, he believed that focusing solely on running the country was more important. Despite this, a group of 215 Democratic Congress members tried (and failed) to find him in violation of the emoluments clause—a part of the Constitution aimed at restricting government officials from receiving gifts from foreign governments without approval from Congress. They argued because foreign officials stay at Trump hotels, the president was receiving financial benefit. A federal appellate court later threw out the lawsuit.

So once the president took office, a seemingly never-ending barrage of impeachment stories alleging various made-up high crimes and misdemeanors started to pour out of the national media. Remember the supposed Russia–Trump Tower scandal, the absurd controversy over the president's decision to fire Jim Comey, or the media crusade against virtually every one of President Trump's early cabinet appointees?

The elite national media have been salivating over the idea of kicking President Trump out of office since before he was even the nominee. I'm sure some journalists are just chasing the dream of being the next Bob Woodward or Carl Bernstein—the next hard-nosed reporter to take down an American president. But some simply want him gone because they hate him. He threatens their influence, their manufactured prestige, and their ability to impose their values and policies on the American people.

There is some media hostility against every administration, but the anti-Trump level has been historic. And it only ramped up higher once he took office. For example, according to the Media Research Center, nightly broadcast news coverage of the administration on ABC, CBS, and NBC from September 24, 2019, to January 1, 2020, was 93 percent negative.[4] This period begins with the day Speaker Nancy Pelosi announced the start of the Democratic impeachment inquiry over a benign phone call between President Trump and Ukrainian president Volodymyr Zelensky. This proportion of negative coverage has been par for the course during the Trump administration. But the impeachment coverage was especially significant because of the amount of time the media spent on it. As the MRC pointed out:

In the first 100 days since Pelosi announced the start of the House impeachment inquiry on September 24 (through January 1), ABC, CBS and NBC have generated a combined 849 minutes of evening news coverage about the subject.

For comparison, after Special Counsel Robert Mueller was named back on May 17, 2017, it took those same newscasts more than twice as long (until December 29 of that year, or 226 days) to register the same amount of airtime for the Russia investigation. In other words, the networks are spending more than twice as much airtime on the Ukraine probe as they did on the Russia probe.[5]

Importantly, the major networks spent so much time talking about the failed impeachment, they largely ignored any other news—especially positive news about the economy. According to another MRC study from February 4, 2020, "For each minute the broadcast evening newscasts spent talking about the president's successful economic programs, viewers heard 77 minutes about the Democrats' impeachment push, a massive disparity. Overall, coverage of the president was 93 percent negative during the last four months, reaching 95 percent negative in January 2020."[6]

It seems to me 77:1 negative coverage does not pass any reasonable test for objectivity or fairness. This was tested again once the coronavirus began to harm economies around the globe, when the media spent a great deal of time and effort trying to place blame for the epidemic on the administration. This sort of blatant bias is not going to help the national press. Most Americans already believe the mainstream media has lost its objectivity. In fact, a

Rasmussen survey from November 14, 2019, found that a full 53 percent of likely US voters believed that reporters were actively helping Democrats to impeach President Trump.[7] Only 32 percent thought reporters were just trying to collect and report the news. This trend is dangerous. If we don't have fair, objective news, we will not keep our free society for long.

The Russia Witch Hunt

As part of the constant media attack, the first major offensive against the Trump presidency was the so-called Russia investigation. For the first three years of his term, the media and Democrats constantly insisted (citing vague, unidentified government leaks) that the Trump campaign colluded with the Russian government to win the 2016 election. This psychosis was born and proliferated mainly because Hillary Clinton and her allies in Washington simply refused to believe that President Trump had won the election legitimately. They decided that something nefarious must have happened, and Russia could be blamed after it became clear that Russian hackers had attacked the Democratic National Committee (DNC) servers in 2016. It was an historic example of political denial. What resulted in this mass denial from Washington was a profoundly vicious inquisition on anyone in the president's orbit. President Trump often referred to the Mueller investigation as a political witch hunt, and I expect most historians will agree with him.

First, Mueller started out with a wildly open-ended mandate from Deputy Attorney General Rod Rosenstein (who was responsible for picking Mueller after the former Attorney General Jeff Sessions recused himself). Mueller was given license to investigate "any links and/or coordination between Russian government and individuals associated with the campaign of President Donald Trump, and any matters that arose or may arise directly from the investigation." We saw the results of this almost immediately.

Mueller was appointed on May 17. Less than a month later, on June 14, his investigation had expanded to include ludicrous claims that President Trump had obstructed justice when he fired Comey (Mueller's friend and former colleague).[8] Mueller became a sort of arch-prosecutor who could spend taxpayer money investigating virtually anything. Indeed, after running through $32 million,[9] most of the indictments that came out of the investigation had nothing to do with President Trump or his campaign.

The second clue that this was going to be an aggressive political witch hunt came when Mueller assembled a team of fifteen highly partisan lawyers, some of whom had direct ties to the Clintons or were known for breaking rules. For example, Jeannie Rhee was a former lawyer for the Clinton Foundation. Andrew Weismann made a name for himself for his work on the Enron Task Force after his conviction of Arthur Anderson was overturned 9–0 by the US Supreme Court because of faulty jury instructions given by the trial judge. Earlier in the case, defense lawyers argued that Weismann and his team had been intimidating witnesses and hiding evidence from Anderson's attorneys. Bruce Ohr was married to Nellie Ohr—who had been hired to do opposition research on candidate Trump by the company that produced the salacious and discredited dossier on which the entire Trump-collusion farce was based. In all, the Mueller team had collectively given more than $55,000 to Democratic campaigns and candidates over a twelve-year period, while they had given Republicans a mere $2,750.[10]

So, Mueller then took his blank-check marching orders, and his partisan hit squad, and proceeded to attack and harass anyone and everyone who knew President Trump. When the special investigation was first announced, I cautioned that President Trump and his team should be extremely careful about speaking with the Mueller team. I said they would analyze and exploit every misstatement, forgotten detail, and imprecise comment.

At the beginning, I warned that Mueller would not find any illegal activity or so-called collusion—but he would aggressively prosecute people for perjury or anything else he could dig up.

This is exactly what happened to former National Security Advisor General Mike Flynn, and former campaign staffer George Papadopoulos—Mueller's first victims. General Flynn was railroaded for not accurately remembering the details of a conversation he'd had with Russian ambassador Sergey Kislyak. Importantly, there was nothing illegal about the incoming national security advisor talking with the Russian ambassador. Flynn simply did not accurately recount the conversation to investigators. This was a case of a decorated military serviceman who simply didn't expect he was walking into political blood sport. Flynn initially pleaded guilty to lying about his conversation to FBI officials—but this was only after Mueller threatened to investigate and indict Flynn's own son, who had nothing to do with the Russia investigation. After the Mueller investigation's failure to find any collusion between Trump's campaign and Russia, Flynn is now seeking to withdraw his guilty plea and clear his name.

Similarly, Papadopoulos was a young staffer trying to make a name for himself. He was charged with lying to investigators about otherwise legal (although perhaps ill advised) conversations he had in London, England, with an Australian professor and a woman who was falsely presented to Papadopoulos as Vladimir Putin's niece. The Left and the media made great hay out of this early Mueller indictment. But Papadopoulos was eventually sentenced to a mere fourteen days in jail for his "violation."

Of course, the most visible charges to come out of the Mueller spectacle were levied against Trump's former campaign manager Paul Manafort and his former business partner Rick Gates. The most important thing to know about the Manafort-Gates cases is that the charges had nothing to do with President Trump, the 2016 election, or any election. They were related to financial crimes and lobbying violations that were said to have occurred long before Manafort joined the campaign. Nevertheless, the media breathlessly followed the case against Manafort and did its best to insinuate that it was somehow related to the president.

Further, the most alarming revelation to come out of the Manafort case was the viciousness with which Mueller would attack and intimidate people just for being connected to President Trump. The day after Manafort willingly testified to a Senate committee about his work on the campaign, Mueller had FBI agents storm Manafort's home in the early hours of the morning. Manafort and his wife were forced to stand in their yard in their pajamas and watch as their home was ransacked. Manafort wasn't a flight risk, and he wasn't accused of any dangerous crimes. There was no legitimate reason for Mueller to use the full force of the government in this way—except to attempt to intimidate Manafort into saying what Mueller wanted to hear.

After Manafort was found guilty of fraud by a Virginia jury, he pleaded guilty to charges levied by the Mueller investigation and signed a cooperation agreement. Then Mueller had Manafort moved to Riker's Island prison in New York. As Dennis Prager wrote for *National Review,* Riker's is a place for barbarous murderers and people who are convicted of torture. There's no justification for someone convicted of white-collar crimes to be sent there.[11] While he was there, Manafort spent twenty-three hours a day in solitary confinement. Even the radical left's darling Alexandria Ocasio-Cortez said that this was inhumane. But Mueller did it because he was conducting an inquisition, and he wanted Manafort to repent and cooperate (in the style of a Salem witch trial).

Similarly, Mueller raided the offices of Michael Cohen, who was one of Trump's personal attorneys. After Cohen pleaded guilty to tax fraud (also unrelated to the Russia-collusion hoax), he spent more than seventy hours being interrogated by Mueller.

Shortly after, Cohen pleaded guilty to lying to Congress about an old Trump Organization business deal to build a tower in Moscow.

Of course, Mueller still had to keep up the appearance that he was focusing on his original mandate, so he did indict thirteen Russian nationals and entities on February 16, 2018 for identity theft, wire fraud, and making social media posts to influence voters. On July 13, 2019, Mueller indicted another twelve Russian intelligence officials for hacking the Democratic National Committee's servers and releasing its emails. Keep in mind, almost none of these charges will go anywhere. The likelihood that the Kremlin will extradite its own intelligence officers to the United States for trial is zero. These were symbolic acts designed to make it look like Mueller was accomplishing something.

With each new indictment or filing throughout the Mueller investigation, the radical Democratic Left, the deep state, and the media continuously congratulated themselves. This was a symptom of their denial over the 2016 election results. This denial was so powerful, it didn't even cease after Mueller released his report—which ultimately made no accusations that the Trump campaign had done anything illegal. For a few weeks after the report's release, the media and Democrats poured over it to see what innuendos they could tease out and spin into political barbs. The Democrats called Mueller in to testify before Congress—hoping that they could get him to say something to keep the dream of collusion alive. He disappointed them.

The Democrats finally lost steam when they realized Americans were tired of the charade. According to an Ipsos/Reuters survey completed in April 2019, only 15 percent of Americans said the Mueller findings had changed their minds about President Trump. In fact, 70 percent said Mueller's findings had no impact.[12] Having lived through this part of history, we now see how striking it is that this investigation took up so much money and energy, how profoundly vicious and hypocritical it was, and in the end how empty the results were.

The tremendous waste was made even clearer when we learned that the foundation of the entire investigation was based on a secret FBI spying operation on the Trump campaign (under Comey) and a bogus piece of opposition research (paid for by the Clinton-run DNC) that was intentionally misrepresented to the courts to continue the illegal spying on former Trump campaign staff. It turns out the FBI had used a phony dossier created by a former British intelligence officer, Christopher Steele, which alleged that President Trump had been involved in a host of salacious activities, as evidence to secure a warrant to spy on former Trump campaign staff. We now know that Steele's sources were almost all Russians whom he had communicated with remotely. Virtually everything was secondhand information that was impossible to verify. FBI agents knew it was flimsy, unverifiable intelligence (at best), but they still used the made-up dossier to trick the Foreign Intelligence Surveillance Act (FISA) court into granting their warrants to keep their illegal spying operation going.

Furthermore, we know that the dossier was paid for by the DNC, which was being run by the Clinton campaign. In other words, the Clintons hired a foreigner to collude with Russians to produce material to influence the 2016 election. Then a cadre of Clinton loyalists in the FBI used this material to allege that the Trump campaign was colluding with Russians to influence the 2016 election. You can't make this up.

A report by the Justice Department Inspector General Michael Horowitz was a critical piece of evidence that there was a real deep state effort to undermine the 2016 election. When the Horowitz report was first released, the Left grabbed on to the fact that Horowitz said starting the initial investigation wasn't inappropriate—citing a very low standard for starting an investigation. But the media and the Left completely ignored the hundreds of pages of the report showing that the FBI continued the investigation after it clearly lacked merit. As Jonathan Turley wrote for *The Hill*:

> This is akin to reviewing the Titanic and saying that the captain was not unreasonable in starting the voyage. The question is what occurred when the icebergs began appearing. Horowitz says that investigative icebergs appeared rather early on, and the Justice Department not only failed to report that to the Foreign Intelligence Surveillance Act court but removed evidence that its investigation was on a collision course with the facts.[13]

The entire Russia collusion narrative was an expression of deep state bureaucrats in our FBI and intelligence agencies who had decided they didn't like the person Americans had elected to be president, and so they were going to do all they could to destroy him. If you were close to Trump, they made your life hell for three years. It was among the most profound abuses of power in modern history—and it set the standard for how Congressional Democrats would operate going forward.

The Impeachment Scam

As the Mueller investigation failed to live up to Democrats' expectations, Speaker Pelosi was under enormous pressure from the radical wing of her party to impeach the president—for anything imaginable. The next opportunity that presented itself was a so-called whistleblower report claiming that President Trump was withholding $391 million in foreign aid to Ukraine unless the government there opened an investigation into a natural gas company that was paying Hunter Biden (the son of former Vice President Joe Biden) $60,000 a month for unclear services. The allegation centered on a telephone conversation between President Trump and Ukrainian President Zelensky. The supposed whistleblower (whose identity Democrats and the media have vigilantly kept anonymous) was not privy to this phone call. His or her allegations were entirely hearsay. Even President Zelensky publicly said there was no pressure from Trump to start an investigation. Yet the radical Democratic Left and the media took the claim as fact. Indeed, Speaker Pelosi announced an impeachment inquiry would begin before she had even read the whistleblower report.

There was a profound irony with this impeachment sham. The Ukrainian company in question, Burisma, had been under investigation before in Ukraine. However, this investigation ended after then–Vice President Biden threatened to withhold more than $1 billion in foreign aid to the country until the former Ukrainian president fired the prosecutor running the investigation. This allegation does not come out of an anonymous whistleblower report— Vice President Biden bragged about it himself to the Council on Foreign Relations on camera.

In his own words to the council, Biden told former Ukrainian president Petro Poroshenko and his aids, "I said, you're not getting the billion. I'm going to be leaving here in, I think it was about six hours. I looked at them and said: I'm leaving in six hours. If the prosecutor is not fired, you're not getting the money. Well, son of a bitch. He got fired. And they put in place someone who was solid at the time."[14]

So, similar to the Comey-Mueller witch hunt, the radical Left was alleging that President Trump used foreign aid to Ukraine to help his political interests while Biden freely admitted he used foreign aid to protect his son's financial interests. Democrats condemned President Trump and refused to say anything negative about Vice President Biden, who as of this writing is the apparent Democratic presidential nominee.

In addition to being based on complete hypocrisy, Pelosi's impeachment circus was entirely partisan and one-sided. Not a single Republican voted to begin the inquiry—and two Democrats joined with the Republican opposition in voting no.[15] At the start of the proceedings Representative Adam Schiff, who led the impeachment process for the Democrats, read a completely made-up transcript of the supposed call between Trump and Zelensky. It was a work of fiction intended to misrepresent the truth on the floor of Congress (Schiff described it as a parody). Schiff suffered no consequences for lying and proceeded to formulate an entirely biased inquiry. Schiff controlled every aspect of the circus. Republicans had to seek approval to bring witnesses, while Schiff could call anyone he wanted. Republican members were silenced when they asked questions Schiff did not want answered. And Republicans were completely left out of the rule-making process for the impeachment hearings.

If you compare the one-sided Schiff model to the two other impeachment proceedings in recent history, it's clear why Schiff's circus was such a failure. In 1973, during the impeachment process for President Nixon, Democratic Judiciary Committee chairman Peter Rodino set a gold standard for fairness. He worked to ensure that the process was serious, sober, and bipartisan. Rodino's process was open—to both the American people and the Republicans in Congress. He ensured that the House minority had a say in the rulemaking. And the impeachment hearings proceeded with the decorum and seriousness that the situation required. As a result, when the House voted to fund the investigation of President Nixon, the measure passed on a bipartisan vote of 367–51. When the House in February 1974 voted to conduct a formal investigation of Nixon and the Watergate scandal, it passed 410–4.

When we began the impeachment hearings of President Bill Clinton in 1998, we used the Rodino model. Republican

Congressman Jim Rogan actually visited with Rodino to get his advice on how to proceed. As a result, Democrats voted with us when moved forward with setting the procedures. When we voted to release the report by Special Counsel Ken Starr (which affirmatively alleged Clinton had committed eleven separate crimes) the measure passed 363–63, with 138 Democrats voting with Republicans.

By contrast, the impeachment hearings against President Trump were completely one-sided. Democrats paraded in a series of witnesses—none of whom had firsthand knowledge of the phone call in question. In fact, the US ambassador to Ukraine, Bill Taylor, acknowledged in his testimony that everything he knew about the Ukraine phone call came from the *New York Times*. Given the complete partisanship of the impeachment, it was no surprise that the Senate quickly voted to acquit President Trump—although Speaker Pelosi did all she could to delay a vote and keep the doomed impeachment story alive. In fact, the House Democrats knew that their impeachment effort would fall apart, yet it appears they were already working on a new effort before the Senate even voted. According to *Politico*:

In a filing to the D.C. Circuit Court of Appeals, House General Counsel Douglas Letter argued that the House's demands for grand jury materials connected to former special counsel Robert Mueller's investigation were still urgent because such evidence might become relevant to the Senate's expected impeachment trial next month.

But Letter went further to note that even apart from the Senate trial, the House Judiciary Committee intends to continue its impeachment investigation arising from the Mueller probe on its own merit.

"The committee has continued and will continue [its

impeachment] investigations consistent with its own prior statements respecting their importance and purposes," Letter wrote in a filing Monday as part of the House's bid to obtain Mueller's grand jury evidence.[16]

In other words, the Democrats have every intention of trying to throw President Trump out of office—no matter what voters decide in November 2020.

Real Abuse of Power

Perhaps the most dangerous thing about the radical Democratic Left's efforts to smear and attack President Trump is the complete erosion of prosecutorial standards. Both the Mueller investigation and the House impeachment hearings operated on standards that were closer to a Soviet police state system rather than an American rule of law system. In both cases, investigators approached their work with the model used by Joseph Stalin's secret police director, Lavrenty Beria: "Find me the man, and I'll find you a crime." Further, House Democrats and some in the FBI have failed utterly to live up to the standard of prosecution set out by former Associate Supreme Court Justice Robert H. Jackson (who served as chief prosecutor of the Nuremberg trials). Jackson cautioned the Conference of United States Attorneys on December 1, 1940:

With the law books filled with a great assortment of crimes, a prosecutor stands a fair chance of finding at least a technical violation of some act on the part of almost anyone. In such a case, it is not a question of discovering the commission of a crime and then looking for the man who has committed it, it is a question of picking the man and then searching the law books, or putting investigators to work, to pin some offense on him. It is in this realm, in which the prosecutor picks some person whom he dislikes or desires to embarrass or selects some group of unpopular persons and then looks for an offense, that the greatest danger of abuse of prosecuting power lies. It is here that law enforcement becomes personal, and the real crime becomes that of being unpopular with the predominant or governing group, being attached to the wrong political views, or being personally obnoxious to or in the way of the prosecutor himself.

This is exactly the pattern that the radical Democratic Left, the deep state, and the national media have followed since the moment Donald Trump became a candidate for president. They hate him. They want him gone. So, together they are working to ruin his presidency—no matter what the American people have to say about it, and no matter what damage it does to the American Constitution.

4.

★ ▬▬▬▬▬▬▬▬▬▬▬▬▬▬▬▬▬▬▬▬ ★

RADICAL DEMOCRATIC BIGOTRY

As the Democratic Left has become increasingly radical, its activists have relied on identity politics, political correctness, and simple insults to suppress legitimate dialogue. They dominate debates and define their opponents as, using Hillary Clinton's term, "a basket of deplorables," who are "racist, sexist, homophobic, xenophobic." Try discussing solutions to America's biggest challenges when you have been defined in those personally destructive terms.

Instead of debating rational, fair, compassionate immigration reform with Republicans, the radical Democratic Left simply says those who oppose open borders and free health care for people in the country illegally are racist. When President Trump announced in September 2019 that he wanted state governors and local officials to affirmatively tell the federal government if they would accept refugees in their states and localities, members of the Left called the policy—as well as Republicans who supported it—xenophobic.

When President Trump protects Americans from the coronavirus pandemic by banning flights from China, he is immediately attacked as racist and xenophobic—even though public health experts applaud his decision as saving American lives.

Those who support Israel's right to defend itself from suicide bombings and rocket attacks from pro-Palestinian terrorist cells are deemed Islamophobic by the radical Democratic Left. Those who support the Boycott, Divestment, and Sanctions movement (BDS) against Israel, such as Representatives Ilhan Omar, Rashida Tlaib, and presidential candidate Senator Bernie Sanders, simply think the Jewish state should be forced out of existence for its own alleged xenophobia. A similar attitude is taken toward anyone who believes that Iran should be heavily sanctioned and penalized for supporting a host of radical Islamic terrorist groups throughout the Middle East, Europe, and Africa.

If you question the fairness of allowing transgender female athletes (those born as men but who define themselves as women) to compete in women's sports, the radical Democratic Left says you are transphobic—despite legitimate, documented evidence of the physical advantages these athletes have over naturally born women. Similarly, if you are a parent who doesn't want your child taught the philosophy of gender fluidity in his or her fourth-grade public school classroom, the radical Democratic Left finds you equally backward and bigoted. If you are simply uncomfortable sharing a public bathroom with members of another gender, you are several varieties of "-phobic."

It has become the natural pattern of those on the left to immediately respond with accusations of bigotry in response to any viewpoint that questions the radical progressive line. Increasingly, there is an "-ist" or "-phobic" word that can be applied to virtually any idea or policy. Identity politics, political correctness—no matter what you call it—has become a tool of thought policing, intimidation, and totalitarianism. It is a cudgel the radical Democratic Left uses to silence enemies and keep its allies in line. Ironically, the Left's passion for designating so-called safe places and avoiding trigger words is the source for bullying and intimidating its opponents.

The most frustrating thing about this phenomenon is that allegations of bigotry by the Left are often textbook cases of ad hominem. Instead of defeating conservative (or even centrist) arguments, the radical Left's strategy is to defeat the messengers and attack their intentions and integrity. This strategy is particularly dangerous for our democracy, because the mainstream media and the academic world appear to be fully invested in supporting their ideological allies—never calling out the radical Left for undermining open debate.

Intolerant Tolerance

The frightening irony behind the Left's aggressive crusade against perceived bigotry is that it leads its members to become bigots themselves.

Vicious opposition to any idea or thought that is outside your worldview leads you to be close-minded, stubborn, and predisposed against anyone different from yourself. According to a recent study published in the *European Journal of Social Psychology*, ethnocentrism (or racism in layman's terms) is just one kind of bigotry. And people who are tolerant and accepting of people of other ethnic backgrounds are just as likely to prejudge or discriminate against others; they just use different qualifiers. In fact, many of the radical Democratic Left's members who protest and attempt to silence conservative speakers—or anyone they claim is racist, xenophobic, sexist, genderist, and so forth—are indulging the same part of human nature which fuels the behaviors they condemn.

According to the study, headed by Boris Bizumic of Australian National University, "We hypothesized that the ethnically tolerant (i.e., people who are anti-ethnocentric and score very low on a measure of ethnocentrism) would perceive people with extremely incompatible values and beliefs as out-groups and would engage in discrimination, prejudice and political intolerance against them."[1]

After four sets of tests involving 507 people in Australia, 265 people in the US, and another 522 people in the United Kingdom, the researchers found that, despite how woke one might be, people most often operate under the primal societal instinct to build in-groups and out-groups. Specifically, the Australian study "showed that the ethnically tolerant perceived supporters of a message in favour of mandatory detention of asylum seekers as out-groups and consequently exhibited discrimination, prejudice and political intolerance against them." Then, the tests in the US and UK "controlled for liberalism," and resulted in the same finding. In all, the test "showed that social identity, and not moral conviction, mediated the link between ethnic tolerance and prejudice. The findings suggest that the ethnically tolerant can be discriminatory, prejudiced and politically intolerant against fellow humans."[2]

Writing on the study, Tom Jacobs put it simpler for the *Pacific Standard*:

> If you're an actual racist, the outsiders you fear and dislike are members of a different ethnic group. But don't think that just because you're free of that particular bias, you are untouched by the unfortunate tendency to reduce individuals into arbitrary categories, and judge them accordingly. Non-racists, it turns out, can also be bigots. . . .
>
> In other words, people screaming "No to racists on campus" may think they're acting out of principle, when in fact they—like the people they are protesting—have simply identified an enemy, and condemned them out of hand.

> To be sure, calling out racism is important, especially in an era when hate crimes are on the rise. But angry

denunciation doesn't change anyone's mind; it just feels satisfyingly self-righteous. And reducing a person to their views on race (which were undoubtedly learned at a very young age) makes it impossible to forge the kind of connection that could lead to productive dialogue.[3]

Now, I am not calling all Democrats bigots—only the ones who relentlessly use ideology-fueled accusations of bigotry against everyone with whom they disagree. I'm also not minimizing bigotry as a problem—or saying that it is unique to the Left. The neo-Nazi and so-called alt-right groups that spewed hate and cruelty in Charlottesville, Virginia, in 2017 are a perfect example of bigotry on the right. However, I refuse to accept assertions that those few hundred people represent the more than sixty million Americans who elected President Trump in 2016—or the many millions more who are registered Republicans nationwide. There is, unfortunately, bigotry in every corner of the social-political spectrum.

However, I am warning that over the last few decades—with the rise of aggressive PC thought policing and destructive identity politics—the Left's movement has become more radical, ideologically isolationist, divisive, prone to blanket statements and stereotyping, and more bigoted. This is not the way to bridge any divides or restore a working order either in Washington or at the local bar. I am not alone here.

In December 2017, Peter Beinart wrote for *The Atlantic*— hardly a right-leaning publication—that if liberals wanted to truly reduce bigotry and improve race relations in America, they should stop reflexively crying "bigot" anytime they disagree with someone. In his piece "Republican Is Not a Synonym for Racist," Beinart warned that liberal "zeal" often backfires and encourages discrimination:

Sometimes, in their zeal to oppose bigotry, liberals defame entire groups. In an analysis of the 2012 election, a political scientist named David T. Smith noted that liberals were significantly more likely than conservatives to say they would not support a Mormon for public office. Why? Smith speculated that the Mormon Church's support for California's anti-gay-marriage initiative, along with Mitt Romney's presidential campaign, had "firmly entrenched a perception among liberals that Mormons . . . have an authoritarian religious agenda." That is, the liberal impulse to oppose discrimination had fostered a discrimination of its own.[4]

The radical Left's blind hatred of all things nonprogressive is more pervasive than you think. It has also led the movement toward reprehensible absurdity.

For example, in 2019, the Heritage Foundation's president, Kay Cole James, was appointed to Google's newly formed Advanced Technology External Advisory Council. It was an unpaid advisory board convened to investigate the ethics of artificial intelligence as the company continues to develop this technology. Google's leadership wanted James on the board, because it wanted a respected conservative opinion. I have known and worked with James for many years. She was perfect for the role.

However, in April of that year, about 2,500 of the famously liberal tech company's employees protested, signing a petition that demanded her removal. It is bad enough that the employees simply didn't want a conservative on the advisory board. But internal messages at Google showed that the hatred of James went much deeper.

In an office message board, one employee called James an "outspoken bigot." Another wrote, "You don't need racists, white supremacists, exterminationists on the board to know their stances. You can just talk to their targets." Yet another employee wrote, "It's so upsetting that some of our leaders overlooked such hateful positions as Kay Cole James and the Heritage Foundation have articulated and regularly advocate for."

When one employee attempted to defend James's placement on the board, suggesting it was snobbery to reject differing opinions out of hand, another quickly responded saying James and Heritage were "dedicated to eliminating LGBTQ+ people from public life" and "treating it like a difference of opinion is simply monstrous and I don't think it belongs on this list, or at Google at all."[5]

Now, those who know James can immediately recognize how vicious and absurd these attacks are. Those who don't know her should know that James is a remarkable, brilliant, seventy-year-old African American woman, who endured and persevered through intense bigotry as she integrated into white schools and literally lived through the civil rights era.

In her own words in the *Washington Post*, she "grew up fighting segregation":

> In 1961, at age 12, I was one of two-dozen black children who integrated an all-white junior high school in Richmond. White parents jeered me outside the school, and inside, their kids stuck me with pins, shoved me in the halls and pushed me down the stairs. So when the group of Google employees resorted to calling names and making false accusations because they didn't want a conservative voice advising the company, the hostility was reminiscent of what I felt back then—that same intolerance for someone who was different from them.[6]

Ultimately, instead of standing up to its mob-like employees, Google simply ditched the entire idea. In an announcement on its website, the company said, "It's become clear that in the current environment, ATEAC can't function as we wanted. So we're ending the council and going back to the drawing board." The company said it would instead find other ways to get outside input.[7] So, rather than impose some introspection in Silicon Valley, the company simply quit this important effort.

As James put it:

> I was deeply disappointed to see such a promising idea abandoned, but the episode was about much more than just one company's response to intolerance from the self-appointed guardians of tolerance.
>
> It was symptomatic of where America is heading. Whether in the streets or online, angry mobs that heckle and threaten are not trying to change hearts and win minds. They're trying to impose their will through intimidation. In too many corners of American life, there is no longer room for disagreement and civil discourse. Instead, it's agree or be destroyed.[8]

James's experience was terrible, but it also shows how damaging the PC-identity politics culture is to our county's founding principles.

Erasing the First Amendment

The national media and many on the left have sounded countless alarm bells over President Trump's hostility toward the press (although he is simply responding to their hostility toward him). They say his criticisms of journalists and particular news outlets are damaging to press freedom. Never mind that he is the most accessible president in my memory—and possibly modern history—and he has done nothing to prevent journalists from writing or reporting whatever they want.

As these so-called defenders of the First Amendment chase shadows over Trump's tough talk toward them, they are largely ignoring the impacts of the radical Democratic Left's efforts to police speech and thought—a much larger, more serious threat to our Constitution's First Amendment and our republic.

Consider the amendment in full:

Congress shall make no law respecting an establishment of religion, or prohibiting the free exercise thereof; or abridging the freedom of speech, or of the press; or the right of the people peaceably to assemble, and to petition the Government for a redress of grievances.

In each one of these clauses (freedom of religion, speech, and assembly) there are many examples of the Left seeking to undermine them.

It only takes a moment's Internet search to find countless examples of conservative speakers being shouted down or threatened into canceling events at colleges, universities, and public forums. The story about Kay Cole James is in this same vein. Further, I detailed a host of examples of the radical Left seeking to silence speech in my best-selling books *Understanding Trump* and *Trump's America.*

Similarly, it's easy to find clear-as-day examples of the radical Left trying to overwhelm or prevent legitimate conservatives from peaceable assembly. One needs only look to President Trump's inauguration to see a smattering of examples where anti-Trump protesters were barring people from entering the Mall grounds— or antifa rioters attacking and harassing people and destroying property downtown.

But here, I most want to focus on the radical Left's emerging persistent attack on peoples' freedom to practice religion. Of course, for decades, fringe members of the Left have sought to prohibit student-led prayer in schools, to cut religious iconography and ceremony out of public life, and to prevent public servants from acknowledging their faiths.

But today, these once fringe members make up a much larger portion of the American Left. In fact, they are part of the large force that's driving the Democratic Party—once pro-faith—in a much more radical, secular direction. Increasingly, these antireligious zealots are working to undermine the free practice of religion in every aspect of our culture and society.

For instance: In February 2019, more than twenty student groups at Yale Law School protested when the Yale Federalist Society scheduled a speech by Kristen Waggoner, an attorney at Alliance Defending Freedom. Waggoner had argued the case of *Masterpiece Cakeshop v. Colorado Civil Rights Commission* before the US Supreme Court.

This was the case of a cake shop owner who declined to make a wedding cake for a gay couple in Colorado after the high court ruled in favor of marriage equality for same sex couples. The cake shop owner said to do so would be an endorsement of homosexuality, which was against his personal religious beliefs. Waggoner argued on the cake shop owner's behalf, and the court ruled in her client's favor.

(Interestingly—and appropriate for this anecdote—the justices didn't rule as they did because it's OK for businesses to deny service to people based on their sexual orientation. The Supreme Court ruled in the cake shop's favor because the government commission was so aggressively hostile to religious views throughout its handling of the case.)

As part of the Yale students' protest, they sent a list of demands to the Yale administration. As Samuel Adkisson, a Yale Law School graduate and former Yale Federalist Society president, wrote for *USA Today*, the students wanted the administration to make it harder for students to work at religious freedom organizations which promoted "discrimination." They also asked that the administration simply deny applications from people who had previously worked at such organizations.[9]

In an amazing stroke of antireligious radicalism, Yale Law School actually went further via a new nondiscrimination policy from its Career Development Office, which assists students and employers with job recruitment before and after graduation. The new policy added "religion" and "religious creed" to a long list of typical characteristics which participating employers are prohibited from considering when recruiting. Employers who don't adhere to the rule cut their recruits off from a set of important financial aid programs at the law school. On its face, this seems normal. However, as Adkisson points out, it seriously and intentionally discriminates against religious students or young lawyers who want to work for religious groups.

According to Adkisson:

> Under the guise of nondiscrimination, Yale Law School has announced it will blatantly discriminate. A student is barred from aid if she works at a synagogue that gives preference to Jewish applicants, but not if she works at an organization that peddles anti-Semitism yet hires all comers. A graduate is blocked from funding if she works for the Christian Legal Society, but not if she works for the Freedom from Religion Foundation. And a graduate is not eligible to receive loan assistance if she is a professor at Brigham Young University, but is eligible if she works for Berkeley.[10]

It would be easy for Yale to say this was some oversight, but it hasn't. In fact, the policy is still on the school's website as I'm writing this in March 2020.[11]

As another example, there is perhaps no political debate in America that involves religion more seriously than abortion. Many who oppose abortion (myself included) do so out of deeply held religious beliefs. Many of us believe that human life begins at conception, that God is the ultimate creator of life, and to end such life is a sin against God and the innocent.

Until relatively recently, this has been true for religious people on all sides of the political spectrum. It was not long ago that many Democrats were pro-life. However, this is changing as the Left is becoming more radical. We saw a clear expression of this when former presidential candidate Pete Buttigieg told a pro-life Democrat there was no place in the party for someone who opposed abortion. In March 2020, one of the last antiabortion Democratic members of Congress, Dan Lipinski of Illinois, was defeated in the Democratic primary. The Left mobilized against him, and his opponent received support from all across the country.

Nevertheless, abortion is the law of the land. Allowing those who choose to do it does not infringe on our religious beliefs—except when it does. Using the tax dollars of pro-life Americans to fund abortions unwillingly puts us in the position of supporting something we believe is wrong. This is why the Hyde Amendment exists. Hyde is a rider Congress adds to the annual spending bills every year that prohibits federal funds from being spent on abortions (primarily through Medicare) except in cases of rape, incest, or when a mother's life is threatened. For many years, this amendment had wide bipartisan support. But not anymore. Remember, at the beginning of the 2020 Democratic presidential primary, former Vice President Joe Biden supported the amendment. Two days after he said so publicly, he changed his mind under massive pressure from the radical Democratic Left.

Further, the passage of the Affordable Care Act in 2010 included a provision known as Section 1557—which would force doctors and hospitals that receive federal funding to provide abortion services and sex-change operations to patients. This meant that virtually every Catholic hospital in the nation would suddenly have to start performing abortions—which the Catholic Church has always opposed.

Thankfully, under President Trump, the Department of Health and Human Services (HHS) is revising this provision to exclude the abortion and sex-change mandate (this comes after several federal courts found the original rule unlawful).

However, outside congressional politics, the radical Democratic Left's response to those who oppose abortion (on religious or basic moral grounds) is becoming nasty. In place of old debates about when life begins, when a fetus becomes viable outside the womb, or when it's reasonable to terminate a pregnancy that puts a woman's life in danger, the radical Democratic Left now absurdly argues that pro-life movements are a tool of white supremacy and are inherently racist.

In fact, the opening line of Alex DiBranco's February 3, 2020, piece for *The Nation* is simply: "The antiabortion movement in the United States has long been complicit with white supremacy."[12] (That's right. The belief that all human life is precious and needs protecting is an expression of pure hate, according to the Left.) In the article, the author spends 3,600 words describing a historical fiction in which antiabortion laws started in the mid-1800s as a reaction to Protestant fear of Catholic immigration to America— and stayed that way through the 1970s. After cherry-picking a few dubious factoids, the author makes the ultimate argument that racist Protestants invented antiabortion laws (they didn't); therefore, antiabortion laws must be racist (they aren't). It is pure baloney. But it's also the latest example of the radical Democratic Left, simply shouting "bigot" instead of engaging in dialogue.

This emphasis on attacking opponents and defining them as "deplorable," and therefore open to attack, went to a new intensity

RADICAL DEMOCRATIC BIGOTRY

when Democratic Senate Minority Leader Chuck Schumer stood before a pro-abortion rally in front of the Supreme Court and said, "I want to tell you, Gorsuch, I want to tell you, Kavanaugh, you have released the whirlwind, and you will pay the price. You won't know what hit you if you go forward with these awful decisions."[13]

When the highest-ranking Democrat in the US Senate starts threatening Supreme Court Justices—by name on the steps of the court, before a rally of fanatic pro-abortion activists—he should be held to account.

Schumer was the personification of the pattern Justice Kavanaugh had warned about during his Senate confirmation hearing when he said:

The Constitution gives the Senate an important role in the confirmation process. But you have replaced "advice and consent" with "search and destroy."

Since my nomination in July, there's been a frenzy on the left to come up with something, anything to block my confirmation. Shortly after I was nominated, the Democratic Senate leader said he would "oppose me with everything he's got." A Democratic senator on this committee publicly referred to me as evil. *Evil.* Think about that word. And said that those that supported me were "complicit and evil." Another Democratic senator on this committee said, "Judge Kavanaugh is your worst nightmare." A former head of the Democratic National Committee said, "Judge Kavanaugh will threaten the lives of millions of Americans for decades to come."

I understand the passions of the moment. But I would say to those senators: Your words have meaning. Millions of Americans listened carefully to you. Given comments like those, is it any surprise that people have been willing to do anything to make any physical threat against my family? To send any violent email to my wife, to make any kind of allegation against me, and against my friends, to blow me up and take me down.

You sowed the wind for decades to come. I fear that the whole country will reap the whirlwinds.[14]

The whirlwind of bigotry keeps growing on the left, and it is encouraged and enlarged by Democratic leaders like Schumer.

5.

★ ▬▬▬▬▬▬▬▬▬▬▬▬▬▬▬▬▬▬▬▬▬▬▬▬ ★

LOVING CRIMINALS, HATING THE LAW

One of the most dangerous trends of the radical Democratic Left is a pervasive desire (or ideological obligation) to vehemently protect people who break the law, contemptuously disregard the rights of law-abiding people, and actively hate those who work in law enforcement. When members of the radical Left talk about crime and punishment, they have a clear formula.

Today's radical Democratic Left insists that those who break laws are to be automatically regarded as victims of systemic flaws or intentional acts of oppression within our criminal justice system. Law-abiding citizens who begrudge people who break the law are heartless, privileged people who are simply too ignorant or self-absorbed to understand the plight of criminals. And police are all vicious, hateful agents of tyranny who are only trying to enforce the flawed system of oppression.

You see this pattern in the Left's arguments against enforcing federal immigration laws and protecting our borders, and you see this in the Left's response to crime in our most dangerous cities.

Sanctuary Cities

One of the most vivid, brazen expressions of the radical Democratic Left's willingness to sacrifice the public's safety to the ideological requirements of its version of justice is in sanctuary laws for people in the country illegally.

Depending on how you define "sanctuary" in this context, there are anywhere from a handful to more than a dozen sanctuary states, and roughly one hundred to five hundred sanctuary cities and counties. The numbers are disputed, because there is no federal legal definition, and some organizations count only jurisdictions with the most aggressively pro-criminal sanctuary laws. Further, there is plenty of overlap between localities that have adopted such laws that are already in sanctuary states. These laws range from simply banning local officers from inquiring about suspects' immigration statuses; to automatically declining requests from US Immigration and Customs Enforcement (ICE) to hold suspects so they can be turned over to federal officers; to actively barring ICE officers from entering local jails, police stations, or detention facilities.

According to the Center for Immigration Studies (CIS), as of February 5, 2020, there were 10 sanctuary states and 172 sanctuary cities or counties.[1] CIS defines a sanctuary jurisdiction as one that

> [has passed] laws, ordinances, regulations, resolutions, policies, or other practices that obstruct immigration enforcement and shield criminals from ICE—either by refusing to or prohibiting agencies from complying with ICE detainers, imposing unreasonable conditions on detainer acceptance, denying ICE access to interview incarcerated aliens, or otherwise impeding communication or information exchanges between their personnel and federal immigration officers.

Now, let me be clear: A great many of the people in the country illegally who benefit from these laws are otherwise law-abiding, peaceful people who are simply looking to make better lives for themselves and their families. Some of them are simply fleeing poverty or violence in their home countries, and our current immigration system is so broken, they make the choice to enter (or overstay their visas) illegally rather than face the horrors of their homes. In some cases, it can take years of paperwork, court appearances, and legal fees for good people to immigrate to America. At this point, the immigration court docket backlogs exceed one million cases, and the courts have no hope of keeping up with the number of people who want to legally come to our country. Congress must fix the immigration system to ultimately solve this problem.

However, there are other people in the country illegally who are not peaceful or law abiding—and they have caused irreparable harm to American lives and communities. I am talking about members of transnational criminal organizations, drug traffickers, and those who buy and sell human beings.

As President Trump pointed out in his State of the Union Address on February 4, 2020:

> Just 29 days ago, a criminal alien freed by the sanctuary city of New York was charged with the brutal rape and murder of a 92-year-old woman. The killer had been previously arrested for assault, but under New York's sanctuary policies, he was set free. If the city had honored ICE's detainer request, his victim would still be alive today.[2]

President Trump was referencing a heinous crime allegedly committed by Reeaz Khan, a 21-year-old Guyanese man who was in the country illegally. According to the *New York Times*, on November 27, 2019, police arrested Khan after he assaulted his father using a broken coffee cup as a weapon.[3]

On the day of his arrest, ICE sent a request to the New York Police Department asking that Khan be held for forty-eight hours so that ICE agents could take custody of him and begin the deportation process. Instead, because of New York's sanctuary policies, Khan was released. A little more than a month later, on January 10, 2020, Khan was arrested again—this time for rape and murder.

Maria Fuertes was beloved by her neighbors. The ninety-two-year-old had been collecting cans in her neighborhood before authorities say Khan attacked and raped her. He then reportedly strangled her and left her to die in the street in freezing weather. She was found and later died in the hospital from horrific injuries—including a broken back, broken ribs, and extensive bruising.

At first, authorities in New York claimed they did not receive the initial notice from ICE, but ICE promptly made their previously faxed request public. It was dated on November 27, 2019. To be clear, I do not blame the New York City Police Department in this; rather, I blame its political leadership. The police are simply being crippled—and the public endangered—by the radical, aggressively pro-criminal reign of Mayor Bill de Blasio.

In fact, according to Nolan Rappaport for *The Hill*, under de Blasio's rule, "The New York Police Department (NYPD) ignored every one of the 2,916 detainer requests it received from ICE in the 12 months ending June 30."[4] The director of ICE's New York field office, Thomas R. Decker, has been abundantly clear how dangerous and damaging the sanctuary policies are for public safety. In a January 13, 2020, ICE statement, he said:

> It is made clear that New York City's stance against honoring detainers is dangerously flawed. It was a deadly choice to release a man on an active ICE detainer back onto the streets after his first arrest included assault and weapon

charges, and he now faces new charges, including murder. New York City's sanctuary policies continue to threaten the safety of all residents of the five boroughs, as they repeatedly protect criminal aliens who show little regard for the laws of this nation. In New York City alone, hundreds of arrestees are released each month with pending charges and/or convictions to return back into the communities where they committed their crimes, instead of being transferred into the custody of ICE. Clearly the politicians care more about criminal illegal aliens than the citizens they are elected to serve and protect.

Unfortunately, this is just one story in one state. In his 2020 State of the Union Address, President Trump pointed out another appalling example on the West Coast of the country. In that case, a man in the country illegally—who had been arrested and released by police five previous times—went on a killing spree in December 2018. As President Trump said:

> Days [after his release], the criminal alien went on a gruesome spree of deadly violence. He viciously shot one man going about his daily work. He approached a woman sitting in her car and shot her in the arm and in the chest. He walked into a convenience store and wildly fired his weapon. He hijacked a truck and smashed into vehicles, critically injuring innocent victims. One of the victims . . . died—51-year-old American named Rocky Jones.
> Rocky was at a gas station when this vile criminal fired eight bullets at him from close range, murdering him in cold blood.

Here, the president was talking about Gustavo Garcia. He was released from jail in California on December 14, 2018. He had been arrested for being under the influence. In this case, too, ICE had requested that Garcia be detained because he was in the country illegally and had an extensive criminal history. In fact, he had reportedly been previously deported twice. However, California's sanctuary law blocked the request.

Three days later, Garcia began an eighteen-hour stretch of maniacal, random violence that spanned six cities outside of Fresno, California.[5] Garcia's rampage included multiple assaults, an armed robbery, at least two murders, a carjacking, a shootout with police, and a high-speed chase—which ended in a multicar wreck that claimed Garcia's life and injured others.

ICE officials later said Garcia's diabolical frenzy could have been avoided had the ICE detainer for his last arrest been honored. Tulare County Sheriff Mike Boudreaux, whose deputies engaged and pursued Garcia, agreed. According to the *Fresno Bee*, "Boudreaux said he is in agreement with ICE's statement and that local law enforcement is 'very frustrated' by how California's sanctuary state law (SB54) has affected their ability to keep communities safe."[6]

Boudreaux explained how, thanks to California's law, Garcia's ICE hold couldn't be honored without a warrant signed by a judge, because he was initially being held for a misdemeanor charge. The *Fresno Bee* reported that "before SB54, Boudreaux said his office would have been able to honor ICE's detainer request, even for a misdemeanor charge, and 'now that tool has been taken from us.'"

President Trump pointed out in his State of the Union that despite these destructive, pro-criminal sanctuary laws, ICE was still doing everything it could to capture and deport dangerous people in the country illegally.

"Last year, our brave ICE officers arrested more than 120,000 criminal aliens charged with nearly 10,000 burglaries, 5,000 sexual assaults, 45,000 violent assaults, and 2,000 murders," the president said.

Further, Senator Thom Tillis has sponsored a bill to allow the victims of crimes committed by those in the country illegally to sue so-called sanctuary jurisdictions for failing to protect the public and their loved ones. The Justice for Victims of Sanctuary Cities Act would force these radical politicians to think twice about continuing their dangerous, lawless policies. The bill clearly defines what a sanctuary jurisdiction is (as I mentioned earlier, this currently doesn't exist in law). It then establishes a legal avenue by which the victims of crimes committed by those in the country illegally can sue sanctuary jurisdictions for compensation. Importantly, the law protects victims and witnesses who may be in the country illegally but are assisting law enforcement with investigations. Finally, jurisdictions that ignore the lawsuits of victims under the law would forfeit certain federal grant funding. Along with Tillis, Senators Chuck Grassley, Lindsey Graham, Joni Ernst, Marsha Blackburn, and Ted Cruz are cosponsoring the bill.

In another very tough move, on January 7, 2020, the Department of Homeland Security announced it would bar New Yorkers from enrolling in the Global Entry and other programs that allow citizens to easily enter the United States. Acting Secretary of Homeland Security Chad Wolf cited New York's sanctuary policies for the decision—specifically, a law passed the previous year that allowed illegal immigrants to obtain driver's licenses, while barring ICE and US Customs and Border Patrol officers from seeing New York's licensing records.

Wolf said driver's license records are critical for ICE agents' ability to verify peoples' identities for the Global Entry program. "[Agents] are using personal data that they get from that database to look up an individual's date of birth, their photo, and they are using that as they build that case. . . . They can no longer do that because of what New York did," Wolf told Fox News.[7]

The sanctuary movement, which got its start in California in the mid-1980s but vastly expanded in recent years, is a perfect example of how the Left seeks to defend criminals while ignoring the public and attacking law enforcement.

Ignoring the Border

Setting sanctuary policies aside, the radical Democratic Left clearly favors criminals over law enforcement officers and law-abiding Americans when it comes to immigration as a whole. Just look at the Left's rabid opposition to President Trump's approach to immigration, which is to deter and stop *illegal* immigration while encouraging and welcoming *legal* immigration on a merit-based system. In other words, President Trump wants to restore law and order to a system that has lacked both for decades.

How anyone can oppose this simple, reasonable approach is remarkable. Yet the radical Democratic Left considers it deplorable. Indeed, Trump's opponents prefer anarchy over law and order. A Harvard Harris poll from 2018 found that 36 percent of Democrats support "basically open borders."[8] This figure will only increase as the Democratic Party becomes more radical.

Even if radical Democratic politicians and activists do not use the exact words "open borders," they advocate policies that amount to the same thing. Abolishing ICE, the federal agency responsible for enforcing America's immigration laws, is now a mainstream position on the left. Representative Alexandria Ocasio-Cortez popularized the movement to abolish ICE in 2018, before other progressive firebrands and potential Democratic presidential candidates such as Senators Elizabeth Warren and Bernie Sanders joined the cause. Soon, Senator Kirsten Gillibrand and New York City mayor de Blasio added their support. Indeed, a Morning Consult/*Politico* poll from 2019 found that a plurality of Democratic voters was more likely to support a presidential candidate who backs getting rid of ICE.[9]

The radical Democratic Left also wants to decriminalize illegal immigration, making illegal border crossing a civil offense, like jaywalking or failing to pay parking tickets. Virtually all Democratic presidential candidates—both so-called moderates and progressives—said as much during the 2020 campaign. And some went even further. Senator Cory Booker promised to "virtually eliminate immigration detention." Sanders vowed to put a "moratorium" on deportations. Warren said students who illegally overstay student visas should be able to stay in America indefinitely. Democrats across the political left also don't want anything to stop those seeking asylum from getting into the United States—despite even some of Trump's critics noting that the system is deeply flawed and overwhelmed with far too many pending cases.[10]

And don't forget Democrats' stated desire to give free health care to people in the country illegally—a plan that, according to the Center for Immigration Studies, could cost $23 billion a year.[11] Add Democratic proposals to grant citizenship to people here illegally, and it becomes clear how radical the Left truly has become. Simply put, they want to reward people for breaking the law.

Clearly, this amounts to lawlessness and anarchy at the border. Dangerous Latin American gangs and Mexican drug cartels would have free reign to increase the flow of drugs across the southern border, terrorizing and destroying American communities. The radical Democratic Left would also make it much easier for these same dangerous people to continue modern-day slavery and human trafficking.

More broadly, the policy of the radical Democratic Left toward immigration would erode any notion of American sovereignty. As President Trump has said, "A country without borders is not a country at all." This should not be a controversial statement, yet Trump's critics do somersaults to portray such sentiments as bigoted and anti-immigrant.

The radical Democratic Left's plan for immigration is a threat not only to national sovereignty, but also to national security.

The coronavirus pandemic, which is spreading across the United States and the world as I write this book, reminds us how dangerous it is to have so many undocumented people in America. There is no good way to monitor them without any documentation, posing an enormous risk for pandemics and, yes, terrorist attacks. No person would let total strangers, some of them violent criminals, freely enter his or her home. The security risk is obvious. Why does this principle not apply to our national home?

The Left's warped vision of immigration stems from a view that rejects assimilation in favor of multiculturalism. President Trump, his supporters, and many of our founding fathers supported the idea that immigrants must assimilate and become American. No matter how multiethnic the country becomes, Americans must maintain a common national identity. Indeed, the president wants to reunify the nation around a common set of values. The radical Democratic Left, however, views American exceptionalism as arrogant and America as systemically racist. America is not one nation, according to this argument; it is just a physical place where many ethnic, racial, and religious groups reside. This line of thinking doesn't lead to social justice or political correctness—it leads to a tribal system of factions vying for power that denigrates the power of the individual.

Given the above description, it only makes sense that the radical Democratic Left doesn't want to secure the southern border. To them, it's a hurdle in the way of mass illegal immigration. Even Democrats who say they want to secure the border rarely offer specific policies for how to do so.

Naturally, much of the discussion around border security focuses on a wall on the US-Mexico border. To the radical Democratic Left, the border wall is a symbol of President Trump's bigotry, a project that must never be realized. Most Americans understand that the idea of a wall along certain sections of the border to keep out illegal immigrants just makes sense. But the

Left's argument against the wall is not about protecting the American people. It stems from blind ideology under which those policing the border are the villains, and those trying to enter America illegally are the heroes.

The radical Democratic Left gets caught up with the wall. Border security entails so much more than a barrier. In addition, the United States can use technology, US Customs and Border Patrol agents, and other capabilities to police the border. Securing the border is ultimately meant to enforce federal laws that are on the books to keep the American people safe and help them economically. It should not be a matter for debate.

Of course, securing the border should be done humanely. The policy of separating immigrant families at the border was a fiasco in 2018. The media showed pictures of immigrant kids in cages andmothers crying for their children—the situation created terrible optics for an otherwise right-minded policy of deterring and stopping illegal immigration. The media largely ignored the fact that the practice started under President Barack Obama. President Trump got no credit when he signed an executive order to end the practice.

President Trump has also shown compassion and flexibility toward illegal immigrants. Under Speaker Nancy Pelosi, the Congressional Democrats would not agree to fund a border wall in exchange for protecting the Dreamers, immigrants who were brought to the United States illegally as children. This shows how radical and uncompromising the Left's position is. Democrats should have taken the deal. President Trump wants to be fair to Dreamers, who came here through no fault of their own. If the radical Left wasn't so set against enforcing federal immigration laws, perhaps the Dreamers could be living here without fear of deportation.

The public debate over immigration between Trump and the radical Democratic Left shows a divide between those who want law and order, social cohesion, and strong national security, and those who want a form of anarchy, multiculturalism, and a false sense of justice. Indeed, to the radical Left, justice is not about following the law, or ensuring people have equal protection under it. Instead, justice is about political correctness and ignoring the law.

Simply put, when it comes to immigration, Democrats are sacrificing the public's safety at the ideological altar of social justice and political correctness—a world without borders in which America is weakened.

Prosecutors Undermining Justice, Weakening the Police, and Endangering the Public

Another way that the radical Left works to protect criminals is by simply ensuring that they face no consequences for their actions. Across the country, an increasing number of radical prosecutors are seeking to undermine our justice system at the local level.

In early January, Supreme Court justice Sonia Sotomayor sent her congratulations, praise, and well wishes to a newly elected local public officer upon his swearing in.[12] While it is highly unusual—although not automatically inappropriate—for a member of America's high court to weigh in on the merits of a politician, Sotomayor's support was deeply concerning. The Obama-appointed judge was not heaping praise on an old classmate or family friend, but to a deeply committed radical who is seeking to eliminate the American justice system as we know it.

Justice Sotomayor was congratulating Chesa Boudin, whom the voters of San Francisco elected last November to be the city's chief prosecutor. Boudin is not a typical prosecutor—or even a typical left-leaning one.[13] He is a former advisor to the Venezuelan dictator Hugo Chávez. He's also the foster child of domestic terrorists and Weather Underground leaders Bill Ayers and Bernardine Dohrn. Boudin's birth parents were imprisoned in 1981 after they helped orchestrate the robbery of a Brinks truck—during which its security guard and two police officers were murdered. His father is still in jail.[14]

Boudin has sought to minimize his parents' crimes and those of the Weather Underground. These crimes include domestic bombings and violence against both police and civilians.[15] [16] He also downplays a host of other criminal acts that ruin communities and neighborhoods across the nation. Yet District Attorney Boudin describes the state incarcerating criminals as "an act of violence in and of itself," saying prison should only be used as a last possible resort for especially dangerous people—although it's unclear what his definition of "dangerous" really is.[17] He says the justice system should easily forgive, or even overlook, a large number of crimes that he refers to as "quality-of-life crimes."

Now, for years, I have worked with Democrats and Republicans to end senseless incarceration of those who are addicted to drugs or struggling with mental health issues (so that they can get real help and become productive, law-abiding citizens). But Boudin is talking about deferring prison for a much wider collection of offenses.

As district attorney, he has said he's simply not going to prosecute people for public urination, seeking or offering prostitution, using drugs (in public or otherwise), or a host of other offenses. He also plans to largely make theft a civil issue. That's right, despite what laws elected local and state legislators in California have put in place, Boudin believes the "district attorney can challenge the legitimacy of laws by declining to bring charges in certain cases."[18] This is to say that Boudin believes the district attorney can play the role of executive, legislator, and judiciary in San Francisco. In effect he would replace the rule of law with the rule of Boudin. This kind of one-man tyranny is the exact opposite of the rule of law on which the founding fathers had insisted. As my former colleague Sean Kennedy and I have pointed out before, this is precisely the flawed logic courts and prosecutors used to delegitimize and essentially condone crimes against African Americans prior to the Civil Rights Act.[19]

Within two days of Boudin assuming office, he fired seven veteran prosecutors who were leading some of the city's most serious investigations. By firing these attorneys, Boudin was throwing away decades of institutional knowledge about the city's gang and drug activities, violent actors, and hundreds of ongoing cases. The prosecutors were largely fired because he viewed them as being too tough on criminals. As a former San Francisco Assistant District Attorney Kimberly Guilfoyle wrote in the *San Francisco Chronicle*, "this isn't just a typical case of administrative shake-up. Rather, it is a dangerous and disruptive move that does a grave disservice to victims and the community."[20] To replace the manpower, Boudin hired his former colleagues at the public defenders' office and other like-minded defense attorneys.[21]

It may not seem surprising that San Franciscans elected a former socialist dictator's aide as their chief law enforcement officer, but Boudin isn't alone. He is part of a much larger pattern happening across the country in which liberal megadonors such as George Soros are pouring money into small, local elections to get radical district attorneys installed nationwide.

In dozens of local district attorney elections across America, Soros and his associates have dumped millions into normally low-dollar, local races.[22] Many of these local prosecutors have also vowed to ignore crimes such as public urination, drug use, public camping, thefts, vandalism, littering, and prostitution. The results have only made these cities and localities more dangerous.

For example, Philadelphia district attorney Larry Krasner took office in 2018 after Soros and his various organizations spent $1.7 million helping Krasner's campaign.[23] Before becoming the top prosecutor, Krasner was well known as a defense attorney who sued the Philadelphia Police Department seventy-five times. For years, he has called American criminal justice systematically

racist, and at his victory party for his primary election, his supporters chanted, "F—— the FOP [Fraternal Order of Police]." In
keeping with his campaign promises, Krasner has refused to prosecute certain crimes involving guns and drugs—and instructed his
subordinates to seek lighter sentences overall.[24]

The result: anarchy in the City of Brotherly Love.

Largely thanks to Krasner's reforms, a profound disrespect
for law enforcement and disregard for the law has proliferated. Six
police officers were shot at by a man during a standoff last summer. Before the situation escalated—while the officers were trying
to serve the man with a warrant—local bystanders threw things
at them.[25]

Pennsylvania US attorney William McSwain described the
tragic event vividly:

> What I witnessed last night was true heroism by the Phila-
> delphia police. But the crisis was precipitated by a stunning
> disrespect for law enforcement—a disrespect so flagrant
> and so reckless that the suspect immediately opened fire
> on every single officer within shooting distance. Only by
> the grace of God did they survive.
>
> Where does such disrespect come from?
>
> There is a new culture of disrespect for law enforce-
> ment in this city that is promoted and championed by Dis-
> trict Attorney Larry Krasner—and I am fed up with it.[26]

As Jennifer Stefano wrote for the *Wall Street Journal*, in a
recent case overseen by Krasner, the defendant, Michael White,
admitted to police and to the jury in court that he killed a man
named Sean Schellenger by knifing him several times in the
back. White then ran from the scene and attempted to hide the
murder weapon. White was ultimately acquitted after Krasner's
office downgraded his primary charge from first-degree murder

to third-degree murder, then finally to voluntary manslaughter before the jury rendered a verdict.[27]

Overall, violent crime in Philadelphia has increased under Krasner.[28] Murders have specifically increased by 13 percent since he was sworn in (they were already at a ten-year high when he took office). Gun violence is up 18 percent.[29] At the same time, Krasner has filed 16 percent fewer felony charges than his predecessor.[30] So, more felonies are being committed in Philadelphia, yet Krasner is pursuing fewer felony convictions. Instead, he is focusing on pet projects. He is working to get a new trial for Mumia Abu-Jamal, who was convicted of killing a police officer. Krasner's deputy prosecutor, Paul George, is Jamal's former defense attorney and Krasner's old law partner.[31]

Again, this kind of thing is happening all over the country in places where the radical Left is entrenching itself. In Dallas, Texas, District Attorney John Creuzot took office in January 2019. According to the *Dallas Morning News*, in April 2019, Creuzot announced he would simply not charge anyone for drug offenses or theft of items worth less than $750.[32] That's right: contrary to state and local laws, Creuzot essentially decriminalized theft. Naturally, both violent and nonviolent crime spiked. The state's largest police union called for his removal from office. Texas governor Greg Abbott had to send state troopers to return order to parts of the city—which caused violent crime to drop 24 percent in short order.[33]

Suffolk County, Massachusetts District Attorney Rachael Rollins declined to prosecute antifa protesters who were arrested for allegedly attacking police in Boston. Further, Rollins has posted a list of violations her office will by default reject—except when a supervisor specifically signs off.

According to her own website, these so-called charges to be declined include:

Trespassing

Shoplifting (including offenses that are essentially shoplifting but charged as larceny)

Larceny under $250

Disorderly conduct

Disturbing the peace

Receiving stolen property

Minor driving offenses, including operating with a suspended or revoked license

Breaking and entering—where it is into a vacant property or where it is for the purpose of sleeping or seeking refuge from the cold and there is no actual damage to property

Wanton or malicious destruction of property

Threats—excluding domestic violence

Minor in possession of alcohol

Drug possession

Drug possession with intent to distribute

A stand-alone resisting-arrest charge, i.e. cases where a person is charged with resisting arrest and that is the only charge. A resisting arrest charge combined with only charges that all fall under the list of charges to decline to prosecute, e.g. resisting arrest charge combined only with a trespassing charge.[34]

Can you imagine living in a community where these crimes are simply ignored—or treated as minor civil violations?

In Baltimore, which has the highest murder rate nationwide, District Attorney Marilyn Mosby has further eroded public trust and safety by alleging—without offering evidence—that "hundreds" of Baltimore police have so-called credibility issues ranging from a willingness to plant drugs and guns on suspects to sleeping while on duty.

The Soros machine is even knocking out Democrats who aren't deemed pure enough. Soros-funded groups backed George Gascón to be the Los Angeles County district attorney. Gascón was seeking to unseat Democrat Jackie Lacey, who is the first African American and first woman to hold the office. Gascón even resigned as the district attorney in San Francisco to oust Lacey— who, incidentally, had the support of Gascón's former colleagues in San Francisco.[35]

While he was in San Francisco (following now Senator Kamala Harris and preceding Boudin as top prosecutor) Gascón presided over a massive rise in property crimes—and a comparably low number of arrests.[36] According to the Los Angeles Association of Assistant District Attorneys, "Gascón's approach to theft crimes is a driving force behind the high crime rate. On streets where the boundary line was between San Francisco County and San Mateo County, thieves would commit car burglaries on the San Francisco side of the border because they would face less punishment."[37] As of this writing, it appears Lacey captured only 49.25 percent of the vote in the 2020 primary. Gascón came in second place, with 27.9 percent of the vote. A third candidate, Rachel Rossi, earned 22.78 percent. This means that a runoff election against Gascón is likely for Lacey in November.[38]

Having said all this, I must note that there is clear merit in analyzing laws and revising the penalties for breaking them. Sometimes, when legislators write laws, they make mistakes— or discover unintended consequences and second-order effects that develop from the laws. I have personally seen this in federal laws that created a vast disparity in federal sentencing for possession of powder cocaine versus crack cocaine. This mistake imposed a huge, unfair toll on many African American communities. We eventually fixed this problem through the legal democratic process. However, it isn't the job of the police or prosecutor to determine when laws are flawed, or to effectively change them through selective enforcement.

The No-Bail Movement

Yet another way that the radical Democratic Left is trying to destroy the American criminal justice system is through a rising movement to eliminate the bail system in America.

First, the bail system is not perfect. In virtually every community in the country, Americans accused of minor offenses—citizens are supposed to be presumed innocent until proven guilty—are jailed for indefinite amounts of time before trial simply because they cannot afford to pay high bail costs. Meanwhile, some Americans who are accused of serious crimes can await their trials in relative freedom because they have the money to do so. This is a system that clearly needs to be fixed—although states should work to fix it rather than Washington.

However, the Left's solution has been to lead a crusade to end pretrial detention altogether. A recently passed New York law has severely curtailed the number of offenses in which judges can impose cash bail. In fact, more than four hundred offenses are no longer eligible for bail in the state of New York. Proponents of the law claim these are only nonviolent offenses—yet manslaughter and assault are counted among them. Citing prosecutorial memos, the *New York Post* wrote, "[The] offenses include most misdemeanors and even some felonies, running the gamut from criminally negligent homicide to peddling drugs on or near school grounds."[39] The law also prevents judges from imposing bail on these charges, regardless of a defendant's criminal history.

Courts in New York began using the new law even before it was officially enacted in January 2020. Almost immediately, you began to see the results—about which many Republicans in the state had warned.

Thirty-year-old Tiffany Harris was arrested on December 27, 2019, after she reportedly slapped three Orthodox Jewish women in Brooklyn. That was a Friday. She was released on Saturday without bail (according to the new law), and then rearrested on Sunday for allegedly punching another woman in Brooklyn. She was again released without bail on Monday—then promptly arrested Tuesday for not appearing in court.[40] In addition to the victims she reportedly assaulted, think of how much time and effort police had to spend repeatedly apprehending Harris. Then also think about how much time and effort the court system had to spend accommodating lawlessness. As the *New York Post* noted, by Wednesday, Harris had generated multiple different arraignment hearings on the docket. These could have been avoided if she had been made to pay a bail after the first arrest (where she attacked three people), or at least been held with bail after the second time she assaulted someone. But the Harris example was just the beginning.

In another New York case, Farkell Hopkins was arrested on New Year's Eve, after he reportedly hit and killed a pedestrian while driving drunk. Hopkins was also released without bail thanks to New York's new law (vehicular manslaughter is also not eligible for bail).

In Long Island, twenty-two-year-old Gerard Conway allegedly burglarized four businesses on December 29, 2019—breaking in through windows and stealing cash registers. He was arrested and released the following day, because third-degree burglary is no longer eligible for pretrial detention or bail under New York's new law. On New Year's Day—shortly after the first alleged burglary spree—he was arrested again for smashing his way into a bagel store and stealing cash registers.

Finally, Paul Barbaritano, fifty-two, was arrested in July 2019 after police found him in an apartment in Albany with reportedly self-inflicted stab wounds. Also in the apartment was the body

of twenty-nine-year-old Nicole Jennings, who had been strangled with a belt and stabbed in the neck. Barbaritano was charged
with manslaughter and held without bail.[41] However, on January
2, 2020, Barbaritano was released under the new bail law (he was
charged with manslaughter rather than murder, so he could no
longer be kept in pretrial detention).[42] The Albany Police Officers
Union responded to the release by saying, "Today New York leaders failed to protect you. . . . This man is alleged to have killed
another human and he is now free, he is walking the same streets
as you and your family members."

Having read those short examples, how would you feel if you
were one of the four women Harris allegedly assaulted? How would
you feel if one of your loved ones had been the pedestrian killed on
New Year's Eve? What if it was your business that got violated by
a serial burglar whom police weren't allowed to keep in jail? What
if it was your daughter who was strangled and stabbed to death?

As I said before, the bail system needs work. But the radical Democratic Left's solution of simply neutering judges and
law enforcement by outlawing pretrial detention or appropriate
bail for hundreds of crimes is not the answer. It is a great benefit for people who commit crimes, but it does nothing to protect
or defend the victims of crimes. Furthermore, it hinders, under-
mines, and endangers the hardworking law enforcement officers
who are trying to keep us safe and uphold the law.

What Actually Works

The strange irony is the radical Democratic Left's approach to
curbing crime is exactly the opposite of what we know works. All
these bad policies aim at letting supposedly minor infractions go
while focusing on major crimes and offenses—or downplaying
things like manslaughter to free up resources. But the more
seemingly small things you let slide, the more lawless communities
feel—and the more major crimes ultimately get committed. This is

the thesis behind the "broken windows"—CompStat policing that turned New York City around under former mayor Rudy Giuliani and Police Commissioner Bill Bratton.

Given former mayor Mike Bloomberg's perversion of CompStat into an aggressive stop-and-frisk system, it is important to draw a sharp distinction. "Broken windows" is *not* stop-and-frisk. Many procriminal advocates like to combine the two to minimize the success of the Giuliani-Bratton system. The truth is, Giuliani had tremendous success and helped make New York remarkably safer. When Giuliani left office, Bloomberg (yes, the one who spent millions to fail at running for president) took the Giuliani-Bratton model—in a likely attempt to put his brand on something—and perverted it into an aggressive system of pseudo-predictive policing. It resulted in massive prejudice, bias, racial profiling—and a tremendous mistrust of police.

"Broken windows" was not about randomly stopping people who lived in high-crime neighborhoods and shaking them down. It was about increasing vigilance on small, everyday offenses—graffiti, littering, public drug use, and so forth. Police didn't focus on trying to predict when these crimes would happen and actively prevent them. They were instead simply determined to observe them when they happened—and to ensure that the offenders knew they had been caught.

This creates two positive outcomes. First, crime is simply less likely to happen in places where people feel a solid sense of order (where potential criminals are certain they will be caught if they break the law). It also puts police in lawful contact with potential fugitives or other suspects in serious crimes. In fact, the first place that Bratton tested the model was in the New York City subway. At the time, the subway had become a refuge for both petty and serious criminals. This was before Giuliani became mayor, when Bratton led the Metropolitan Transit Authority Police. Giuliani later elevated Bratton to police commissioner when he became mayor in 1994.

As NPR reported in an interview with George L. Kelling, one of the criminologists who developed the academic theory behind "broken windows":

> [Bratton] focused first on cleaning up the subway system, where 250,000 people a day weren't paying their fare. They sent hundreds of police officers into the subways to crack down on turnstile jumpers and vandals.
>
> Very quickly, they found confirmation for their theory. Going after petty crime led the police to violent criminals, says Kelling: "Not all fare beaters were criminals, but a lot of criminals were fare beaters. It turns out serious criminals are pretty busy. They commit minor offenses as well as major offenses."[43]

In fact, according to the National Bureau of Economic Research, "During the 1990s, crime rates in New York City dropped dramatically, even more than in the United States as a whole. Violent crime declined by more than 56 percent in the City, compared to about 28 percent in the nation as a whole. Property crimes tumbled by about 65 percent, but fell only 26 percent nationally."

If we are serious about stopping crime in our major cities, investing in and sustaining a fair, rational immigration system, and making sure that our neighborhoods remain safe, we must prioritize our justice system to protecting law-abiding citizens, supporting police, and deterring criminals.

The radical Democratic Left's path leads only to emboldened criminals, more victims, fewer police, and anarchy.

6.

★ ═══════════════════════════════════════ ★

THE RADICAL 200

The real House Democratic Party is far more radical than the liberal media version.

The liberal media is desperate to keep Nancy Pelosi as Speaker. They know that means they must protect the House Democrats who were elected in 2018 in seats Trump carried in 2016—or in seats that were close and might flip in 2020 with a strong reelection campaign.

So, the liberal media has created a false narrative in which there is a small radical wing, personified by Representative Alexandra Ocasio-Cortez and the squad, and a larger, supposedly centrist wing, composed of all the marginal incumbents. This is designed to allow the marginal members to run campaigns claiming, "We aren't those radical left-wingers." This is a technique Democrats have been using since the nomination of radical Senator George McGovern in 1972. Back then, there was some truth to the claim. Southern and midwestern Democrats voted much more conservatively than their liberal wing.

However, today this "I'm not like my radical party" claim is simply not true. This is another example of fake news. There is no significant number of House Democrats who exist in a moderate wing. When you examine the records for voting, cosponsorships, and resolutions, it is striking how radical virtually the entire House Democratic Party is.

In fact, there are two-hundred-plus radical Democrats serving with Speaker Pelosi, AOC, and the squad. There is a solid radical core among the House Democrats that includes more than two hundred members. For perspective, that's 200 out of 232 total House Democrats. Consider how the media describes the entire House Republican membership (197 members) with mention of the Freedom Caucus (about thirty members). For brevity, I am only picking more than a dozen examples of genuine radicalism that had 200 or more Democrats behind them. There are other examples at the website www.trumpandtheamericanfuture.com, and I will be adding more after the book goes to print so the website will be updated to reflect the continuing radicalism of the House Democrats.

The truth is, for virtually every House Democrat, you could make a poster labeled "They are all the same," that had Speaker Pelosi on one side, AOC on the other, and the local Democrat in the middle. The record would prove this time after time. There is no moderate House Democratic Party: there are only the radicals and a tiny remnant of the nonradicals.

This drift toward the left fits with the entire pattern of the modern Democratic Party. On March 7, 2020, Myra Miller and Dave Winston of the Winston Group wrote, "A majority of Democratic voters are now self-identifying as liberal (51 percent) over moderate (38 percent)—a stark contrast to the composition of the party when Democrats won the majority in 2006 in which the party was more moderate (51 percent) than liberal (38 percent). Ever since then, the Democratic Party's steady trajectory toward identifying as liberal over moderate has not changed."[1]

So, the House Democratic Party is simply following the same movement to the left as self-identified Democrats in general.

The Militant Pressure Campaign

In a legislative body, there are three ways for an activist base to coerce other members to conform with activist policies and language if they disagree: Internal pressure, including committee assignments, favors, and social patterns; the threat of a primary from the activist side of the party; and dominating the language of the general movement, which defines the party.

First, internal pressure. Majorities have substantial power to reward or punish members with everything from committee assignments, the ability to travel on congressional delegations, the ability to get bills or amendments made in order on the floor, the ability to raise money from a national network, and a host of other advantages or disadvantages.

When I was a junior member of Congress, President Ronald Reagan was advocating a series of policies that were splitting the House Democrats. For example, the big Reagan tax cut of 1981 attracted ninety Democrats to abandon their liberal leadership and side with President Reagan. Liberals and their leadership decided they would grind down the conservative Democrats, who were called the Blue Dogs. After a few years, one of the conservative Democrats came to me on the House floor and said he wanted to switch parties. He was sick and tired of the liberals attacking him over every vote and constantly threatening to take away his committee assignment. Then, Texas Congressman Phil Gramm got so fed up with liberal pressure, he resigned from his seat and successfully ran as a Republican to fill his own seat in a special election. Over a decade or so, the number of conservative Democrats shrank, and their replacements found it much easier and rewarding to vote with the liberals.

Second, the threat of a primary from the activist wing of the party. Often, members are moved more by the threat of a primary than by the challenge of the general election. At one point in the late 1980s, Jack Kemp and I were advocating sweat equity for public housing residents. We were fascinated by the reforms of British prime minister Margaret Thatcher, which had turned about 40 percent of British public housing into privately owned properties, so their owners developed a real interest in property—and in sound policies.

We were in the middle of a heated debate on the floor, with liberals attacking the idea of the poor being able to earn their apartment through sweat equity. As one liberal put it, without recognizing the irony, in New York a sweat equity program would turn poor people into millionaires and then they wouldn't be poor anymore. I was standing on the back rail amazed at this turn of the debate, and a senior Democrat from an inner-city district turned to me and said (I'm paraphrasing from memory), "You know, there is a lot of merit to Kemp's idea."

"Well, then," I suggested, "why don't you vote yes. You are senior enough you might bring a lot of Democrats with you."

He looked at me quizzically and said, "Let me explain my district. I will never have a general election opponent who matters. My district is totally safe in a general election. However, if I vote with Kemp, I will anger the public employees' union that represents public housing workers. They will field a candidate against me just to teach me not to vote with the Republicans. I will have to raise $500,000 [today it would be $5,000,000] and then spend four months campaigning. I will win, but it will have messed up my life. Right now, I plan to be on the beach in the Bahamas for the summer. I have to ask myself if this vote is worth that much work in a hot summer campaign on my neighborhood pavements, and the answer is no."

The recent vote for impeachment in the House was, in part, a byproduct of this kind of primary threat. A lot of marginal Democrats, who knew their districts were not happy with impeachment, also knew that the money and activist energy in the Democratic Party is all on the left. Voting against impeachment would guarantee primary fights.

In 2020, Congressman Dan Lipinski was defeated in a Chicago primary, because he was one of the few pro-life Democrats left in office. His father, Bill Lipinski (whom I served with) had held the seat from 1983 to 2005. Dan had succeeded him and held the seat for fourteen years. They both represented an old-fashioned, Polish, Catholic, right-to-life belief. In 2018, Lipinski narrowly defeated his liberal challenger. In 2020, she beat him 48 percent to 46 percent. Left-wing activists and donors from across the country wanted to defeat Lipinski. There was no room for dissent in the House Democratic caucus.

The Democratic presidential debates have made clear how radical the Democratic Party is becoming. It is that unity on the left that compels even swing district members to vote much more radically than their constituency would want.

Additionally, the language dominance of the general movement, which defines their party, further pressures members to move to the left.

Elected officials exist within the intellectual and linguistic framework of their parties. When I first started running for office, Republicans were generally against tax cuts. In fact, they had vigorously opposed President John F. Kennedy's 1963 tax cuts. However, in the mid-1970s, an energetic young Republican congressman named Jack Kemp began advocating tax cuts to create jobs and spur economic growth. At first, he was almost alone. Then he convinced a presidential candidate, Ronald Reagan, to be in favor of a dramatic tax cut program to get the economy growing.

Even with President Reagan's strong commitment, there were still a number of skeptical Republicans. The Republican leader Howard Baker said, "It is a riverboat gamble." The economic growth under Reagan began to convince the GOP that we were the tax-cutting party. We had the largest capital gains tax cut in history in the Contract with America. No successful Republican national leader has been for tax increases—or against tax cuts—in the last forty years.

Similarly, the rise of identity politics, the growth of the unrestricted abortion movement, the gun control movement, the support for illegal immigration, the increasing hostility toward police in favor of criminals, the need to attack the successful and call for redistributionist tax increases, the requirement to be for radical policies on climate change—all these patterns are now baked into the Democratic Party. It is a rare elected Democrat who can disagree with many of them and survive politically.

The intensity of the Left's hatred for Trump has combined with the increasingly totalitarian pressure on campuses and in newsrooms to create an environment in which it would take an extraordinarily courageous House Democrat to deviate from the party line. As I have mentioned, Theodore White's observation that liberal ideology turned into a liberal theology explains the intensity of belief on the left. It has hardened into an almost religious requirement for uniformity. Now, forty-eight years later, the liberal theology has grown more radical and extreme in its willingness to impose its views on every American. This intensity has a huge effect on incumbent House Democrats, who are bombarded by the news media, left-wing activists, and their colleagues in the House. Remember: their staff members (who draft much of the legislation) are subjected to the same pressure and bombardment to tow the party line.

The Winston Group paper I mentioned earlier, which is titled "Biden and the Moderate Lane," captured the dramatic rise of liberalism as the core value of the Democratic Party. The paper reports that Democrats have shifted 13 percentage points toward the left (one out of every four moderate Democrats switched from moderate to liberal). This was driven by the dominance of the activist left, the language of President Barack Obama and his team, and the reaction to President Donald Trump. It is in this rising tide of liberalism among Democrats that the shift toward radicalism among House Democrats can be best understood.

The Proof

Ihavechosensomekeyexamplestoshowtheradicalismandsolidarity of the House Democratic Party. There are many other examples, which can be found at www.trumpandtheamericanfuture.com. However, for this section, twelve radical votes or cosponsorships should be enough to make the case that more than 200 of the 232 Democrats in the US House of Representatives are truly radical.

I first got intrigued with this idea of a monolithic left-wing House Democratic Party when I noticed a roll call vote on May 17, 2019. At that time, 227 Democrats voted against protecting women's sports under Title IX in favor of opening up women's events to transgender women (those born as men who define themselves as women). Only one Democrat voted against weakening Title IX. Given how important Title IX and the development of women's athletics has been, I thought this was a dramatic change worth studying.

Then I ran across a bill that 208 House Democrats (including AOC and the squad) had cosponsored. It was HR 860—a bill that included a nearly 20 percent increase in the Social Security Tax. Under this bill, people with a $50,000 annual salary would pay $1,200 more a year in FICA taxes. The average American would pay $8,400 a year in Social Security and Medicare taxes combined. I wondered how the average Democrat could go home and defend a 20 percent increase in the Social Security tax. It would hit low- and middle-income workers especially hard.

These two examples convinced me there was a herd mentality building in the House Democratic Caucus that was going to lead them over a left-wing cliff. As I began examining key votes, the evidence grew and grew. Here is a select list of tough-to-defend-or-explain votes. Even more will be available at the website I have mentioned.

On November 15, 2019, House Democrats voted to allow the Export-Import Bank to subsidize Chinese Communist Party–owned state companies, even if they were subverting United States foreign policy, were a national security risk, and were undermining American economic strength. Roll Call Vote 623 shows 217 out of 232 House Democrats voting to permit subsidy of the Chinese Communist systems.

On May 5, 2019, House Democrats voted to implement the Paris climate accord—even if it would outsource American jobs to China. Roll Call Vote 183 had 213 Democrats voting for Chinese jobs over American jobs.

On February 8, 2019, House Democrats voted to allow the Veterans Administration to pay for childcare workers who had been charged with sexual offenses, offenses against a child, a drug felony, or a violent crime. Look up Roll Call Vote 74. It shows 213 Democrats voting to put children at risk.

February 27, 2019, House Democrats voted against requiring notification to Immigration and Customs Enforcement (ICE) when a person in the country illegally tries to buy a gun (which is itself already against the law). For Roll Call Vote 98, there were 208 Democrats who voted not to tell ICE when illegal aliens try to illegally buy guns.

On June 2, 2019, House Democrats voted against reporting to ICE illegal immigrants who were members of illegal street gangs.

In Roll Call Vote 239, there were 220 Democrats who voted to protect illegal immigrant street gangs over law enforcement and public safety.

On March 8, 2019, House Democrats voted in favor of allowing illegal immigrants to vote. In Roll Call Vote 117, a total of 227 Democrats voted to give people in the country illegally the ability to cancel out the votes of American citizens.

On June 27, 2019, House Democrats voted against requiring state election officials to identify foreign nationals who handled voters' ballots or voting machines. In Roll Call 427, there were 218 Democrats who voted to protect foreign nationals involved with our elections.

On January 3, 2019, House Democrats voted to fund the United Nations Population Fund, which sponsors abortion and sterilization programs. The same vote reversed the Trump administration's Mexico City policy, which was first instituted by President Ronald Reagan and cut off American taxpayer funding for abortions overseas. Roll Call Vote 10 had 232 House Democrats voting for abortion and sterilization.

On May 17, 2019, House Democrats voted to break Title IX's protection of women athletes by allowing transgender women to compete. The record for Roll Call Vote 216 shows 227 Democrats voting to favor transgender women over natural women.

On January 10, 2019, House Democrats voted to cut rural broadband pilot projects designed to create the infrastructure to bring modern wireless networks to rural America. For Roll Call Vote 24, there were 228 Democrats who voted against progress for rural America.

On October 29, 2019, House Democrats voted against supporting the natural gas mining industry, which has created 1.7 million jobs and helped America achieve energy independence. In Roll Call Vote 589, there were 221 House Democrats who voted against American oil and gas production.

On December 18, 2019, House Democrats voted to impeach President Trump despite a lack of evidence. Roll Call Vote 695 showed 229 Democrats voting to impeach (only two voted against) while all 195 Republicans voted against in the most partisan impeachment vote in American history.

The Fight against Israel

An amazing pattern among the radical House Democrats is the depth of their anti-Israel bias and anti-Semitism. Democratic president Harry Truman was the leader who heroically recognized Israel as a country—despite the opposition of his senior advisors. Democrats for two generations were strongly supportive of Israel. Now support for Israel has decayed in the Democratic Party, and among the most radical members an overtly anti-Israel bias is now obvious.

However, the breadth of hostility to Israel really shows up when it comes to the global Boycott, Divestment, and Sanctions (BDS) movement, which seeks to economically and psychologically isolate Israel. This movement is a real threat to the survival of Israel, because it consistently sets up the image that Israel is unacceptable, and the Palestinians are victims who need to be supported no matter how much they engage in terrorism.

There were three efforts in the House to offset the Boycott, Divestment, and Sanctions movement. In every case, House Democrats were overwhelmingly in favor of hurting Israel.

On April 4, 2019, on a vote to assert that it is in the national security interest of the United States to oppose the BDS movement, the House Democrats voted overwhelmingly—226 Democrats against Israel. That was Roll Call Vote 152.

On May 23, 2019, an attempt to block foreign tax benefits to companies that have any subsidiary engaged in the boycott against Israel was rejected by House Democrats with 220 "no" votes. This was Roll Call Vote 230.

On July 24, 2019, on a motion to stop taxpayer-funded pension plans from boycotting Israel, 226 House Democrats voted against protecting Israel (and for that matter the taxpayer-funded pension plans, by prohibiting them from earning a higher return from Israeli companies). That was Roll Call Vote 152.

The striking thing about these three votes is how consistent the House Democrats are. These are not just the votes of AOC and the squad. These are not just the votes of the handful of Muslim and left-wing members who are historically anti-Israel. This is nearly the entire House Democratic Party as a virtually unanimous monolith siding against Israel—our closest ally in the Middle East. It is a good example of how radical virtually all of the House Democrats have become.

I hope this outline has sufficient proof for you to accept that describing the radical two hundred House Democrats is not an exaggeration.

As you can see in the votes I listed, there were a consistent two-hundred-plus out of two-hundred-thirty-two Democrats voting on ideas which most Americans simply reject. Despite the best efforts of the liberal media to redefine them as moderates, every one of these House Democrats can be accurately described as a radical.

7.

AN ECONOMY FOR ALL AMERICANS

When I set out to write this book, I was looking forward to the chapter on the economy. I had intended for it to be an incredibly positive and robust chapter. However, as I am writing this in late March 2020, the world's economies are taking a beating. Markets are violently reacting to the massive disruption caused by COVID-19, the coronavirus that started in China and has swept across the globe since December 2019.

The United States' markets are no exception. Many companies are having to scramble to fill gaps in supply chains that have been snarled by quarantines and other public health measures to stop the spread of the virus. This has resulted in a constant stream of bad economic news, which feeds concern, which spooks investors, and which then results in bad economic news. It is a negative feedback loop, and America will come out of this OK only if President Trump and his team can figure out how to break the cycle.

As of now, it appears they will be able to. Trump appointed Vice President Mike Pence to lead a task force to deal with the

American response to the virus. President Trump has been hugely helped because the first three years of his presidency provided a remarkably strong economic foundation. So, despite the current turmoil, the economy under President Trump has been historically strong. If we had not had three years of strong growth and jobs, the coronavirus impact might have been much worse.

If the Trump administration is successful in responding to the outbreak, this could be a particularly valuable victory for the president that will no doubt help him in the 2020 election. Many on the radical Left and in the political establishment—including former Vice President Joe Biden—spent much of their breath before Trump took office (and early in his term) claiming he would destroy the economy.

For example, in January 2016, Moody's Analytics chief economist Mark Zandi told *Politico*, "If Trump's policies were enacted it would be some form of disaster for the economy. If you force eleven million undocumented immigrants to leave in a year, you would be looking at a depression. It would not help the people he is talking to, they would be the first to go down."[1]

In August 2016, Biden told a crowd that then-candidate Trump would have "loved Stalin"; said the now-president's plans were un-American; and said Trump didn't understand the economy. According to Biden, "This guy doesn't care about the middle class, and I don't even blame him in a sense, because he doesn't understand it. He doesn't have a clue."[2]

Shortly after Election Day, Paul Krugman wrote for the *New York Times* that "we are very probably looking at a global recession, with no end in sight. I suppose we could get lucky somehow. But on economics, as on everything else, a terrible thing has just happened."[3]

In support of these predictions, a little more than a month after President Trump had won the election—but not yet taken office—the broad national media began priming the pump to try to sow economic anxiety over his presidency.

As one of many examples, on December 27, 2016, Peter Hans for *Forbes* warned:

> Turns out, nine of the past 10 U.S. recessions occurred under a Republican president. With, one exception under Jimmy Carter in 1980, which lasted just six months.
>
> The Great Recession was already a year old when Barack Obama inherited it from George W. Bush, and it ended six months into his presidency.[4]

On March 17, 2017, months after Trump's inauguration, Anna-lyn Kurtz for *Fortune* captured the Democrat's feverish, destructive hopes—and then offered them a megaphone—when she wrote, "Donald Trump is setting up America for economic doom, at least according to Democrats, it seems."[5]

By December 26, 2017, Robert Shapiro for Brookings Institute wrote that a recession in 2018 was almost certain, and Trump would be badly hurt politically:

> Four years of rapid job growth have brought the unemployment rate to 4.1 percent—well below the Federal Reserve's estimate of "full employment"—so future job creation almost inevitably will slow down. More generally, the record of the last two years on GDP growth, business investment, consumer spending and personal disposable income all show an expansion considerably weaker than the 1990s cycle at a comparable point (1999).[6]

It turns out, there was no 2018 recession. Further, the 4.1 percent unemployment figure was not the floor. (As I started writing

this book, the unemployment rate was hovering around a fif-
ty-year low at 3.5 percent, and it had been for months—although
it is clear we will have a huge spike in unemployment in response
to the public health steps to defeat the coronavirus. Already, it
increased to 4.4 percent in March.)

By November 23, 2018, Derek Thompson with *The Atlantic* felt
he needed to up the ante. Recall at that time the surging Trump
bull market had shown one if its first corrections. The Dow Jones
Industrial Average had dropped more than 500 points. This was like
chum in the water for the hordes of mainstream journalists who were
eager to report on anything that hinted at a President Trump failure.

With dramatic flourish, Thompson wrote, "After the Dow Jones
Industrial Average sank 550 points on Tuesday, the past few weeks
qualify as no mere correction, but as one of the worst stock melt-
downs of the past few decades. Some analysts say it could get worse."[7]

Of course, nothing got worse in the near term. In fact, a few
days later, the DJI had soared nearly 2,000 points.[8] There was
another slight dip in December 2018, but it quickly rebounded and
continued an upward trend. It turned out; the two late-2018 dips
only provided investors with opportunities to buy low.

On August 28, 2019, Tara Sinclair, an economist at George
Washington University, predicted to the *New York Times* that
there was "potentially a self-inflicted-wound type of recession. . . .
But how deep that gash goes depends on many other characteristics of the economy and the policy response thereafter."[9]

Once again, the so-called experts were consistently wrong,
and Trump was right. In fact, prior to the coronavirus outbreak,
US markets had increased by 50 percent since Trump's election.
This added more than $19 trillion to household wealth.

As the US economy has flourished since the beginning of
Trump's presidency, these same supposed experts have done their
best to ignore or avoid talking about the benefits of the Trump
economy. Now, as the reaction to the coronavirus is causing real

pain to many people (physical, emotional, and financial), all the national media can do is dream up ways to make it somehow Trump's fault. All are missing the fact that without Trump, things could have been much worse economically for America.

Jobs and Wealth

Perhaps the biggest success story of the Trump economy has been its remarkable ability to get Americans back to work. Before the coronavirus pandemic forced many parts of the economy to grind to a halt, unemployment had been at sustained, record lows for months.

Before Trump took office, figures from the US Bureau of Labor statistics show that unemployment had been hovering around 5 percent going back to September 2015. The moment President Trump won the election, it dropped from 4.9 percent in October to 4.7 percent in November, as businesses expressed their relief at not having a continuation of the Obama years in Hillary Clinton. Since January 2017, when Trump took office, unemployment has steadily declined. By the end of his first year, it had dropped from 4.7 percent in January to 4.1 percent in December. In 2018, it dropped further to 3.9 by December. In 2019, the trend continued—but it seemed to hit a floor of 3.5 percent.[10]

For perspective, the United States hadn't experienced 3.5 percent unemployment since 1969—a full half-century ago—and did so only briefly.[11] In 2020 figures, this means only 5.79 million Americans in the workforce don't have jobs, while 158.76 million do have jobs.[12] Importantly, this decline in unemployment is being felt by Americans from virtually every walk of life. Before the coronavirus pandemic, unemployment rates for African Americans, Latino Americans, and Asian Americans are all at record lows. And with the right policies, we will recover these historic rates within a year *if* we follow Trumpian policies and do not let Washington insist on doing really destructive things.

African Americans in particular have seen a tremendous run of success in finding work in the Trump economy. At the end of February 2020, African American unemployment was at 5.8 percent. This is higher than the national average, but it is well below historic rates for Black Americans. In fact, it's almost half the twenty-year average of 10.3 percent for the group.[13] It is also 1.2 percentage points below the pre-Trump record low of 7 percent, achieved in April 2000. In fact, the Trump economy beat the 2000 record in December 2017 and continued to lower the record figure for Black Americans in April 2018, May 2018, and August 2019. The new historic record is now 5.4 percent.

Hispanic and Latino Americans have enjoyed a similar trend. The pre-Trump record for Latino and Hispanic unemployment was 5 percent—last hit in March 2007, according to US labor statistics. This record was beaten in June of President Trump's first term, wherein Hispanic unemployment fell to 4.9 percent. Five new records have been set since then, leaving the current record at 4.2 percent for Hispanic and Latino Americans.[14]

Asian Americans were seeing 2.5 percent unemployment according to the February 2020 job figures—well below the national average and a half percent higher than the May 2018 record low for Asian Americans of 2 percent.[15]

With these kinds of employment figures for American minorities, it is difficult to understand the radical Democratic Left's absurd claims that President Trump and his policies are discriminatory or racist. On the basis of employment alone, Trump has overseen an economy that has been better for Black, Hispanic, and Asian Americans than any other president in history. Similarly, American veterans have seen unemployment rates that matched or were close to the national average. Those with disabilities, and those without high school diplomas, have also seen new record high employment under President Trump. Importantly, women now make up the majority of the US workforce, with the lowest female unemployment rates in the Unites States since 1953. Finally, millennials have flourished. In fact, we have a record number of people aged twenty-five to thirty-four in the workforce, and their wages have been growing by 5 percent each year. On average, for his first term, until the Wuhan virus hit, President Trump had presided over the lowest period of unemployment that has occurred under any US president since we started tracking the statistic.

At the same time as the unemployment records are being made, the Trump economy has been creating jobs at a steady clip. Under President Trump, 3.5 million people have joined the workforce. The February 2020 jobs figures showed an increase of 237,000 jobs—much higher than so-called experts expected. Overall, the Trump economy's job creation success has included 1.2 million new manufacturing and construction jobs. And this is set to expand, as roughly 12,000 new factories have been built or are under construction. The coronavirus emergency has suspended this scale of expansion, but with the right policies there is every reason to believe it will resume once the virus has been defeated. This downturn is caused by a virus—not a systemic error or failing in our economic systems.

All this activity has helped bring real median income in the United States to a record high of $63,179—surpassing the 1999 record of $61,526.[16] As Daniel Kurt for Investopedia put it on February 5, 2020:

> Actually, the latest figures are better than they've been for years. Based on recent U.S. Census Bureau figures, there's room for optimism. The median household income in 2018 was $63,179, which is a 0.8 percent increase from 2017. . . . This was the second annual increase in a row, while the increase in 2017 was the first annual increase since 2007 when the Great Recession left millions of Americans without work.[17]

So, more Americans are working, and they are making more money. As of now, the home ownership rate appears to be rebounding after falling from a high of 69.2 percent in 2004 to a trough of 62.9 percent in the second quarter of 2016. President Trump was elected, and the housing market finally started recovering from the 2008 crisis. According to economic data at the Federal Reserve Bank of Saint Louis, by the end of 2019, home ownership had moved up to 65.1 percent.[18]

All these trends were built on the strong foundation of President Trump's early years in office. The 2017 Tax Cuts and Jobs Act, the massive deregulation effort, and his aggressive pro-American trade positions have created an environment for Americans to succeed. Taken together as a gestalt, they form an incredibly effective economic policy. Despite how the media distorts (or ignores) these figures, I expect historians will largely view President Trump as wildly successful. I also think that American voters in November 2020 are unlikely to ignore that more of their friends and family have jobs and are doing well financially (provided the coronavirus challenge is met). And remember: we entered the coronavirus crisis from a position of strength precisely because of these policies.

Defeating Deception

The members of the radical Democratic Left have done—and will continue doing—everything possible to claim the Trump economy is good only for millionaires and billionaires. They are just plain lying. They tried the same thing (and arguably were successful) in smearing the 2017 tax cuts.

The lies were so blatant, and so bad, even the *New York Times* had to acknowledge the deception. Writing in April 2019, Ben Casselman and Jim Tankersley wrote: "If you're an American taxpayer, you probably got a tax cut last year. And there's a good chance you don't believe it."

Citing a survey taken that month, 40 percent of Americans polled did not believe they received a tax cut, only 20 percent said they did, and a small number thought their taxes went up. This is despite, as the writers pointed out, "not even one in 10 households actually got a tax increase."

As Casselman and Tankersley put it: "To a large degree, the gap between perception and reality on the tax cuts appears to flow from a sustained—and misleading—effort by liberal opponents of the law to brand it as a broad middle-class tax increase."[19]

In the story, Tax Policy Center senior fellow Howard Gleckman told the paper, "The Democrats did a very good job. . . . They were able to put that into the public perception, and the reality has been unable to break that perception."

Gleckman's own center found that 65 percent of Americans got a tax cut, only 6 percent paid more in taxes, and the rest had no significant change. Even the most hostile pro-tax think tanks had to acknowledge the truth. As Casselman and Tankersley wrote:

So did the Institute on Taxation and Economic Policy, a left-leaning think tank that was sharply critical of the law. In fact, that group went even further: In a December 2017 analysis, it found that every income group in every state would pay less on average under the law in 2019.[20]

The tax cut lies are a perfect example of how the radical Democratic Left has tried to simply fib its way out of the conversation when it comes to the Trump economy. It has taken the same tack on Americans' movement away from welfare and toward work.

As President Trump noted during his State of the Union on February 4, 2020, "Under the last administration, more than ten million people were added to the food stamp rolls. Under my administration, seven million Americans have come off food stamps, and ten million people have been lifted off of welfare."

Many on the left have tried and failed to nitpick around this announcement. Some claimed that rather than being "lifted off of" welfare, these ten million were "cut off" welfare. Sarah Jones, writing for *New York* magazine, wrote that "people didn't stop using food stamps because their economic circumstances had drastically improved. The percentage of Americans on food stamps shrank because the Trump administration changed eligibility standards. The president took help away from people who needed it."

The change in standards Jones is referencing was a move by President Trump to strengthen work requirements for able-bodied, working-age adults who do not have dependents. Federal rules already say that people in this category must work at least twenty hours a week or enroll in training or educational programs to receive food stamp benefits for longer than three months. However, before the Trump administration rule, many states could waive these requirements if unemployment in the state was 20 percent higher than the national average. Since unemployment was already at a historic low, this was allowing many states to waive the rule when there was not a pressing need. President Trump's rule would bring the unemployment requirement to 6 percent, according to the *Wall Street Journal*.[21] The change would affect only roughly 755,000 able-bodied adults who do not have dependents. This is a small slice of the 36.4 million Americans who receive food stamp benefits.

Despite claims by Jones (and Representative Alexandria Ocasio-Cortez) that the president was callously booting people off government assistance, the *New York Times*'s Jim Tankersley and Lola Fadulu wrote on February 20, 2020, that "for now, the evidence supports Mr. Trump's contention that an improving economy is more responsible for falling food stamp rolls than Mr. Trump's attempts to limit access."

The reporters immediately added that the president planned to tighten requirements in the future. However, in a thriving economy it makes sense to raise the eligibility requirements for assistance. These programs are intended to help people get back on their feet—not keep them in perpetual government dependence.

Dottie Rosenbaum, a researcher at the Center on Budget and Policy Priorities, told the paper: "The decline in poverty levels since the end of the Great Recession has been the single largest factor in recent SNAP participation declines. . . . This shows the program is working as designed."[22]

The fact is, in three short years, millions of people have brought themselves off the welfare rolls, because they had the opportunity to rise and work. The Trump economy has been a hugely positive force for lower-income Americans—and importantly, it is starting to be a real challenge to the Franklin D. Roosevelt–Lyndon B. Johnson model of giant government welfare programs.

A US Census Bureau report, *Income and Poverty in the United States: 2018*, which was published on September 10, 2019, found that President Trump's policies were moving America in the right direction. Overall, the poverty rate fell to 11.8 percent in 2018— which was well below 2007 figures for the first time in eleven years.[23]

In fact, poverty rates for African Americans (21.2 percent) and Hispanic Americans (18.3 percent) are at all-time lows. The president's critics will note that these rates are still well above the 11.8 percent national average—but they are dropping.

To help this trend continue, the administration has created almost nine thousand opportunity zones to spur business and growth in communities that need jobs the most. As a result, home values in these areas have increased by $22 billion—improving the financial security of thirty-five million Americans. Senator Tim Scott was critical in developing this policy.

Trade

If the coronavirus has taught us anything, it is that President Trump and many members of his administration have been absolutely right to push China on trade. It is abundantly clear now that decades of bad deals and fundamental misunderstandings about China's global strategy mean that we are far too dependent on China for vital sectors of our industries, including medical supplies and medicines.

Thankfully, President Trump and his team have been diligently working through a series of trade deals with China to go step-by-step and undo decades of bad policy. So far, after the first phase of the US-China trade deal was signed in January, China agreed to buy $200 billion worth of American goods and services from the agriculture, energy, and manufacturing sectors. With the outbreak of the coronavirus, we will have to wait and see when a phase two deal is struck and what it entails.

The president was able to get to this first deal after a long campaign of intense, and serious trade tariffs—which virtually everyone in the national media and on the left said would hurt trade and never lead to an agreement. As CNBC's Jim Cramer pointed out, once again, President Trump was right, and the so-called experts were wrong. Cramer has long supported President Trump's approach to China—because he understands China's long history of taking advantage of deals, which had no consequences. As Cramer said on *Squawk on the Street* just before China signed the deal, "I keep wondering when people are going to recognize that it is historic that tariffs did succeed. . . . Tariffs were not supposed to work."

But China is far from the only trading relationship President Trump has corrected. As Peter Navarro, who is an assistant to President Trump on trade and manufacturing policy, pointed out in September 2019 in the *Wall Street Journal*, President Trump's decision early on to terminate the Obama-negotiated Trans-Pacific Partnership (TPP) was right on point.

Navarro pointed out that the TPP would have caused American car makers to bleed money, and the United States already had existing trade agreements with more than half of the countries included in the deal. As Navarro noted, "Of the remaining five countries, Japan accounts for almost 90 percent of their combined gross domestic product, and President Trump recently completed a deal with Japan on the first stage of negotiations. America lost nothing from exiting the TPP."[24]

Then, of course, President Trump led negotiations on the US-Mexico-Canada Agreement (USMCA), which the Canadians ratified in mid-March 2020. Democrats and the media criticized President Trump for seeking to replace the former North Atlantic Free Trade Agreement (NAFTA) for much of his early term. Yet in the end, the agreement Trump and his team negotiated was highly bipartisan. As the *Washington Post* reported, "Bipartisan majorities in Congress approved the trade deal by wide margins, with the package sailing through the Senate, 89 to 10." Only a handful of members voted against the bill, including former Democratic presidential candidate Senator Bernie Sanders.

Despite enormous bipartisan support, Speaker Nancy Pelosi held the deal hostage in the House in an effort to keep success away from the president as he endured the Democrat-invented impeachment trial. Pelosi's effort eventually failed after she ran out of excuses to hold up the bill and it became clear she was slow-walking the agreement for nakedly partisan reasons. We won't know how much the revised trade deal with our neighbors will help the US economy until the coronavirus is contained, but it is widely expected to be a boon for US workers.

The New Coronavirus

As I mentioned earlier, I'm writing this in late March-early April 2020. I can't predict what the impact of the new coronavirus on the world's economy will be by the time this book publishes in June. Right now, the virus was recently declared a pandemic by the World Health Organization. There are more than 338,104 reported cases of the infection worldwide. The virus has now spread to South Korea, Iran, Italy, the United States, the United Kingdom, much of Europe, and many other countries.[25] No doubt, when you read this, the number of cases will be much higher. I am watching the progress of the virus in Italy, where my wife, Callista, is the United States ambassador to the Holy See, and we are in the middle of Italian efforts to contain and stop the epidemic. The self-isolation rules and other steps Italy has taken have slowed the virus but not turned the corner as of March 22, when I am writing. Hopefully by the time the book is published, Italy will be free of the epidemic.

The threat of the virus has affected the economy as much as public health. Partly due to general panic (and mostly due to real supply chain disruption in China) markets, including those in the United States, have been incredibly volatile. We have seen steep drops in the stock market, the Federal Reserve has lowered rates by a half percent, and the ten-year US Treasury note yield dropped below 1 percent for the first time in history.

None of this necessarily means we are heading into a prolonged economic downturn. But it is a big shock to the system. After all, China is the world's second-largest economy. General Secretary Xi Jinping is trying so desperately to make this a short-term issue that the Chinese Communist Party delayed its annual leadership meeting—which rarely happens. If it turns out that the Chinese economy is really collapsing, President Trump and the Congress will have to work hard to keep US economic momentum going. In many ways, what we are seeing play out is proof that the foundational assertions behind the American economy President Trump and Republicans have been building since 2017 are correct. We have outsourced too many vital parts of our supply chain, we are far too heavily dependent on investment in China, and we need to be much more strategic and America-focused in our dealings abroad.

This is part of the reason shortly after the markets started to turn, I suggested that the White House should put together a one-time short-term tax incentive for companies (including American ones) to migrate vital parts of their supply chains into the United States. The need to keep economic momentum is also likely what spurred President Trump's suggestion that congressional Democrats pass a temporary cut to the payroll tax. These two steps—and others to follow—could help the United States stay ahead of global downturns and help insulate our economy from the woes of the world.

By the time you are reading this, I genuinely hope that the coronavirus trouble is over, that a vaccine is well in development, and that the global economy has regained its momentum and success (with the coronavirus representing a minor correction). However, if the world is still grappling with this particularly infectious (although not historically deadly) virus, I hope that the Democrats in Congress have put partisanship aside and have joined with President Trump to ensure that American lives and the American economy are as safe and successful as possible.

On March 6, 2020, Peter Coy with *Bloomberg Businessweek* wrote: "Let's just say it: The longest economic expansion in U.S. history may already be over, killed by Covid-19."[26] Setting all politics aside, let's hope he is wrong like all the other doomsayers.

After all, it is possible that we will have a steep economic decline during the crisis of the viral threat to public health—and then an equally fast recovery after the virus has been defeated. That V-shaped decline and recovery was the pattern of the 1920 to 1921 depression. The recovery was so fast that the depression was not driven into public memory, unlike the much longer depression of 1929 to 1933 and extremely slow recovery of 1934 to 1942.

The best advice for the Trump administration in trying to recover quickly once the pandemic is defeated is a brilliant study by James Grant, *The Forgotten Depression: 1921: The Crash That Cured Itself.* If we follow the right policies and reestablish the Trump economic growth principles, we will recover amazingly fast once the virus is no longer a threat.

8.

★ ━━━━━━━━━━━━━━━━━━━━━━━━━━━━━━━ ★

FROM EDUCATION
TO LEARNING

The extraordinary crisis of the new coronavirus may be forcing changes that have long been necessary in moving our system from education to learning. Driven by rational fear of the pandemic, schools at every level are shifting to distance learning, away from classrooms and campuses.

The result is going to be a volume of new information about how people learn, and what new technologies make possible. These new capabilities for distance, autonomous, and self-paced learning have been growing steadily since the end of World War II. I remember my father taking courses by mail when he was assigned to army posts that did not have access to the material he wanted to learn. Back then, such courses took the form of a written package sent through the US mail. It was a chance to learn, if you were dedicated, diligent, and disciplined. However, it was a challenging and lonely process—and many people could not bring themselves to complete such a lonesome program of study.

Over time, the rise of personal computers, the Internet, inexpensive video (every smartphone is a movie camera), and more experience with distance and autonomous learning have built tremendous capabilities for people to learn more skills faster and more conveniently. Importantly, people can now learn things that are focused on what they think they need for their jobs or their careers. It is tailored learning.

The emergence of these new systems of learning has been fought at every step by the keepers of the old order. Remote learning systems have faced relentless accreditation challenges, roadblocks for government funds, and constant ridicule by establishment academia. There has been a concerted effort to delegitimize degrees offered by distance learning institutions. The entrenched ideologies, interest groups, and bureaucracies of the old order have consistently fought against the emergence of virtually any new methods of learning.

The resistance has been understandable. From the standpoint of bureaucratic education and guild-based higher education, the rise of new systems means a tremendous shift in power. Who now defines value in education, the teacher or the student? It also represents a tremendous threat to resources as old institutions see new adversaries for funding. Finally, new systems could signal a collapse in prestige and social status. Who will define what a degree is worth? The university—or the student or employers?

In every aspect of the education bureaucracy, from the K–12 public school machines to the guilds of higher education, it has been the teaching class that has dominated—and defended its turf against innovation. The amazing thing about this reactionary hostility to change in education is that it has occurred in a period when the established education system itself is decaying. Every day there is new evidence that traditional education is failing to perform its mission to create educated, competent citizens capable of working and participating in self-government.

For the last sixty years our K–12 systems and centers of higher education have been drifting away from the patterns that once made them the envy of the world. Slowly, they are ceasing to be the engines of human capital development that have made America the most inventive, innovative, entrepreneurial, and productive society in history.

The sixty years of decay have been especially obvious in the K–12 public school systems. As early as 1983, the Ronald Reagan administration issued a report, entitled *A Nation at Risk*, which warned that

> the educational foundations of our society are presently being eroded by a rising tide of mediocrity that threatens our very future as a Nation and a people. What was unimaginable a generation ago has begun to occur—others are matching and surpassing our educational attainments.
>
> If an unfriendly foreign power had attempted to impose on America the mediocre educational performance that exists today, we might well have viewed it as an act of war.[1]

The examples of costly inner-city schools failing completely—and remaining unreformed—are striking. The Baltimore school system is incredibly expensive. According to May 21, 2019 US Census data, Baltimore spends $16,184 per student—the fourth-highest spending school in the nation. (The national average is $12,201.)[2] However, as Sanford Horn wrote for *The Federalist* on August 2, 2019, Baltimore has more than a dozen schools in which not a single student passed state exams:

> Project Baltimore reported that in 13 of 39 city high schools, zero students were proficient in math. Zero. Let that sink in for a minute. In six more Baltimore high schools, only

1 percent tested proficient. In roughly half the schools, 3,804 students attempted the exam, with a mere 14 proficient in math. Not 14 percent, 14 actual students. It's no wonder the poverty rate in Baltimore is 22 percent.

Incompetent so-called leaders and teachers' unions have corrupted the public school system. They hide behind tenure while indoctrinating students instead of educating them, condemning the next generation to the consequences of the corrupt and broken system they created . . .

As Sanford said, nothing gets changed, because the teachers' unions and the education bureaucracy oppose any effort to eliminate mediocrity and move toward achievement. From the viewpoint of the teachers' unions, the school systems work because they pay salaries on time. If there is a major problem with these failing systems, according to the union, it is the failure to give raises to teachers who are failing to teach.

The lack of learning is so bad that in some places we should not use the words "teachers," "schools," and "students." If you have a building that houses a thousand young people who are not learning enough to pass a state exam, how can you call the building a school? I don't know what new word we should use, but "school" doesn't work. If you have adults paid full time to work in that building, but none of the young people for whom they are responsible can pass the minimum state achievement test, they clearly are not teachers. Again, I don't know what we should call them, but it isn't "teacher." If you are one of the young people trapped in the building that is failing to prepare you for a job—or the basic duties of citizenship—you are clearly not a student.

I outline this breakdown in language because we have failed to come to grips with how bad our K–12 system has become in some places. We cannot compete with China, or the world at large, if we cannot educate the next generation of Americans. They must be able to learn new jobs, and have full understanding of the world in which they live. Right now, we produce so few K–12 students competent in science, technology, engineering, and math that seats in these programs at our best universities are being taken by foreign students who can meet the requirements.[3]

This collapse of our education system was already a crisis thirty-seven years ago when *A Nation at Risk* was published. Because our competitors have continued to improve and invest in effective learning, the gap has become greater and the threat to our national security much more dangerous.

Every effort to reinforce success in learning outside the traditional public bureaucracies is met with enormous hostility from the teachers' unions, the bureaucracy, and the radical Democratic Left. For the unions and the bureaucrats, this fight is about money, power, and status. The more attention we pay to outside competing models, the less importance the traditional systems will have and the less money they will be able to coerce from the public. I use the word "coerce" because teachers' union strikes are direct coercing efforts to inconvenience parents to the point that they will pay whatever it takes to get the schools open.

Consider the eleven-day teachers' strike in Chicago in October 2019. In this case, the teachers' union left more than 300,000 public school students without access to learning for nearly two weeks. In return, they coerced the mayor into promising to shrink classes, hire more support staff and nurses—and grant a 16 percent blanket raise to teachers over the next five years.

This walkout followed a series last year in Oklahoma, West Virginia, Los Angeles, and Denver. As Randi Weingarten, the president of the American Federation of Teachers, told the *New York Times* on October 31, 2019, "This is now a strategy."[4]

Evidence that Catholic and other religious schools, charter schools, and even home schooling can be more effective than the bureaucratic unionized system seems to be irrelevant to the unions and bureaucrats. The political power and social status of the old order are brought to bear to stop any successful competition.

The failure of the old system to teach children from lower-income and minority neighborhoods has become so obvious that parents in Black and Latino communities increasingly favor school choice. The tens of thousands of parents who want their children in better schools but have not been able to get them there has become a political movement that is helping pro–school choice Republicans gain votes in communities that have not previously identified with them.

In Florida, Ron DeSantis became governor in part because 19 percent of African American women voted for him against a Black candidate who was against charter schools and totally committed to the teachers' unions. Their children were more important than their past worries about Republicans.

It is clear that a major choice in 2020 is between the teachers' union–dominated Democratic Party and the pro–charter school, pro–school choice Republicans. If the Democrats get control of the White House, they will continue to try to kill any choice except their teachers' union allies. The Democrats want to return to a public bureaucracy monopoly of learning (except of course for their own children, who usually go to elite private schools).

The performance failure of K–12 big city bureaucratic schools has been matched by the ideological conquest of higher education by left-wing ideologues. President Reagan used to say "It isn't so much that liberals are ignorant. It's just that they know so many things that aren't so." The things that "aren't so" are now the requirements for passing classes, getting graduate degrees, getting hired by colleges, and getting promotions—including tenure. The radical Democratic Left has created a complete, insular fantasy world in higher education.

Furthermore, as the authoritative nature of false knowledge sinks in, it becomes harder and harder to challenge. Theodore

H. White captured this phenomenon in his book *The Making of the President 1972* when he talked about the transition from the liberal ideology to the liberal theology. What had once been an open set of values subject to challenge and modification had hardened into a quasi-religious commitment to "the revealed truth of the left."

The result of this two-generation collapse of traditional education has been two profoundly different disasters. On the one hand, we have far too many young people who can't read, write, or do arithmetic. Given the absence of those capabilities, they certainly can't prepare for further study in science, technology, engineering, and mathematics, which is so central to our economic and national security survival.

On the other hand, among those young people who are going to competent K–12 schools, far too many are going on to higher education, where they are brainwashed into an ideological view of the world which makes good citizenship and practical, common sense problem-solving impossible.

This dual failure is undermining America's human capital.

We have a generation of young people who literally don't have the skills necessary to compete in the world. They will be unable to keep up with our international competitors. Unless this collapse of K–12 education is dramatically and decisively reversed, the United States will find itself in an economic and national security crisis. We also have a generation of young people who have a fair number of educational skills but who have been indoctrinated into a series of dangerous, destructive, and dysfunctional beliefs.

To make matters worse, the major teachers' unions and the education bureaucracy have now adopted many of the most radical ideas and values of the academic Left. And they are driving them down all the way to preschool and kindergarten.

As Henry Olsen wrote for the *Washington Post* on May 12, 2019, California lawmakers decided to teach gender expression and identity to kindergarteners. As Olsen put it:

The California guidelines are quite clear about what is to be taught and why. Page 45 of the K–3 guidelines states: "While students may not fully understand the concepts of gender expression and identity, some children in kindergarten and even younger have identified as transgender or understand they have a gender identity that is different from their sex assigned at birth." The idea that 5-year-old children can be trusted to "know" their gender identity is unbelievable; 4-year-olds still exhibit firm beliefs in magic.

Keep this in mind: At the same time California is seeking to instill liberal values in its youngest students, its high school graduation rate in 2018 was 83 percent—but slightly less than half (49.9 percent) of its graduates met *minimum requirements* to attend California colleges and universities.[5]

Left unchallenged, this left-wing, union-bureaucrat-led process will lead to a divided country with poor students with no skills, and middle-class or wealthy students with a totally warped understanding of reality. Such a country cannot compete economically with better-educated countries. Nor could it sustain a modern defense system against competitors with dramatically more educated scientists, engineers, and technologists.

Furthermore, this kind of propagandized education system would produce citizens whose view of how the world works would be so out of touch with reality that it would be virtually impossible to have rational debates about policy options. Founding father and President Thomas Jefferson actually warned about this danger in an 1816 letter to Charles Yancey when he wrote, "If a nation expects to be ignorant and free in a state of civilization, it expects what never was and never will be."[6]

A major break in the education monopoly of the Left began to occur with the rise of the school choice movement in Wisconsin in the 1980s. Polly Williams, a Democratic state representative and single mother who had been the Jesse Jackson presidential campaign's leader in Wisconsin, worked with Republican governor Tommy Thompson to create a school choice program for Milwaukee. That breakthrough led to the spread of a school choice movement across the country—and to the rise of charter schools, both public and private, as an alternative to the bureaucratic schools, which were widely seen as failing to educate.

In addition to school choice, there has been a steady increase in homeschooling with an estimated three million children now learning in a family environment (often in a co-op with other families). The more radical the bureaucratic schools have become, the more people are seeking alternative methods of educating their children.

The other great driver of educational change has been the growing gap between what educators want to teach and the skills and knowledge employers need. Educators teach what interests them and makes them happy. In their minds, their highest-value product is a new, younger version of themselves. They define value by what they value. However, the interests of educators may have nothing to do with the interests of employers. In fact, being supposedly educated may actually make someone less employable and capable of doing productive work.

In their two great works, *Future Shock* (1970) and *The Third Wave* (1980) Alvin and Heidi Toffler took direct aim at the industrial school system, which had become the standard. They noted that if the goal was to produce reliable, obedient factory workers, having people show up on time, sit in rows staring at the boss (the teacher), and doing what they were told was a good model. However, the Tofflers warned that as the information age replaced the industrial age, workers would no longer be valued primarily by the ability to do routine, repetitive things in an organized manner.

Peter F. Drucker made the same point in his seminal work *The Effective Executive* (1966) when he asserted that in the information age, routine industrial work was going to be replaced by knowl-edge workers. Knowledge workers could not be managed in the sense of the industrial era. Instead, knowledge workers had to be led, because their engagement had to come from within and could not be coerced from without. You could measure activity on an assembly line. You cannot measure knowledge by looking at activity. You must measure it by output—and optimizing that output from knowledge workers requires leadership rather than supervision.

The Tofflers and Drucker were describing a revolution that is gradually sweeping through society—despite the powerful, bitter resistance of the great bureaucracies and interest groups that want to cling to their power and privilege from the industrial era.

The industrial era was a relatively short period in human his-tory. Prior to industrialization, most learning was done at home and on the job. Then education was industrialized into schools, classes, and hierarchical structures. Now, with the transition from industrialization to information, the process of learning is gradu-ally reverting to its preindustrial forms.

The near universal reaction to the coronavirus has been to scatter learning from its schoolroom and campus focus. The pan-demic has forced us to experiment with distance learning on a scale that would have seemed impossible in January 2020. Now it is a virtually universal experiment. From preschool to graduate school, the pandemic has forced students and teachers to separate and try a variety of new ways of learning.

By the end of the summer, we will be questioning many of the principles, costs, and structures that have come to define the industrial era bureaucratic system. I expect that the new informa-tion technologies are going to prove amazingly powerful in allow-ing an explosion of learning.

Just as Amazon uses information technology that allows you to browse well over a million products and pick the one you want, the new world of learning is going to have similar flexibility and personalization. Here are some principles to begin to define information age learning:

Everyone learns at a different pace and in different patterns. We need to develop new systems for ranking knowledge. The rigid grade level structure may now be inappropriate. Some people learn quickly. Others learn slowly. People will learn faster and more completely if their learning relates to solving a need they have at that moment (think of learning to ski when you are on a slope versus reading about skiing in the summer).

Google and YouTube have created the opportunity for just-in-time learning. I often find myself functioning as my own research assistant. Thirty years ago, I would have rejected doing so as being too slow. Now, with my iPad, I can move from this page to do some research and back to apply it to this chapter faster than I can ask someone else to do it.

Employers and income-producing opportunities will replace academic accreditation as a statement of value. Mike Rowe pointed out on my Newt's World podcast that a welder can make $160,000 a year with no student debt, while his or her cousin is making $60,000 a year or less with a liberal arts degree and tens of thousands of dollars of student debt.[7] Sebastian Thrun cofounded Udacity to develop microcourses that fit the needs of potential employers.

People still find themselves stymied trying to learn things, but mentors (rather than traditional teachers) will be the key human resource for learning. Udacity, even though it is an online learning system, matches up each student with a mentor. Part of the difference is the mentor is available online via video conferencing software like Skype, Zoom, and a host of other Internet-based systems.

Learning will occur your entire lifetime. There will be no sense of high school, undergraduate, graduate, and other hierarchical levels. You may need to know one set of things in your twenties and a totally different set of things in your forties. A PhD, MD, or lawyer who decides to take up cooking or open a winery is not going down the education ladder. Such people are learning what is appropriate for what they want to do at that moment. In his 1961 book, *Excellence*, John W. Gardner wrote: "An excellent plumber is infinitely more admirable than an incompetent philosopher. The society which scorns excellence in plumbing because plumbing is a humble activity, and tolerates shoddiness in philosophy because it is an exalted activity, will have neither good plumbing nor good philosophy. Neither its pipes nor its theories will hold water."[8]

People will learn and do at the same time, and they will alternate learning and doing. Being cloistered in a particular educational bureaucracy for four or six years will become less and less common.

The convenience of the learner will rival the convenience of the teacher in scheduling and organizing learning. Bureaucratic education was organized around the convenience of the academic class. In many colleges, a particular "must have" course is offered only once a year. If the class is full, you may have to stay in school an extra year just to get that one required course. Students are expected to be in a particular room at a particular time at the convenience of the faculty member. All this will change as the information age puts more and more power in the hands of the learner. Think of the shift from having to go to a movie theater at a specific time to being able to call up movies on demand. This shift will gradually occur as we transition from education bureaucracy to information age individualism.

The emerging introductory systems on the Internet will move on from dating and social interactions to hobbies, interests, and incomes. The polarization of Ivy League versus non–Ivy League described by Charles Murray in *Coming Apart* will gradually diminish as activity interests, job interests, and learning interests online bring people together without having to spend enormous amounts to be socialized on a particular campus.

None of these changes will be completed overnight. However, the combination of the obvious collapse of entire school systems' effectiveness, with the rise of new systems of learning, make the transition almost inevitable over time. America will be better off the faster we can migrate to the new, more powerful individualized systems.

9.

★ ▬▬▬▬▬▬▬▬▬▬▬▬▬▬▬▬▬▬▬▬▬▬▬ ★

COVID-19 WOULD KILL MEDICARE FOR ALL

In the early days of the Wuhan virus outbreak in the United States, Senator Bernie Sanders and other hard left Democrats made the argument that the national emergency was exactly why we needed government-run health care. They warned that the private health care sector would use the outbreak as an opportunity for price-gouging and that Americans who got sick would end up bankrupt or even be left to die because they were unable to get coverage.

Only days later, we saw just how wrong they were.

As I am writing this book, the fallout is still unfolding. However, the turning point in the battle may prove to be the day President Trump stood in the Rose Garden with leaders from America's health care companies to make clear that all the resources of America's massive private sector would be brought to bear to fight the virus.

In fact, it has been the private health sector's ability to surge and adapt quickly to the crisis that has thus far minimized deaths in our country. America's pharmaceutical industry went from being a punching bag for left-wing politicians to being our greatest hope for treatments and a vaccine. America's private health insurance companies rapidly waived all copayments for virus testing and treatment and made it clear they would take care of their customers. And our private hospital system (both for-profit and nonprofit varieties) went from a source of outrage over high prices to the heroic front-line warriors risking their own lives in our battle against the virus. They are saving thousands of lives and dealing with an unprecedented influx of patients needing respiratory care.

Throughout the crisis, government has had a vital role to play, but it was not to run the health care system. Instead, government has served as a facilitator and coordinator. In fact, many of the most vital steps President Trump took involved getting the government out of the way. He waived many bureaucratic rules that would have otherwise prevented our health care system from adjusting to the crisis. Most significantly, he instructed the Food and Drug Administration to issue new guidance for running clinical trials during the emergency, cutting out several bureaucratic steps that would delay the process of finding a cure. He also waived Medicare rules that prevented patients from using telemedicine, which has proved to be an important way for seniors to see their doctor for routine care without risking exposing themselves to the new coronavirus and other illnesses.

Where there were failures in responding to the virus, it was mostly on the part of bureaucratic government—most significantly in distributing adequate testing capabilities in the early days of the outbreak. *The Washington Post* ran an investigation into the early testing failures that showed how the government's arcane web of bureaucracy prevented scientists from helping. After spending more than 100 hours filling out forms to develop new testing kits and emailing the applications to the FDA, one scientist was told that the agency could not accept the submission because it needed to be put on a CD-ROM and mailed to the agency.[1]

In fact, it was the private sector that stepped in to fill in the gap. For example, on March 19, 2020, Bright MD freely offered its AI-powered virtual health screening platform called SmartExam to hospitals, so they could quickly screen and evaluate potential COVID-19 cases. This freed up much-needed resources. The week of January 24, 2020, the health care software company Epic updated its system to help doctors screen and document the travel of patients with the virus, and detect cases and trouble areas nationwide. The company also created new software to allow doctors to easily alert patients to infected zip codes near them. As a final example, the company Buoy Health updated its risk-assessment and triage software tool to help quickly identify high-risk patients. This information could be shared across the system. As of now, Buoy has informed and de-escalated 87 percent of patients in the system who had COVID-19-related concerns.

As states where the virus hit the hardest struggled with a lack of available hospital beds, it was their Certificate of Need laws—which dictate when and where hospitals can be built—that received scrutiny for decades of limiting supply.

This is not to say that America's health care system does not have serious problems. Most significantly, it costs way too much. It is extremely wasteful, rife with middlemen, and doesn't spend nearly as much energy keeping people healthy as it does treating people who are sick. I will examine in detail in the following chapters these and other problems that make the health marketplace completely dysfunctional in the United States. More important, I will show how President Trump's leadership is helping to accelerate our transition to a new-model health system, which is already producing much better health outcomes at about half the cost of the current one.

But it is first important to understand why the radical Democratic Left's government-run health care solutions are unacceptable and dangerous—especially in light of the public health emergency we are living through.

Price-Setting Leads to Shortages, Waiting Lists, and Lost Lives

Government-run health care—whether it is Bernie Sanders–style Medicare for All, "public option" plans like that of former vice president Joe Biden, or Nancy Pelosi's HR3 plan on drug prices—inevitably leads to scarcity. And scarcity in health care leads to lost lives. During a public health crisis like COVID-19, this maxim is truer than ever.

Scarcity is the inevitable result of big-government health care plans because they all rely on price-setting or the closely related global budgeting (in which the government will not let total spending on health care in a state or country rise above a certain amount). Rather than market-based competition, they use these government systems as the tool by which they control costs.

Price-setting is exactly what it sounds like. The government determines what it thinks is a fair price for a product or service, and sellers are required by law to charge that amount. There are two big issues with the government setting prices.

First, there is simply no way that a collection of bureaucrats sitting in Washington knows enough to set the right price for anything. Prices serve an important purpose, which is to establish a measurement of value that society places on a product or service. In functioning marketplaces, prices are determined by thousands, even millions, of independent transactions between buyers and sellers. This process is organic, extremely complex, and can't be dictated by a third party.

A panel of government bureaucrats, no matter how smart, will invariably overvalue some things and undervalue others. When this happens, the undervalued services or products become scarce, and the overvalued ones become more abundant than needed.

The reason why government price-setting in health care inevitably leads much more to scarcity than abundance is because the government is a major payer in health care. So its bias is always to underpay for budgetary reasons. While it is true that private sector insurance overpays for much of health care, for reasons I will explore elsewhere, it is also true that Medicare underpays. One estimate is that Medicare pays for only 87 cents of every dollar of hospital costs.[2] The Centers for Medicare and Medicaid Services, which run the program, estimate that more than two-thirds of hospitals lose money on Medicare inpatient services.[3]

The second problem with the government setting prices is that it dramatically stifles quality improvements and other innovation. If a health care provider is going to get paid the same amount regardless of the quality of the service it provides, what is its incentive to do a good job? What is its incentive to innovate?

If you want an example of how much slower government moves than the private sector when it comes to incorporating new technologies, look at telemedicine. Platforms like Teledoc that allow virtual doctor visits are becoming very popular, especially among younger Americans. Telemedicine is ideal for routine medical consultations; it saves patients time and prevents them from having to sit in a waiting room with a bunch of other sick patients.

Almost all the major insurance carriers cover telemedicine. Meanwhile, until a few months ago, Medicare still covered telemedicine only in limited circumstances. After the outbreak of the Wuhan virus, President Trump was able to use emergency authority to make telehealth options available to everyone on Medicare as a measure to keep seniors safe from exposing themselves unnecessarily. However, the expansion is only on a temporary basis. In fact, the administration had already put a process in place that would expand coverage of telehealth to more people, but the only way it was able to do it was by classifying it as "virtual medicine," with "virtual check-ins," instead of "telemedicine."

It shouldn't take a national emergency such as the coronavirus pandemic to quickly adapt to new health care technologies, treatments, and options. It also shouldn't take engaging in bureaucratic loopholes and legal wordplay. Yet this is the sort of intransigence we should come to expect the more government pays for health care.

The Particular Danger of Price-Setting with Drugs

This principle is especially true when it comes to pharmaceuticals. The drug pricing system in America is screwed up in a million different ways. This has led to huge sticker prices for new drugs, outrageous price increases on old drugs, and totally unaffordable out-of-pocket costs for Americans who fall through the cracks of insurance. Again, I will address this issue elsewhere. But first it is important to understand why the approach of Biden, Pelosi, and Sanders is so dangerous.

They all use different approaches, but their plans are essentially the same. Through various mechanisms, they would allow Medicare to determine how much drugs are worth and force the manufacturers to sell them at those prices. The result will be a dramatic drop in investment in biopharmaceutical research as the venture capital ecosystem that funds research and development dries up. It will simply no longer be financially worth it for them to invest. The ultimate result is fewer new therapies and treatments— at exactly the moment we need them the most.

For instance, the Council of Economic Advisors estimated that HR3, the drug pricing bill passed by House Democrats in 2019, could lead to as many as one hundred fewer new drugs being available to Americans over the next decade (about one-third of expected).[4] It also estimated that the economy would lose $1 trillion in value during that same time.

To be clear, there are many measures we can take to lower the cost of prescription drugs without sacrificing innovation. In fact, done right, market-oriented reforms can decrease prices while *increasing* innovation. But to do that, we cannot allow the government to dictate prices. We know this because of what has happened to pharmaceutical research and development in Europe.

In the 1980s, European countries imposed price controls on drugs through their single-payer health care systems. The result was an almost immediate flight of capital, research, and development from Europe to the United States. In 1990, Europe accounted for almost 50 percent of global R&D, while the United States accounted for 33 percent. By the end of the decade, those percentages had basically flipped: 37 percent in Europe and 48 percent in the United States.[5] The difference is even starker on a per capita basis: European drug companies invest about one-fourth per capita on research and development as US companies.[6]

Price controls don't just result in fewer drugs being invented; they also lead to fewer existing drugs being made available. Otherwise prosperous European countries like Denmark and France have access to fewer than half of the new drugs introduced in the last decade. In the United States, patients have access to nearly 90 percent.[7]

Government-Run Health Care: Scarcity When We Need Health Care the Most

At the time I am writing this, it is almost certain that Joe Biden will be the Democratic nominee for president in 2020. However, it was Sanders's single-payer, government-run health care plan called "Medicare for All" that defined the Democratic Party's approach to health care. Last year, over half of House Democrats signed on to support a single-payer, government-run health care plan.

A single-payer health care plan like Medicare for All would throw all Americans off their current insurance—even if they are happy with it—and put them on a government-run and taxpayer-financed health plan. This would come with a huge middle-class tax increase to pay for the plan's estimated price tag of anywhere between $20 trillion and $40 trillion over the next decade (the truth is nobody really knows how to calculate these costs). Single-payer health care plans like Medicare for All would also devastate America's hospital system.

Estimates are that Bernie Sanders's Medicare for All plan would reduce hospital revenue by a net $200 billion per year, and that 90 percent of all hospitals would lose money. Average hospital margins across the country are already low: about 7 percent, and roughly 25 percent of America's hospitals lose money every year.[8] These hospitals are disproportionately public and located in rural areas. They accept more patients on Medicare and Medicaid than other hospitals, which is why they lose money.

This means that even though the largest financial losses under Medicare for All would be on those hospitals that accept a larger percentage of private-payer patients, the impact would be the most devastating to those who are already losing money or operating on very tight margins. It would push them into the red—or further into the red—and force many of them to close. So, despite the Democrats' egalitarian rhetoric on health care, it would be poorer and rural Americans who would be hardest hit by big-government plans. The Democrats' plans would end up shuttering the hospitals these Americans depend on most. What good is being covered for health care if you don't have any health care facilities nearby?

As bad as this result would be under normal circumstances, imagine America's response to the Wuhan virus under government-run health care. It would have meant fewer hospital beds when we need them most—and those shortages would have been felt most by the poor. This is exactly what has happened in Europe under their single-payer systems. Most of the European countries have thus far suffered a much higher fatality rate among infected people than in the United States. A big factor in that difference has been hospital capacity.[9]

It also would have meant a far less robust pharmaceutical eco-system to develop treatments for the coronavirus. Several of the early treatments identified are existing drugs used to treat other illnesses. Who knows if they would even exist under a single-payer, government-run health system?

Biden's Plan: Single-Payer, Government-Run Health Care in Slow Motion

Biden will deny that his health care plan would lead single-payer, government-run health care. He spent much of the campaign portraying his approach as a more reasonable approach than that of Sanders. The mainstream media, which was desperate to beat Trump and saw Sanders as a liability to that goal, dutifully took its marching orders from the Biden campaign and described his plan as "moderate." But it is not moderate. It would be the most aggressive permanent expansion of government since the Great Society. And the truth is that in the long run, the practical impact of his plan is the same as Medicare for All.

Biden says that instead of "starting from scratch" and kicking people off their private insurance, he wants to "build on the suc-cess of the Affordable Care Act" by introducing a "public option" to the Obamacare exchanges. A public option is a health plan run by the federal government.

Recall that a public option was considered and rejected during the debate that led to the passage of Obamacare. It was the same hard-left Democrats who now support Sanders and single-payer health care that were fighting for the public option back then. That's because a public option is a Trojan horse for single-payer.

Biden's campaign says his public option would be "like Medi-care" and would save money for patients by "negotiate[ing]" lower prices from hospitals and doctors. But Medicare doesn't negotiate rates with individual providers the same way that private insurance does. Instead, it relies on a panel of experts to determine what it thinks an appropriate fee should be, runs that fee through a formula that accounts for geographic cost of living differences, and then sets the rates. Doctors and hospitals don't have the option to propose a better offer; it is a "take it or leave it" proposal. In fact, about 20 percent of doctors do not participate in Medicare. But most do, because it covers everyone over sixty-five.

Biden's campaign is deliberately vague on whether his public option would use Medicare payment rates and whether doctors who accept Medicare could decide not to accept the public option. But these are incredibly important details. They determine whether his public-option plan will be a one-way trip toward hundreds of millions of Americans losing their preferred insurance plan and having no choice but to join Bidencare. This would cause a crisis in medical availability across the country as hospitals close, doctors retire, and young people decide not to go to medical school.

If the Biden plan is for his public option to negotiate payment rates the way an insurance company does—in other words, to compete with private insurance on an even playing field—then it is unlikely that it will be any less expensive than its private sector alternatives.

If, however, the Biden public option takes Medicare's payment rates and imports them over to his public plan, then it will need to convince doctors to accept those payment rates. And why would they accept? The plan would need to have tens of millions of people enrolled nationwide before it could obtain the sort of scale where it would make sense for a doctor to accept that sort of "bulk" discount. This means that even if the Biden public option did use Medicare rates, its network of doctors would be tiny—narrower than the already narrow networks of private plans in Obamacare. People don't just buy insurance based on price, they also look to see if their doctor or hospital is covered. Even those without a regular primary care doctor who do sign up are unlikely to stay long when they get sick and find out it will take thirty days to get an appointment.

The most likely scenario—the only one that could make the public option "work," in terms of it being a more superficially attractive alternative to private plans—is that the Biden public option would use Medicare rates and force every doctor and hospital that accepts Medicare to accept it as well.

Faced with a competitor that plays by a different set of rules, private-sector insurance would collapse, and everyone would be forced into the public option. This is because the Biden plan explicitly allows businesses to satisfy their legal requirement to offer a health plan by pushing their employees into the public option. So, employer-provided private-sector insurance would evaporate as well as in the individual marketplace.

Don't be fooled. The result of Biden's "moderate" public option plan is single-payer, government-run health care with all its devastating consequences in terms of hospital closures, lower quality of care, and less innovation.

The Affordable Care Act at Ten

It is also important to understand that when Biden says he wants to build on the imagined success of the Affordable Care Act, he is proposing to erect a skyscraper on a cracked and broken foundation. Ten years after the Affordable Care Act, the most significant result of Obamacare has been to make health insurance less affordable, not more. By 2017, average premiums had doubled in the individual marketplace since the year before Obamacare's main regulations went into effect.[10] They increased by another 26 percent in 2018 before President Trump's reforms allowed states to create stabilization pools and other tools to stop the bleeding.

Premiums declined by 1.5 percent in 2019.[11] Average deductibles for silver plans had also climbed to over $4,000 by 2017.

These huge cost increases hit middle-class Americans the hardest. Under Obamacare, Americans who make more than 400 percent of the poverty line are ineligible for subsidies. CMS Chief Seema Verma uses the example of a sixty-year-old couple in Grand Island, Nebraska, earning $70,000 per year. They're just above the threshold for subsidies, which means that they must spend $38,000 per year on premiums. That's over half their income, and they could still be responsible for up $11,100 in out-of-pocket expenses. One health economist, Robert Laszewski, was cited in a recent *Forbes* article by John C. Goodman as noting that a family of four in Northern Virginia is paying $19,484 in premiums plus a $6,500 deductible—essentially having to pay $25,984 before receiving any meaningful benefits from the insurance.[12]

Furthermore, most of the plans available feature extremely narrow networks of providers that exclude the best doctors. As Goodman has written, Obamacare turned plans available in the individual marketplace into private-sector versions of Medicaid plans, or "Medicaid with a high deductible." Goodman notes that there is not a single health plan in the Dallas–Fort Worth area available on the Obamacare exchanges that includes the University of Texas Southwestern Medical School, widely considered one of the best research hospitals in the country. There is also not a single Obamacare plan in all of Texas that covers treatment at MD Anderson Cancer Center in Houston. What good is being able to get insurance if you have a preexisting condition, if there are no good doctors covered to treat that condition?

One big reason Obamacare caused the huge spike in premiums and deductibles in the individual market is that the measures it put in place to supposedly control premiums failed. Take the medical loss ratio (MLR) rule.

The MLR rule requires that insurance companies in the individual and small group market to spend at least 80 percent of the premiums they collect on medical claims. The threshold is 85 percent in the fully insured large group market. Failing to meet that threshold requires that the insurer issues rebates to plan members. The goal is to keep premiums in check by limiting insurance companies' profits. But like many of Obamacare's rules that sound good, it is harmful in practice. A percentage cap means that insurance companies have more room for profit if the underlying health claims spend is bigger. So the rule creates an incentive for insurance companies to pay higher prices to providers for medical services. It also lowers their incentives to police health care fraud. A recent investigation by Pro Publica detailed just how little effort insurance companies put into preventing fraudulent claims.[13]

Two recent studies showed that insurance companies that were previously below the MLR threshold made up the difference through a rise in claims costs rather than by lowering premiums.[14] Another study suggests that insurance companies engage in a high degree of manipulation of their financial information to overestimate claims to put themselves into compliance.[15]

At Gingrich 360, we had a discussion with a company that partners with patients and insurance companies to save money by finding lower-priced health care providers. They told us that one of the main concerns they have heard from insurance companies is that their service may work too well. If the insurance company lowers their medical claims too much, they would fall short of the MLR rule and they would have to lower premiums.

However, by far the biggest reason Obamacare caused such huge increases in premiums and deductibles was because of the burdensome requirements imposed on plans under the guise of protecting patients. Most Americans agree that people with preexisting conditions should be guaranteed the right to purchase affordable insurance. This is one of the few components of Obamacare upon which Republicans and Democrats agree. In fact, many states had already created guaranteed coverage pools for people with preexisting conditions before the passage of the law. These plans featured a wide network of available doctors and comprehensive coverage—precisely the features that someone who is sick or prone to get sick would want.

Obamacare could have taken the approach of supporting states in these efforts by providing additional funding to subsidize the costs of these plans or even requiring the states that did not have such a program establish one. This way, taxpayer funds would have been directed at those who needed the most medical care. We could have guaranteed coverage for those with preexisting conditions without raising premiums and deductibles for everyone else in the individual marketplace.

Instead, Obamacare imposed blanket requirements on all insurance sold in the individual marketplace that forced middle-class Americans to bear the brunt of covering the health care claims of the sickest of their fellow citizens. The law did this first by preventing insurance companies from engaging in underwriting, which allows plans to raise or lower premiums based on a person's expected medical expenses; and second, by requiring that plans cover a variety of medical services that many healthy Americans may not want or need covered.

The practical impact of these requirements was that insurance became more expensive than it was worth for most Americans shopping in the individual marketplace. The only people who were getting a good deal were those who were already sick and knew they would receive value from the plans, and relatively low-income people who were having their premiums subsidized to a great degree.

It's no wonder then that as premiums and deductibles climbed and provider networks became narrower, the number of Americans enrolled in the individual marketplace who were ineligible for subsidies fell. They simply couldn't afford the Affordable Care Act plans. Even many who could afford high premiums chose not to enroll because they were such a bad value. This of course, exacerbated the problem, because as fewer healthy people enrolled, the ratio of sick people to healthy people became higher, which drove up premiums and deductibles even more.

President Trump: Providing Relief from Obamacare

Despite this clear record of the Affordable Care Act's failure to deliver on its central promise, President Trump and Republicans were criticized for "undermining" Obamacare by repealing the individual mandate as part of the 2017 tax cut. But for Americans who were being given a choice between a tax penalty or buying insurance that wasn't worth the money, repealing the mandate was a relief.

Instead, thanks to President Trump's leadership, these individuals and families could avail themselves of new, more affordable plans. Obamacare had some exceptions to the rules that were the primary culprit of driving up premiums and deductibles for everyone. One of those exceptions was in short-term, limited-duration plans. However, Obama's Department of Health and Human Services reduced the maximum length of the plans to three months.

President Trump and his team at HHS recognized these plans as an opportunity to reintroduce affordable insurance back to Americans who did not receive insurance from their employers. They changed Obama's HHS rules to increase the maximum duration of the plans to 364 days and made them renewable for up to three years of coverage. These plans can have premiums as much as 60 percent below what is available in the Obamacare exchanges, according to analysis from the Congressional Budget Office and the Joint Committee on Taxation.[16]

These plans became critically important during the Wuhan virus pandemic. According to Brian Blase, a former White House

Special Assistant to the President, one company that offers short-term plans saw a 165 percent increase in enrollment between February and March 2020. Ninety percent of the new enrollees were previously uninsured. Blase pointed out that because of the expanded unemployment benefits passed as part of the emergency legislation, many newly unemployed people did not qualify for subsidies on the Obamacare exchanges. This made short-term plans with their lower premiums a much better option.[17]

President Trump also allowed companies the option to satisfy Obamacare's coverage requirement by giving their employees pretax money in a health reimbursement arrangement (HRA), which they could then use to purchase individual coverage on the exchanges. This reform took effect in 2020, and it will finally allow employers to help pay for health care coverage for their employees that is portable. If a person likes his health plan, he can keep it if he changes jobs, since it belongs to him, not his company.

The next step should be to adopt the idea of John Goodman, a health economist, to combine these two reforms by allowing the sale of short-term plans on the exchanges so they can compete against the bloated Obamacare plans. This step would likely take an act of Congress.

Trump's HHS also issued rules allowing groups of small businesses and other entities to band together and negotiate as one with insurance companies for coverage. These Association Health Plans will give millions of more Americans more affordable options than what is available now that Obamacare has made a mess of the individual marketplace.

Finally, President Trump also gave states more flexibility to create their own solutions to lower premiums in the individual marketplace. The Trump HHS issued waivers to those who submitted plans to take the Obamacare subsidies and allocate them in a more optimal way. As a result, many states created reinsurance programs that function like what existed before Obamacare.

In fact, one of the big reasons Obamacare premiums stabilized at a national level in 2019 was due to the success of state-issued waivers to lower premiums.

A New Hope

The rush among Democrats to adopt government-run health care, whether it is all at once like Sanders or through a Trojan horse like Biden's public option plan, is an admittance of failure. It shows that even they recognize that the Affordable Care Act failed to deliver on its central promise: to make health care affordable. This is because it failed to control the underlying cost of health care. But their solution of price-setting is a one-way street to hospital closures, waiting lists, lower-quality health care, and less medical and biopharmaceutical innovation.

Fortunately, our choice is not between the status quo and the Democrats' big-government health care disaster. There is another approach that would supercharge America's supply of health care, deliver even more innovation, and lower costs by as much as 50 percent. What's more: This approach is not a theory. It is already happening, and President Trump has noticed.

10.

★ ▬▬▬▬▬▬▬▬▬▬▬▬▬▬▬▬▬▬▬▬ ★

AMERICA'S HEALTH CARE
REBELLIONS, PART I

Imagine your four-year-old daughter wakes up at midnight, crying. She's running a small fever and she keeps tugging at her ear. You recognize the symptoms immediately: an ear infection.

If this was the America of 2020, your daughter's ear infection would mean staying up all night, then making a bleary-eyed, early-morning drive to the urgent care clinic on the other side of town (because the two clinics closer to where you live aren't in your insurance network). Then, after forking over a $25 copay, it means sitting in a waiting room with other sick people for forty-five minutes before finally being seen for three minutes by a doctor, who is somehow more frazzled, tired, and rushed than you are. Then, after getting a prescription for antibiotics, it's off to the pharmacy, where after waiting an additional forty-five minutes for the prescription to be filled, you're shocked to find out you have to pay $20 instead of the $10 you paid last time at the same pharmacy for the same drug. By the time you get home, you're exhausted, stressed out—and you and your child have been exposed to who knows how many germs and viruses during the ordeal. Naturally, you get sick as well, and your daughter's ear infection ends up causing you to miss three additional days of work. A few weeks later, you receive a bill. You owe an additional $174 for the urgent care visit. Even though you went to an in-network provider, you haven't reached your insurance deductible yet. That night your daughter wakes up at midnight with a sore throat and you steel yourself to repeat the ordeal.

Now, imagine that your daughter's late-night cries occur in the America of a few years after a revolutionary series of reforms made by President Trump and a bipartisan coalition of lawmakers at the federal and state levels. These reforms—accelerated by the Wuhan Virus epidemic—radically changed the American health care experience.

Here's how different the patient experience is in the America of 2025:

Instead of being woken up at midnight by your daughter's cries, you get an alert on your smartphone sent from a device around her wrist that she is running a fever. Once you recognize the telltale signs of an ear infection, you pull out your smartphone and activate an app that pulls up all the doctors who are on call for these minor emergencies, lists how much they charge for a virtual medical assessment, and details how much your insurance company will cover. There are no in- or out-of-network doctors—you can choose anyone you want depending on how much you want to spend. You choose a doctor who has an average patient review of 4.2 stars and charges a little *less* than your insurance company will cover (because you're a smart shopper and the difference will be credited to lowering next month's premium). Within seconds, you are video-chatting with the doctor.

You explain what's going on and use a home health kit that integrates with your phone to allow the doctor to peer into your child's ear from hundreds of miles away. She agrees it is an ear infection, writes a digital prescription for antibiotics, and suggests giving her some children's ibuprofen to help with the discomfort.

You receive the alert in your app that the prescription is waiting, thank the doctor before ending the video conference, and then pull up the notification. Just as when you chose the doctor, your app lists all the different pharmacies that carry the drug, the price they charge, and how much your insurance will cover.

Again, there are no in- or out-of-network pharmacies. And it's a good thing. You are about to tap screen to select your normal pharmacy that charges less than your insurance company reimburses. Then you notice that a rival pharmacy has added a rush delivery option promising to have your daughter's prescription to your front door in less than six hours. Competition is fierce between pharmacies nowadays, and they're finding creative new ways to attract customers and make extra money. With the added rush delivery charge, this option costs about $5 more than your insurance will reimburse—but the extra expense means your daughter getting medicine sooner. Worth it!

You make your selection, give your daughter some children's ibuprofen, and get her ready for bed. The entire process, from pulling up the app to purchasing your soon-to-be delivered medicine, took about twenty minutes. Also, at each step in the purchase process, the app calculated the difference between your total bill and how much your insurance company will cover. There are no surprise bills.

When your daughter wakes up the next morning, her medicine is waiting for her. You give her another dose of ibuprofen and bribe her with a cookie to choke down the chalky antibiotic.

You Deserve Better

I chose to begin this section of the book focusing on a typical patient experience in the American health care system. Much of the focus of debate in Washington over health care centers on such horror stories as medical bankruptcies, people dying because they can't afford their insulin, overtreatment, and medical errors.

Meanwhile, defenders of the American health care system point to the miracle treatments being developed that cure genetic diseases and harness the body's own immune systems to fight cancer. They point to the fact that America has the most highly skilled specialty surgeons in the world, and that if you have a serious illness, statistically speaking you will have a better medical outcome here than anywhere else.

These points are all important. The horror stories need to be acknowledged and addressed. The miracle breakthroughs and cures need to be encouraged and made available to all. The heroic and knowledgeable doctors of America need to be celebrated and rewarded for their passion and skill.

But focusing on extreme examples can obscure just how bad the average patient (or customer) experience is in America when compared with what we expect from any other industry. We can't address the extreme examples without fixing the fundamentals.

When tackling any problem, it is often useful to pose the question, "If we were starting from scratch, would we do this?" No way. If we were starting from scratch, there is:

- No way patients wouldn't know the price of treatment until after they receive it.
- No way a single medical provider would have dozens of different prices for a single medical procedure.
- No way your bill for health care services would come in separate pieces over the course of months.
- No way a patient with insurance could end up with tens of thousands of dollars in medical debt because they got sick while traveling or chose an in-network hospital but were treated by out-of-network doctors.

- No way our medicines would cost us wildly different amounts at different pharmacies at different times, depending on what kind of insurance we have.
- No way our patient records would be held captive by our medical providers, making it difficult and time-consuming for us to gain access to see them, much less share them with different providers or loved ones.
- No way we would tolerate up to 400,000 deaths from medical errors per year—the third-leading cause of death in America.[1] This is about three to six times the number of deaths than are currently projected from the Wuhan Virus pandemic.
- No way we would tolerate a system that overtreats patients to the tune of $750 billion per year—unnecessary medical care that actually makes patients sicker instead of healthier.[2]
- No way we would allow a fraud rate of up to 10 percent in health care—over $300 billion in theft every year.[3]
- No way our health insurance would depend on where we work. And that it would change every time we changed jobs.
- No way we would design a health care system in which our choice of insurance would come at the expense of our choice of doctor. Or that we'd design a system in which the health plans guaranteed to be available for those with chronic illness were the most likely to exclude the best doctors and medical systems at treating those conditions.
- No way we would tolerate non-physician insurance adjusters overriding the best judgment of doctors on what health care is best for you.

This is just a smattering of the absurd—and to be blunt, deeply unethical and exploitative—behavior that is considered standard practice in the health care industry. To be clear, there are millions of dedicated, committed Americans working in health care.

This includes not only doctors and nurses but also the executives and managerial-level men and women who help run hospitals and insurance companies. Most of them are mission-oriented people who got into health care because they wanted to help people. In fact, at Gingrich 360, we work directly with some of these people to help improve the health system.

However, the experience of history teaches us that good people operating in a bad system will take part in bad actions. And tragically, this is exactly what happens every day in the American health care system. One of the most appalling examples is the number of hospitals that are suing and garnishing the wages of low-income patients and their families due to unpaid medical bills. One of these patients is Lisa Lester. Her husband was a patient at Mary Washington Hospital in Fredericksburg, Virginia. He was on Medicare, but it didn't cover everything, and the bills kept mounting. The couple explored putting him on her company's insurance plan (ironically, she works for a medical billing company), but it would have cost an additional $1,400 per month—more than half her paycheck. When Lisa's husband died in 2018 of congestive heart failure, he had accumulated over $10,000 in unpaid bills.

Lisa was one of over twenty thousand patients and their families sued by Mary Washington Hospital from 2013 through 2018. For reference, the population of Fredericksburg is only 28,000. The hospital sued so many people that for years, one day per week in the local courthouse was dedicated solely to Mary Washington cases. In 2017, Mary Washington garnished the wages of more than 1,500 patients.

At Gingrich 360, we learned about Lisa's story from Patient Rights Advocate, a nonprofit organization that advocates for transparency in health care. This group, led by life science entrepreneur and proponent for patients rights Cynthia Fisher, has made patient access to information and real price transparency a key focus of their efforts. They were in the courthouse in December 2018 when Lisa's case was up. They were there encouraging patients to contest the lawsuits and offering to represent them. (It turns out that when these poor patients show up to the courthouse with a lawyer, the hospital is much more willing to cut a deal or even drop the suit entirely.) They also filmed patients telling their stories. You can view them at the Patients' Rights Advocate website.

Public outrage over Mary Washington's billing practices led the hospital to announce it would stop suing patients in 2019. However, recent news stories have highlighted several similar cases throughout the country. Methodist Le Bonheur Healthcare in Memphis, Tennessee, which, like Mary Washington Hospital, is a nonprofit that does not pay state or federal taxes, filed 8,300 lawsuits from 2014 through 2018.[4] Patients in Coffeyville, Kansas, are being sued by Coffeyville Regional Medical Center and other local hospitals over unpaid bills, having their wages garnished and even being sent to jail for failing to appear in court.[5] UVA Health System in Blacksburg, Virginia, another nonprofit, sued patients 36,000 times for more than $106 million from 2013 through 2018. One lawsuit was over a $13.91 bill. During that period, the hospital earned more than $554 million in net revenue. About one hundred of the lawsuits per year were against UVA Health System's own employees. That means UVA was garnishing the wages of its own employees to pay for the medical care they received at the hospital where they worked.[6] It's a story reminiscent of early twentieth-century coal miners who ended up owing the coal companies money because their wages weren't enough to cover the cost of the medical care, burial insurance, equipment, and other fees they were forced to purchase from the company store.

Most of these patients, like the Lester family, are employed and have insurance, but they cannot meet the deductible and coinsurance. When Carlsbad Medical Center was asked by the *New*

York Times to comment on the fact that it had sued almost three thousand patients since 2015, the hospital responded with a statement saying, "The majority of accounts from which we seek to collect payment are patients with insurance who have not fulfilled their deductible, co-paying, or co-insurance responsibility set by their health insurance plan."[7]

While it is true that most hospitals are not this aggressive in suing patients, the recent focus on the practice is having an impact. One of the biggest takeaways from recent focus groups we have done on health care is that Americans are empathetic people. We view health care as a moral issue as much as a pocketbook one. When Americans of all socioeconomic backgrounds see that low-income patients with insurance are being sued, having their wages garnished, and even being sent to jail over medical debt, it is clear to them that the American health system needs serious changes.

Americans also understand that even those who are not in medical debt are having more and more of their money consumed by health care premiums. (Remember, the portion of your insurance premium paid by your employer is part of your compensation. If it wasn't going toward premiums, it could be more cash in your paycheck.) Americans also understand that even while they pay for expensive health insurance, there are so many holes in the system that they are still a few strokes of bad luck away from financial ruin due to a medical emergency.

Given this exploitation and dysfunction, it is understandable that so many Americans want the government to take over. But government-run health care like Medicare for All, the public option, or even efforts to simply fix Obamacare are ultimately dead ends. To the extent that they offer any additional financial security or predictability, it comes at huge and unacceptable cost. They result in higher taxes, yes, but more important, also in lowering the quality and availability of our health care. What good is it to have so-called free health care if you can't see a doctor when you need one? How can health care be a right, as so many of the radical Democratic Left claims, if the government refuses to cover the newest and most effective treatments? This is the experience that Americans on Medicaid, veterans dealing with the US Department of Veterans Affairs, and even some on Medicare experience every day. It is also the experience of citizens of other countries with nationalized health systems. It is not one we want to replicate here.

Fortunately, there is another rebellion happening against the health care status quo. Instead of turning to government to take over, a ragtag group of physicians, medical entrepreneurs, patient advocates, and innovative business leaders are creating a new-model health system by returning to the basics of what works in America.

These acts of rebellion are scattered and uncoordinated, but they are already delivering astonishing results. In fact, this rebel health care alternative is producing vastly better health for patients at about half the cost of America's health care status quo.

Tragically, for many years, the successes of these health care rebels have been ignored by the political system. That changed on January 20, 2017 when Donald J. Trump took the oath of office.

Rebellion Number 1: Ending Secret Pricing and Bringing Transparency to Health Care

One of the greatest strengths of President Trump is that he goes outside of the typical Washington channels for information. This drives the news media (and likely his staff) crazy but it allows him to avoid the Beltway groupthink that continually fails to produce solutions that match the scale of America's challenges. This hunger for big solutions and willingness to consider untraditional points of view is what led President Trump to the health care rebels, and the cornerstone of their—and now his—strategy to deliver real change in health care: radical transparency.

Dr. Keith Smith is one of these health care rebels. He is an anesthesiologist and the managing director of the Surgery Center of Oklahoma. Back in 2009, Dr. Smith made a truly radical decision. He posted prices online for all the surgeries the center performs. If this doesn't sound radical to you, it's probably because you are comparing what Dr. Smith did to what is considered normal (in fact, mandatory) in every other industry in America. But due to the way the health care system has evolved in America, most health care providers keep their prices secret. In fact, most doctors and nurses have no idea what their prices are at all.

This is because health care providers don't just have one price for a service, they have dozens. And these prices can vary wildly depending on the patient's circumstances—most significantly, whether he has insurance and what carrier he uses. To make things worse, the prices for services are disaggregated into component parts. For instance, the price for treating a broken arm is actually the sum of at least four different prices: one for the Xray, one for the application of an arm splint or cast, one for the doctor visit, and then one for the doctor to treat you. And that's if they're *not* nickel-and-diming you.

The opposite is true for the Surgery Center of Oklahoma, and the small but growing number of health care providers who are following its lead. If you have your smartphone or computer nearby, open your browser and go to its website: surgerycenterok. com. You simply click on the part of the body that needs attention, choose a procedure from a drop-down list, and receive the price. Now try finding that same information on the website of your local hospital. Chances are you'll spend a lot of time and find no answers.

Dr. Smith's prices for surgical procedures aren't just easier to understand because they are public. They're also "bundled." They include the initial consultation, the facility fee, the surgeon's fee, the anesthesiologist fee, and uncomplicated follow-up care. They don't include hardware or implants necessary for the procedure, because those can vary by patient. However, the prices for those are provided after the initial consultation, prior to the surgery, and with zero markup.

Why is it that Dr. Smith and the Surgery Center of Oklahoma can list one easy-to-understand price for their services while others cannot? Simple: Dr. Smith doesn't individually negotiate with dozens of different insurance companies. His prices are the same for everyone (apart from some free or greatly discounted care he provides to the poor). Furthermore, he doesn't accept payment from insurance companies, because dealing with their claims departments is too big a hassle and consumes resources that could instead be spent treating patients. Instead, his patients pay cash up front, choosing to either forgo insurance entirely (this can make sense for patients with insurance if they have a high deductible) or seek reimbursement from their health coverage provider afterward.

In the eleven years since Dr. Smith published the Surgery Center of Oklahoma's prices online, he has changed them only four times—each time lowering them. Meanwhile, in the commercial insurance market for large-employer plans, the price of knee replacements increased by 74 percent from 2003 through 2016, according to an analysis by Peterson-Kaiser Family Foundation. The same analysis showed that overall health care prices paid by large employers have increased by 21.6 percent from 2008 to 2018.[8]

This leads us to the truly amazing thing about the prices at the Surgery Center of Oklahoma. Besides being public and easy to understand, they are also about *half* of what commercial insurance pays on average for the same procedures. In fact, it may be more accurate to say that they are half the price *because* they are public and easy to understand.

Joe DeSantis is the chief strategy officer at Gingrich 360 and is my main advisor on health care policy. His experience with a recent interaction with the health system perfectly captures how the byzantine, opaque system of health care pricing in America is failing US patients and driving up costs.

Joe and his family are insured under his wife's employer's preferred provider network plan. Earlier this year, his nine-year-old son was suffering from heel pain, so they took him to a podiatrist. In addition to prescribing orthotics and physical therapy, the doctor said his son should wear a walking boot for two weeks to help the inflammation die down. A few weeks later, Joe received the explanation of benefits from his health insurer. Here are the key data points:

Service Description	Provider Charges	Allowed Charges	Your Responsibility	Paid by [Insurer]
OFFICE VISIT	$249.00	$98.00	$20	$78.00
XRAYS	$70.00	$37.49	$0	$37.49
XRAYS	$70.00	$37.49	$0	$37.49
MEDICAL EQUIP	$585.00	$185.07	$0	$185.07
MEDICAL EQUIP	$585.00	$185.07	$0	$185.07
MEDICAL EQUIP	$559.00	$230.62	$0	$230.62

The two Xrays were for each foot. The first two "MEDICAL EQUIP" items were for each orthotic. The third was for the walking boot. At first glance, it may look like this is where Joe's insurance really earned its keep. It negotiated about $2,118 in charges down to $773.74 and covered all but $20. But some simple research shows that these benefits are not as good as they appear.

First, Joe called the podiatrist's office and asked how much an appointment would be if he were paying cash rather than going through insurance. He was told $200. So that's already less of a discount than claimed. He then went to MDSave.com, a website allowing patients to pay cash for health care services. He found a nearby imaging center that charges $60 for Xrays. He also found a service called Upstep that creates custom-made orthotics by sending the mold material used to create the feet casts to your home. Cost: $229.00 for the pair. Finally (and here is the kicker), he looked up the walking boot his son was given by the podiatrist. He quickly found it on sale for $49, marked down from *$99*. Not the $559.00 the provider charges—and not the $230.62 paid by the insurer.

This means that in the transparent, cash-pay health care economy, Joe's son consumed $599 in health care services and products—nearly $175 *less* than what his insurer actually paid (with the $20 copay) in the complicated, opaque system of provider networks. The cash price was about 23 percent less than the insurer-negotiated so-called discount.

This pattern of cash prices beating insurance-negotiated prices holds true throughout health care. Worse, it gets more pronounced the more expensive a procedure is. Larry Van Horn is an economist from Vanderbilt University. He took data from over one billion commercial insurance claims and compared the allowed charges (the insurance-negotiated prices) with the prices patients paid using the aforementioned MDSave website. He found that patients using MDSave paid, on average, 39 percent less for medical procedures than commercial insurance.[9]

The implications of this figure are staggering. In 2017, the United States spent $3.5 trillion on health care. Commercial insurance paid for about 34 percent of that amount, and hospital and physician services account for about 53 percent of all health care spending.[10] This means that if commercial insurance paid the same as cash-paying patients for hospital and physician services, we would save *$246 billion per year*. This would translate to about a 21 percent reduction in health insurance premiums: a $1,509-per-year saving for individuals and $4,321-per-year savings for families.

Larry's work also revealed the chief culprit for insurance overpayment for health care procedures: massive price variation. In markets that are functional and work to benefit consumers, prices for similar products tend to coalesce within a narrow range. For example, a three-pack of Crest 3D White toothpaste costs $9.99 on Amazon.com, whereas a three-pack of Colgate Optic White costs $10.96—about a 10 percent variation. The manufacturer's suggested retail price (MSRP) for basic model 2020 minivans for sale in the United States ranges from $27,400 for the 2020 Kia Sedona to $33,745 for the Chrysler Pacifica—about a 20 percent variation.

Larry found that for cash prices in health care, the mean spread between the bottom and top quartile of cash prices is 22 percent, which roughly matches what we see in normal marketplaces. However, for insurance-negotiated prices, the average spread is 77 percent. Digging into Larry's data is even more illustrative. It shows that for relatively inexpensive procedures such as lab tests and Xrays, the bottom quartile of insurance-negotiated prices *are* generally lower than the bottom quartile of cash prices. The top quartile of prices, however, are much higher compared with the top quartile of cash payments.

As the procedures become more expensive, the insurance advantage for the bottom quartile of prices disappears. Meanwhile, the top quartile of insurance-negotiated prices for the procedures remain much higher than the top quartile of cash prices. This means that the more expensive a procedure is, the less likely insurance is to pay a better price than a cash-paying customer, and the more likely insurance companies are to massively overpay in real dollars.

Larry's analysis is not the first to show the problem of price variation in health care. Another study from 2015 by Blue Cross Blue Shield showed that the price insurance paid for a total knee replacement in Dallas, Texas, ranged from $16,772 to $61,584.[11] Of course, some variation in price can be expected due to high-risk patients. But those should be a few exceptions at the high end of the spectrum that make only a modest impact on the average price. The same study pegged the national average for knee replacements at around $31,124.

There is also wide variation in average prices among markets. A Kaiser Family Foundation analysis of insurance data showed that the price paid for total knee replacements averaged from $23,000 in the Louisville, Kentucky, area to $50,000 in the New York City area. Similar variations in prices paid by insurance within and among markets exist for most other medical services, from MRIs to pharmaceuticals to hip replacements. These wide variations in prices raise obvious questions: Why doesn't everyone in Dallas go to the $16,000 facility? Why don't New Yorkers fly to Louisville to get their knees replaced and save $25,000 minus the cost of airfare and lodging?

The reason is secret prices. Secret prices are a byproduct of the way insurance companies construct provider networks, which are the list of doctors you are allowed to use if you want your insurance to help pay the bill (or have it count toward your deductible). These networks don't just restrict our choice of doctors, they also prevent us from making informed choices within those networks about health care providers. This leads to higher prices.

Insurance companies and health care providers have similar reasons for wanting prices to be secret. For insurers, the secret prices are the supposed proprietary ingredients with which they make their health plans. An insurer that negotiates lower prices with providers will be able to charge lower premiums, giving them a competitive advantage. They don't want these rates disclosed, because then their competitors in the insurance space will demand the same rates.

Hospitals want the prices to be secret for a similar reason. Hospitals start with a so-called chargemaster price for services and procedures and then negotiate a discount with the insurance company. In truth, the chargemaster price is a fantasy number that is merely a starting point for negotiation. Nevertheless, the provider doesn't want the negotiated rate made public, or else they believe they will have to give the same price to everyone.

In theory, provider networks should be saving us money despite the secret prices. Insurers should be able to leverage the fact that they represent tens or hundreds of thousands of patients to get the best possible prices from most of the local health care providers. Meanwhile, the higher-priced providers who won't negotiate a competitive rate are left out of the networks, so patients don't use those facilities. This combination of bulk purchase discounts and leaving out the highest-priced providers should create the optimal balance between low premiums and choice of doctors for patients.

In practice, it doesn't work this way. The reason is that providers, particularly large, dominant hospital systems which have the highest prices, have more leverage over insurance companies than the other way around. Insurance companies succeed by enrolling enough people to accurately predict claims for the coming year. The more people they enroll, the more confidence they have in those predictions, and the better they can set appropriate premiums. But big health care systems can exploit this to their advantage. They understand that when customers choose health insurance, they aren't just looking at premiums and deductibles, they also look to see if their doctor or hospital is in network. This is doubly true for human resources professionals who choose company health plans. Their incentive is to keep employees happy as much as it is to keep spending under control. Switching a company plan to one that doesn't cover people's doctors, or the nearby hospital, is a surefire way to generate employee backlash if it is not handled correctly.

Large hospital systems exploit this leverage in ways that go beyond charging higher prices. For instance, they will insist "on all or nothing" inclusion of their services in networks. This means that if the insurer wants the system's hematology specialists in network (which may be the only local options available for patients) they also need to include the hospital's imaging services and orthopedic surgeons, even if there are much-lower-priced local providers for those services.

They will also include anti-steering clauses in their contracts to prevent the insurer from pushing patients toward lower-priced providers. Even without these clauses, providers know that thanks to secret prices, patients will resent the insurance company for pushing them to higher-value providers, because they can't see for themselves the difference in price.

The result of secret prices is that in 17.7 percent of the American economy—$3.6 trillion—customers are making decisions absent of price considerations.[12] Many academics and those in the health care industry refer to this problem as patients being "price insensitive." What they mean is that because insurance is paying the bill, patients have no incentive to choose lower-priced providers.

But this characterization is incorrect. In fact, patients are very sensitive to price. Patients feel the impact of prices while still in the deductible phase of their coverage, during which they are responsible for paying 100 percent of the price the insurer has negotiated with the provider. This means that if a resident of San Francisco needs a lower back MRI and has a $7,000 deductible, according to a 2016 analysis by ClearHealthCosts.com, they could end up paying between $475 and $6,221.[13] Patients feel the impact of prices after they reach their deductible because they still must pay coinsurance until reaching their out-of-pocket maximum of $16,500. In the MRI example, above, a 20 percent coinsurance is the difference between $95 and $1,244. Patients feel the impact of prices because even after they reach their out-of-pocket maximum, higher prices lead to higher premiums.

The problem is that patients feel this impact *after* making their decision rather than at the point of sale. Patients also feel the impact of prices because they put off getting care when they need it. A 2018 University of Chicago poll showed that 44 percent of Americans skip doctor visits because of cost, 40 percent "skipped a recommended medical test or treatment in the last 12 months due to cost," and 32 percent were "unable to fill a prescription or took less of a medication because of the cost."[14] This is the medical impact of patients being blindsided by charges they cannot see in advance.

Prices also impact patients outside the clinical experience. Money spent on health care is money that can't be saved for college, invested, or even used for basic necessities like food and clothing. Premium increases in employer-sponsored plans is money spent that can't go toward higher salaries. So, no. Patients are not "price insensitive." They are price blind. And that's because the health care industry has put a blindfold on them, leaving patients powerless against a relentless escalation of health care prices and insurance premiums that is leaving them poorer and in worse health.

But this is about to change. Enter President Trump.

THE PRICE-TRANSPARENCY REVOLUTION

Secret pricing is the underlying dysfunction behind the skyrocketing cost of health care in America. It is responsible for the out-of-control increases in health insurance premiums as well as rising out-of-pocket costs: deductibles, copays, and coinsurance. It is responsible for the narrow insurance networks that limit patients' access to the doctors of their choice. It is responsible for the hassles of prior authorization in which the insurance company inserts itself between the patient and the doctor. It is responsible for price-gouging and surprise medical bills. It is responsible for the fraud, overtreatment, waste, and administrative bloat—which are eliminated in other markets through clear prices and competition for customers.

Attempts to address these problems in a piecemeal fashion will ultimately fail. The Band-Aid solutions will ultimately be overwhelmed by the underlying dysfunction. In June 2019, President Trump signed a groundbreaking executive order to finally put a stop to secret prices and return power back to patients. The order instructed HHS to develop rules that would require hospitals, other health care providers, and insurance companies to make all their prices public. Those prices include all their negotiated rates as well as their self-pay cash rates. HHS finalized the rules for hospitals in November, and the rules for insurance companies should be finalized in the spring of 2020.

Importantly, this information is required to be made available in real time in a machine-readable format. This will allow third-party developers to create apps that allow patients to shop not just for the lowest-priced provider within insurance networks, which will make patients more aware of how much more it will cost them to get care in a big-hospital system, but also compare negotiated rates among providers when making a decision on what insurance to buy. This is extremely important information if you are choosing between high-deductible plans. It is also useful information when deciding whether traditional insurance is worthwhile at all. Many people may find that having a catastrophic plan and then self-paying for most routine health expenditures works best for them.

The rule is being challenged in court by the hospitals. If it survives, it could be one of the most sweeping and consequential reforms of health care in history. It would be an enormous step forward in creating a genuinely functional free market in health care.

WIDER TRANSPARENCY: QUALITY

In our early 2020 focus groups on health care at Gingrich 360, we spent a good amount of time talking about what it means to make the health system more transparent. Prices came up a lot, but Americans view a transparent health system in much broader terms.

For instance, many participants see quality transparency as a natural and necessary partner to price transparency. This makes sense. You want to know what you are paying for. Right now, quality transparency in the health system is incredibly difficult. The US government collects a fair amount of data via Medicare, but the way it reports the data is spread out among several different programs and uses conflicting standards. It is also not presented in the most understandable way.

One of the biggest holes in the data is on independent surgery centers. This is important because many patients assume that they should go to a brand-name hospital system for their surgeries, because people tend to trust brand names as a signal of quality. In fact, most academic studies of these independent surgery centers show that they provide remarkably high-quality care at much lower prices than hospitals.[15] They're less expensive, because they tend to specialize in a few different procedures, allowing the centers to cut out unnecessary expenses. They have high quality, because they perform the procedures so often the surgical teams become good at them. Fewer complications also lead to lower prices.

Having easily comparable, quality data on independent surgery centers and hospitals will allow patients to see that the lower price at the surgery centers does not mean lower quality. Getting more patients to utilize these centers will be a critical step in eliminating unnecessary spending in health care.

Websites like Leapfrog, ProPublica, and US News and World Report also report quality ratings on hospitals and doctors. But most of them rely on surveys to collect the information, meaning that health care providers are sharing only the information they want to share. The various methodologies can also be confusing. Still, there is a fair amount of data on quality already. I recommend Leapfrog Group's Resources and Tools section, which you can find online, and lists the best resources available.

Fortunately, we are on our way to a big improvement in patients' ability to access quality information about their health care options. That's because President Trump's health care transparency executive order didn't stop just with prices. It also instructed HHS to develop a system for quality transparency in health care providers so patients can understand what they are buying.

Developing a consensus on what measures of quality will be used and how it will be reported will be a real challenge. As you can imagine, there are many different measures that could be used. Further, some metrics are hugely important to some procedures and largely irrelevant to others. And patients also need to be able to see quality data on individual doctors, not just overall scores for a given facility. If a hypothetical hospital employs nine excellent doctors and one terrible one, it likely has a pretty good overall score.

Just because it will be difficult, however, does not mean it should not be done. Americans deserve to know if they are choosing the best care.

WIDER TRANSPARENCY: ELECTRONIC HEALTH RECORDS

During the focus groups Gingrich 360 conducted on health care, we asked participants to describe what a transparent health system would look like. We expected lots of discussion on prices and quality—and there was. But we were surprised by the intense focus of participants on wanting access to their health records.

Around the same time, a close friend of mine described to me her experience trying to change doctors from one in a big Washington, DC, hospital system to one located near her new home. She eventually got so frustrated with the experience that she sent one of her employees down to the hospital to sit in the records office and refuse to leave until she was given copies of her records.

By law, patients are guaranteed the right to obtain a copy of their medical records. However, the process of obtaining them is so cumbersome and outdated that at a practical level, patients are still unable to really utilize them.

First, patients must pay to get them. Every state has its own rules about what a reasonable fee is, but in general, patients must pay the hospital a $15 to $25 search fee to find the records, and then pay a dollar per page on top of that. If you are someone with chronic illnesses, this can add up to a lot of money.

Second, too much of the process is paper-based. The official request is often required to be mailed or faxed to the doctor's office, which makes it more time-consuming for the patient, and the records are returned on paper as well. This makes transferring your records to a new doctor difficult, because providers are using electronic health records now.

In the early 2000s, I was one of the chief advocates of electronic medical records. One of the biggest problems the health system faces is a lack of care coordination. Patients go from doctor to doctor to deal with different specialists for different conditions, and they don't always know what the other doctors are doing. This leads to waste in the form of duplicated tests, procedures and paperwork, as well as medical errors, such as two doctors independently prescribing drugs that interact badly.

Electronic health records were supposed to fix this. The vision was that it would work like a bank card. It doesn't matter where you have a bank account, you can get money from any ATM in the world. We imagined that a patient would walk into any hospital or doctor's office, pull out a card, and the provider would be able to see his or her pertinent information.

Today, we have electronic health records, but this vision of convenient interoperability has not borne out. First, we did not anticipate the degree to which hospital systems and the major electronic medical record companies would collude to make the different health records systems inoperable. This was done explicitly to trap patients in a health system by making it as difficult as possible to move to a different one. It also traps doctors, because it makes it difficult for them to bring their patients with them when they move.

Second, the electronic health record interacted with health care's arcane and labyrinthine billing system in a truly destructive way. The number of different fields that doctors have been required to fill out is making the electronic health records indecipherable to patients. It is also adding significantly to doctors' workload and is interfering with the patient-doctor relationship, because the doctor's face is behind a screen for the entire appointment. Some doctors are now hiring electronic scribes to walk with them from appointment to appointment to record all the different data points.

There has been some success with electronic health records. They have helped improve care coordination within health systems, because all the different doctors working under the same umbrella have access to, and are adding to, the same record. They have also enabled health systems to better track health outcomes, because the uniform digitization of the data enables more rapid and systematized analysis. Furthermore, many patients can access some of their patient information, such as test results, via propriety portals that are built into each hospital or doctor's office's electronic health record system. But they cannot download that data, so the vision of patient empowerment to move between providers is still missing.

There is no reason why in this age of instantaneous access to data located anywhere in the world that patients should have their medical information trapped in one location, with their only recourse being to have to pay potentially hundreds of dollars to receive printed copies of their own records.

Fortunately, in addition to prices and quality ratings, President Trump's executive order on health care transparency instructed

HHS to create rules that would guarantee patients instant access to view and share their medical records. HHS released the final rules in the spring of 2020. They set standards for application programming interfaces (APIs) that would allow patients to use third-party apps to store and share their medical records with other doctors or loved ones. This is the vision of patients being in control and allowing any doctor access to their records that we conceived of in the first decade of the twenty-first century, just updated for the age of the mobile phone. Instead of a card, it is an app.

President Trump's approach will improve health care quality, since doctors from different health systems will now be able to access the same patient information to avoid duplication and errors. It will also supercharge his administration's rules on price and quality information, because it will allow for truly seamless shopping among providers for health care services and procedures. The fewer practical barriers that patients face when switching between providers, the more price and quality ratings can promote competition.

Transparency of price and quality, and real-time access and ability to share your patient information: This is a health system that puts patients in control of their health, a system that will make health care more affordable and allow Americans to get the care they need when they need it.

11.

★ ▬▬▬▬▬▬▬▬▬▬▬▬▬▬▬▬▬▬▬▬▬▬▬▬▬▬ ★

AMERICA'S HEALTH CARE REBELLIONS, PART II

Transparency in health care will be a huge catalyst to catapult health care into the 21st century. It will accelerate innovation, lower prices, and improve quality. Ultimately it will save lives and save money. But it is just one of five rebellions necessary to improve health care in America. I discuss the next two in this chapter.

Rebellion Number 2: Taking Control Away from the Middlemen

Transparency in price and quality combined with real-time access to one's medical records is the foundation of a new American health care system, because it enables an entirely new approach for interacting with the health system. For instance, once providers are posting transparent prices, the layers and layers of middlemen in the health system that add little to no value while increasing costs can begin to be excised.

Taking control away from the middlemen is the second act of rebellion in health care. In some cases, this means removing them completely. In other cases, it means insisting that they become much more transparent, so they are delivering real value.

One of the main fronts in this rebellion is in employer health plans. A growing number of companies have grown tired of annual increases in traditional health insurance premiums. However, instead of taking the approach of most companies over the past decade—increasing deductibles so employees take on more of the cost—these companies have opted to take more control over their employee benefit dollars.

Many large companies and unions already self-insure and have been doing so for decades. They pay directly for their employees' health care but still rent an insurance company's provider network and their negotiated rates. They do this because it is the easiest way to protect their employees against balance billing—when a provider charges a patient the difference between what a health plan will pay and their chargemaster price. They also use the insurance companies to process the health claims. This arrangement between self-insuring companies and health insurance companies is why even though you may work for a large company that self-insures, your insurance card probably still has the name of a major health insurance company.

While companies are saving a little money by adopting this model, they are not taking full advantage of the potential of self-insuring. By relying on the insurance company to process the claims, the companies are not seeing the enormous price variation among providers in the network.

They are also not catching all the fraudulent claims. Fraud in health care is an enormous problem. Estimates are that up to 10 percent of health care spending—over $300 billion—is from fraud.[1] I wrote the foreword to a book called *Stop Paying the Crooks* by Jim Frogue, which goes into this problem in detail. It shows how Medicare and Medicaid are unable to keep up with all the fraud and how it costs taxpayers hundreds of billions a year. However, recent reporting suggests that the problem may be even worse in private insurance.[2] Insurance companies are simply not incentivized to rigorously police fraud because it is simply easier to pass on the costs to their customers.

However, there is a growing recognition among business leaders in America that they need to start taking more control over their health care expenses. Companies are hiring third-party claims administrators—or processing the claims themselves—so they can see which providers are delivering the best value. And some have gone so far as to directly contract with providers, entirely getting rid of the insurance company networks.

The result is an emergence of a much more proactive form of self-insurance, in which employers steer their employees to the lowest-cost, highest-quality providers in the networks, with benefits like no copay, no deductibles, and even cash bonuses. It is being adopted at large companies that already self-insure, and by mid- and small-size companies. Companies employing this approach are already achieving huge savings—not to mention making their employees much healthier, happier, and more financially secure. Here is the approach of this new model:

- Know and monitor your claims data to understand the price variation in your marketplace.
- Engage and inform your employees about your company's health care costs and show them the big differences in prices among providers.
- Incentivize your employees to use low-cost, high-quality providers by waiving copays and deductibles and offering other bonuses for shared savings—including higher salaries from decreasing the overall health expenditure.
- Contract directly with price- and quality-transparent surgical centers such as the Oklahoma Surgery Center. If there are none nearby, pay travel expenses with cash incentives for your employees and caregiver to go to one.

- Hire or contract with on-site or nearby primary care providers to be the provider of choice. Be sure that their service includes telemedicine for 24/7 access to a doctor. Monitor the increased use of primary care, decreased hospitalizations, and overall improved health, well-being. and morale of the employees.
- Contract with price-transparent pharmacy benefit managers.

Nationwide price and quality transparency will supercharge this approach. Patient Rights Advocate has been collecting success stories of companies who have been offering much better health coverage to their employees at a fraction of the cost by applying this model.

One of these success stories is Employee Solutions in Plano, Texas. After switching to this model in 2015, their monthly employee expenses dropped from about $800 per month to $450 while also lowering their employees-out-of-pocket expenses. In other words, both the employer and employee are saving money.[3]

Another is Stauffers of Kissel Hill, a grocery and garden store in Lancaster, Pennsylvania. Stauffers has begun steering its employees to price-transparent providers through incentives like no copay, no deductible and cash bonuses for choosing high-quality, low-price providers. The program saves the business 60 percent per procedure, on average. Right now, the program is optional for their employees. They estimate that if all employees participated it would save the company 41 percent on health care costs—or about $1.3 million per year.[4]

One of the keys to making these plans work is active employee engagement and making sure employees are sharing in the benefits. Without properly explaining to employees why they are being steered to certain providers, employees will just feel like they are being micromanaged. Employees need to understand the enormous differences in price among providers and understand that every dollar spent on health care is a dollar that would otherwise be in their paycheck. So transparency is key, and employees need to be rewarded financially with higher salaries and other benefits. For instance, the Phia Group in Massachusetts, which itself advises companies on how to set up health plans following these principles, buys its employees two years' worth of diapers and wipes for having their babies at a community hospital instead of at the larger, more expensive teaching hospital in Boston.[5]

One barrier to this form of proactive self-insurance is that it is still necessary for the employer to buy reinsurance (also called stop-loss insurance) to protect itself against extremely high-cost claims. Reinsurance costs much less than traditional health insurance, but unlike the small-group market for health insurance, it can be underwritten. In other words, the amount an employer pays for reinsurance is dependent on the health status of its employees. So, a small company with just a few employees with particularly acute chronic illnesses could find that the approach would not save money due to the reinsurance costs being higher than the savings from steering its employees.

Fortunately, there are ways that small businesses can band together to spread out the risk more evenly. One way is an association health plan of self-insured employees—sometimes called a "captive." BevCap Management is a group of thirty self-insured beverage distributors. The average employee deductible in its plans is $750, versus a national average of $2,000; the average health care cost per employee is $8,500 per year, versus a national average of $14,000; and its pharmacy expenditure is 8 percent to 15 percent of claims, versus 18 percent to 22 percent on average.

Last year, President Trump took a big step to give many more small businesses the opportunity to save money on health plans. Until recently, it was difficult to qualify to join an association health plan. The businesses had to be in the same industry and geographic area. President Trump acted to significantly loosen these rules, giving many more small businesses the opportunity to create customized insurance plans for their employees. This new capability will dramatically increase the number of companies able to take advantage of this new model.

If you are an employer that wants to get more control over your health care costs, or if you're a citizen who wants to better understand this new approach, I recommend checking out the Health Rosetta at https://healthrosetta.org/employers/. The site has introductory courses and materials that can help you determine if self-insuring and direct contracting make sense for you. And Health Rosetta can work with you to help set up a plan for your employees.

Even if self-insuring does not make sense for your company (in fact, my small company looked at it and decided against it for the time being), Health Rosetta has resources for finding good insurance brokers. Many insurance brokers are not being up-front about the fact that they are being paid by the companies that hire them *and* the insurance companies whose plans they sell—a big potential conflict of interest if not disclosed. Dave Chase, the founder of Health Rosetta, has created a code of conduct for brokers and developed a network of them who agree to abide by it.

THE MIDDLEMEN BETWEEN US AND THE MEDICINES WE NEED

Pharmaceuticals have an even bigger middleman problem than other health care providers. This is because of the introduction of an additional player to the process of receiving treatment: pharmacy benefit managers (PBMs).

Like health insurance, PBMs do serve a legitimate purpose. And unfortunately, like insurance, the way their business model evolved has added layers of complexity, which are being exploited to add unnecessary costs that are hitting patients hard.

Here is what pricing and payment for pharmaceuticals would look like without PBMs:

- Step 1: Drug manufacturers set a sticker price for medicines, referred to in the industry as a list price.
- Step 2: Drug wholesalers negotiate a bulk discount, and then sell to pharmacies at a price somewhere between what they paid the manufacturer and the list price of a drug. This price is called the average wholesale price (AWP).
- Step 3: Pharmacies then dispense the medicines and are paid by a combination of the patient's copay and the patient's health plan at a rate they negotiated.

This is similar to the pricing and payment process for the rest of health care. The addition of a wholesaler is natural, because drugs are mass-produced, whereas medical services are provided one at a time. This system is complicated but makes sense and is theoretically manageable.

This hypothetical, simpler system does have a problem though. Even though individual health plans may cover tens or hundreds of thousands—and in some cases, millions—of people, the plans still don't have the same scale that national pharmacy chains have. For example, CVS will fill more than one billion prescriptions this year alone.[6]

That's where PBMs come in. They aggregate as many health plans as possible as clients. Then they use the fact that they represent so many potential customers to negotiate a steeper discount with the pharmacy chains than a single health plan could on its own. So rather than a pharmacy submitting a claim to an insurance company—like a doctor would for a medical service—pharmacies are submitting a claim to the PBM, who then pays the pharmacy their contracted rate. Then the PBM sends a bill for the medicine to the health plan client at a markup, a practice called "spread pricing."

How much of a markup, you might ask? In most cases, nobody knows. But the health plan is OK with this arrangement because it assumes that whatever price it agreed to pay the PBM for the drugs is less than what it could negotiate from the pharmacy directly. In addition, having one price to pay for a medicine is more predictable than many different prices from different pharmacies.

If this mind-set sounds familiar, it should. It is the same mistake that so many self-insuring companies make by not rigorously inspecting their claims data and steering their employees to the highest value health care providers.

Spread pricing is particularly problematic for what it does to the price of generic prescription drugs, which cost pennies to manufacture but can still end up costing hundreds of dollars after making their way through the PBMs. While generic drugs only make up 23 percent of total drug spending, they account for 90 percent of prescriptions dispensed.[7] So, for PBMs, which make their money from health plans based on how many prescriptions they process, generic drugs are where the money is made.

One place where it is possible to determine the impact of spread pricing is in Medicaid, since much of the data is public. The Massachusetts Health Policy Commission compared the prices being paid for drugs in its regular Medicaid program, which does not allow spread pricing, with the prices in the managed-care Medicaid program, which does. The commission found that PBMs were adding $15.97 per drug to the program. What's truly disgusting is that the study found that the biggest markups were being imposed on drugs used to combat the opioid crisis. PBMs overcharged the state a total of $252,536 for naxolone, which is used to treat overdoses.

And they charged 111 percent more for buprenorphine, which used to help people taper off opioids.[8]

You can also imagine the position in which the spread pricing model puts pharmacies, particularly the smaller, independent ones. Small pharmacies have less leverage to negotiate discounts from wholesalers than the large chains, and then they have to negotiate rates with giant PBMs. Three PBMs (Caremark, Express Scripts, and OptumRX) handled about 75 percent of all prescription drug claims in 2018.[9]

As a result, independent pharmacies are often forced to accept reimbursement rates from the PBMs that barely—and in some cases fail to—cover the acquisition cost of the drug. Small pharmacies are forced to do so, because if the PBM represents the dominant health plan in the area, it can threaten to remove the pharmacy from the network. More than four hundred independent pharmacies have sued OptumRX over its pricing practices for generic drugs.

This sort of heavy-handed negotiation might be justified if it saved patients money on their drugs. But many generic prescription drugs are so cheap that the PBM-assigned copay for a patient can sometimes be higher than the price of the drug if the patient had just paid cash directly to the pharmacy. This is even more common in cases in which a patient is still in their deductible phase of insurance and he or she must pay the full list price of the drug. One analysis shows that patients' out-of-pocket expenses for drugs exceed the cash price of drugs 23 percent of the time, with an average overpayment of $7.69.[10]

In these cases, when patients pay more out-of-pocket than the PBM-negotiated rate with the pharmacy, the PBM will sometimes demand the extra money back from the pharmacy after the fact—a practice known as a claw back.

The Republican Congress recently passed, and President Trump signed, a law that released pharmacists from so-called gag clauses in PBM contracts that previously prevented them from telling patients if they can save money by paying cash. Still, even with this small additional layer of transparency, patients face a no-win scenario. Either they pay more out-of-pocket than the drug costs, or they can save a few dollars by paying cash—but they can't count the purchase toward their deductible. Adding insult to injury, they're paying for insurance they aren't using.

Also, keep in mind that Caremark is owned by CVS, and Walgreens has launched its own PBM. So pharmacists at many big pharmacy chains may be trained to never volunteer to tell you if you can save money by paying cash, since it could mean less money to their total corporate bottom line. You must remember to ask.

The PBMs spread-pricing business model is a bad enough problem on its own because of its inflationary effect on the price of generic drugs. But it is on the price of brand-name drugs that PBMs have had their most destructive impact. The reason is that PBMs don't just negotiate prices for drugs with pharmacies. They also create programs that help reduce their clients' overall drug expenditure by influencing doctors' and patients' decision making. One tool is creating drug formularies on behalf of their health plan clients. A drug formulary is a tiered system of different levels of coverage for different drugs. As an example, to encourage greater use of generic drugs, a lower-cost, generic drug would be preferred on the first tier with a low copay, while the brand-name version would be on a higher tier with a much higher copay—or possibly not be covered at all. PBMs will also create step-therapy rules, which require a patient to first try a lower-cost medicine to treat a condition. Only if it fails is the more expensive drug covered.

This insertion of the PBMs between patients and doctors can be frustrating. However, you can understand the health plan's motivation to not pay for a high-priced drug if there is a lower-priced alternative.

Why pay for the Cadillac Escalade when all you need is a Chevy Cruze to commute to work?

However, this power to prioritize certain drugs over others creates complicated conflicts of interest. That's because the health plan clients are not the only ones paying PBMs. The PBM middlemen are also being paid by the drug manufacturers. Drug manufacturers will often offer volume-based, percentage rebates to the PBMs to prioritize their drugs on the formularies used by the health plans the PBMs manage. By offering bigger rebates, a drug manufacturer can get its higher-priced drug on a preferred formulary tier, even if there are lower-priced alternatives. Rebates, discounts and other price concessions totaled $175 billion in 2019.

It is important to understand that rebates are not discounts negotiated on behalf of clients; they are actual cash payments made directly to the PBMs from the drug manufacturers. This means that the PBM is being paid by both the health plans and the drug manufacturers. Furthermore, the amount of these rebates are closely guarded secrets. You would think this would be considered a conflict of interest (or perhaps some sort of racketeering). But surprisingly, health plans are OK with this rebate arrangement. This is because the PBMs keep only a portion of the rebates and pass the rest back to their clients. So, health plans are making money off this arrangement too. PBMs argue that it is OK if a drug with a more expensive list price is higher on a formulary than a cheaper one, because the rebate system means that the net cost is lower to the insurance company. This means that patients benefit from lower insurance premiums. But there are two enormous problems with this arrangement. The first is the incentive it creates for drug manufacturers to constantly raise their list prices in order to offer bigger rebates to PBMs in exchange for higher placement on their formularies. This has a huge impact on the amount patients pay at the pharmacy counter. Imagine two competing drug manufacturers that each sell a treatment for the same condition. One puts its drug at a list price of $100 and offers the PBM a

25 percent discount. The other manufacturer puts its drug at a list price of $150 and offers a 50 percent discount.

In this scenario, the net to the manufacturer is the same, but since the PBM is receiving double the rebate on the higher-priced drug, it places it on a preferred formulary tier instead of the lower-priced drug. Lower copays lead to more sales, meaning the drug manufacturer (and PBM) make more money.

Naturally, the competing drug manufacturer will respond by *raising* the price of its drug and offering a larger rebate to compete with its rival—precisely the opposite of what a manufacturer would do to be more competitive in a normal, functioning marketplace. This scenario is not hypothetical: it is exactly what has happened with insulin. Over the past decade, the list prices of the most prescribed insulins have tripled even though they are the exact same products.[11] But even as prices have skyrocketed, the net prices have fallen. For instance, Eli Lilly raised its price for Humalog by 52 percent from 2014 through 2019, but over that same period its net price fell by 8 percent.[12] Sanofi raised its list price for insulins by 140 percent from 2012 through 2019, but during that time the net price fell by 41 percent.[13]

But if net prices are falling, what is the problem?

The problem is that patients' out-of-pocket costs are often determined by the list price of a drug, not the net price. So, patients are being slammed at the pharmacy counter with costs totally disproportionate to the real value of the medications. The dramatic rise in the list price of insulins has occurred during the same period that Obamacare caused a huge increase in the proliferation of high-deductible health plans. So until a patient meets his or her deductible, the patient is often paying the full list price of the drug at the pharmacy counter to count toward his or her deductible. This is why out-of-pocket costs for the insulin Lantus have increased by 62 percent since 2012 despite the net price falling by 37 percent.[14]

In response to intense criticism of the high price of brand-name insulins, Eli Lilly created a half-priced version of Humalog in 2019. Novo Nordisk introduced a half-priced version of its insulin Novo-Log and NovoLog Mix in 2020. But you won't find these half-priced

versions on most health plan formularies, because they result in lower rebates to the PBMs.[15]

To make insulin more affordable, manufacturers are beginning to experiment with direct-to-patient sales that bypass insurance altogether. Sanofi created a $99-per-month subscription service for its insulin—which is about what insulin cost before the escalation began. However, to qualify for the program, you cannot have prescription drug insurance. This is likely because PBM contracts prevent the manufacturers from selling directly to patients covered by the plans they represent. Imagine a drug price system so messed up that the only way diabetics can get affordable insulin is by dropping their prescription drug coverage. Insurance companies are moving to put out-of-pocket caps on insulin for their customers. However, this is a Band-Aid solution to the middleman problem in drugs. Insulin is the most visible example of the impact of the distorted drug pricing system, but its impact is felt on all drugs. In 2018, Sanofi paid out 55 percent of its gross sales in rebates. A pharmaceutical industry–funded study showed that nearly half of spending on brand-name medicine goes to the supply chain and others.[16]

It only makes sense to focus on ways to cut out middlemen in as many parts of the health care supply chain as possible. This would simplify our systems, improve access to needed medications and lower costs for Americans.

FIXING WARPED DRUG PRICING

Fortunately, there is a growing backlash against abusive PBM practices that has spurred demand for a much simpler type of

PBM business model. This model gives clients the benefits of scale to negotiate discounts from pharmacies and manufacturers and helps set up programs to encourage health plan participants to choose more affordable drugs—without the destructive spread pricing and rebate systems that are driving up costs. After an audit revealed how much CVS Caremark was marking up the cost of generic drugs in the Ohio Medicaid program, they were fired by the state's largest Medicaid managed-care provider.

Ohio passed new rules requiring all PBM contracts in Medicaid to use a fixed administrative fee per prescription filled instead of spread pricing, and a 100 percent pass-through on all rebates. While the early results from the change have not yet shown taxpayer savings, it has resulted in higher payments to pharmacies, keeping money in the local economy rather than going to a giant corporation headquartered in Rhode Island.[17]

The Trump administration has also helped put pressure on PBMs to be more transparent by changing the rules that govern Medicaid managed-care plans. The new rules require these plans to account for the money they are receiving from their PBMs drug rebates when calculating their medical loss ratio. The administration initially proposed a much more radical step in Medicare, which was to require a 100 percent pass-through of drug manufacturers' rebates to patients.

This would have turned back-end rebates into upfront discounts for seniors and provided relief at the pharmacy counter. So if a PBM negotiated a $50 rebate on a $100 drug, the patient's out-of-pocket cost would be based on a $50 price tag rather than a $100 one. Though some private-sector insurance is already doing this, requiring 100 percent pass-through in Medicare likely would have spurred all private-sector insurance to do the same. Unfortunately, the administration dropped the proposal. Seniors would have saved enormous amounts of money at the pharmacy counter in exchange for just a few extra dollars a month in premiums, but the federal government's subsidy of those premiums would have increased significantly. I think this was a mistake. In addition to the incentive it creates for drug manufacturers to raise their prices so they can offer larger rebates to PBMs, the current rebate system is a bizarre inversion of how health insurance should work. Sick patients end up paying more at the pharmacy counter so that healthy patients can have lower premiums. This doesn't make any sense.

Fortunately, there is bipartisan legislation in the US Senate that will produce some reform. The bill, from Republican Senator Lamar Alexander and Democratic Senator Patty Murray, would ban spread pricing and require 100 percent pass-through of rebates to PBM clients. Many self-insured companies are demanding changes from the PBMs that are managing their health plans' pharmaceutical spending. In fact, one of the key components of the type of proactive self-insurance described earlier is using a transparent PBM. One of the most effective of these transparent PBMs is a grocery store chain. HEB is one of the largest privately owned companies in America. It has more than three hundred stores, located mostly in Texas. And it also operates a 100 percent transparent PBM that delivers real savings and accountability to clients. HEB has pharmacies in its stores, but unlike other major pharmaceutical chains that also operate a PBM, it is not "double dipping" by taking profits at both ends. All the discounts the PBM arranges through itself and other pharmacies are passed through 100 percent to the clients.

Some independent PBMs are keeping the spread pricing and rebate model, but they do so with radical transparency. This way clients know exactly how much the PBMs are earning. One example is a company called MedImpact that I worked with when I was running the Center for Health Transformation. MedImpact has been serving its clients with this model for thirty years.

When the middlemen are in control, the middlemen profit at the expense of the rest of us. When we are in control and know the facts, we can make the decisions which are best for us and best for our pocketbooks.

Rebellion Number 3: Health Care Over Sick Care

Taking control away from the middlemen synergizes with another act of rebellion in health care. For many doctors, the insurance-dominated, fee-for-service financing model has become a self-destructive spiral. To afford the massive overhead required to operate a clinic or hospital, doctors are forced to rush from patient to patient to rack up as many billable services as possible. This in turn, creates more paperwork to process all the billing with insurance companies, so doctors must spend even more time filling out forms and more money on administrative help. This increases overhead, which leads to having to rush through even more appointments. It's a destructive cycle.

In recent years, a lot of attention has been focused on the problem of physician burnout. Symptoms include exhaustion, cynicism, and a lack of compassion for patients. Health systems have been taking steps to try to reduce these symptoms through less stressful hours and other improvements to work-life balance.

However, Drs. Simon Talbot and Wendy Dean argue that what doctors are experiencing is not a sign of working too much, but instead of "moral injury."[18] This is a term first applied to soldiers returning from war who were grappling with the moral implications of their actions. If comparing the ethical conflict that doctors go through to that of a soldier in war seems extreme, consider the fact that physicians commit suicide at twice the rate of members of the military. In fact, the suicide rate among physicians is higher than that of any other profession.[19]

Drs. Talbot and Dean argue that doctors are experiencing a similar conflict between their ethics and what they must do to survive in the health system as soldiers do during war. Most doctors enter the profession because they have a calling to help people.

However, once they become doctors, they find that they cannot provide the quality of care they feel obligated to provide. This is because the convoluted business of health care produces conflicts between their moral obligation to put their patients first and practical reality that they are paid by insurance companies, or the large health systems that employ them.

This conflict is especially dangerous for primary care doctors. More than any other medical specialty, the objective of a good primary care doctor is not just to get their patients healthy, but also to *keep them that way.*

Doing so requires having the time needed to really get to know their patients and their unique circumstances. Research shows that more than 80 percent of health outcomes are from factors outside the clinical setting.[20] Things like food quality, access to transportation, and whether a patient is socially isolated all play a major role in a person's health—and these aren't things that can be fixed with a prescription.

Unfortunately, primary care doctors are being forced to spend less time with patients when they should be spending more. Independent primary care doctors are faced with so much administrative overhead caused by regulations and having to deal with health insurance bureaucracy that they are selling their practices to large health systems. The health system handles the administration, but the primary care doctor finds themselves devalued. This is because primary care operates with relatively low profit margins compared with other areas of health care.

As Dave Chase, the founder of Health Rosetta, has written, this has turned primary care into "the milk at the back of the store." Primary care doctors are what brings in customers, but the system makes money on all the other things that they end up purchasing as part of the interaction. So, for the business side of health care, the objective of the primary care doctors is to refer patients to the services that make the most money, such as imaging, testing, surgeries, and specialist examinations, rather than to help patients.

This is the heart of the moral injury that primary care doctors are facing. If they remain independent, they become overwhelmed with the administrative component of health care and can't spend the time they need with patients. If they join a health system, they are valued based on how many patients they get to consume health services rather than avoid them by staying healthy. Fortunately, a new health care model for primary care is emerging across the country that is better for doctors and for patients.

DIRECT MEDICAL CARE

We already covered how some surgeons are no longer accepting insurance and simply offering one low price to all patients on a cash-pay basis. In fact, there are many more primary care doctors who have done the same. However, rather than charging per visit, they are creating a membership model that gives patients unlimited visits and consultations per month, as well as many other benefits.

This rebellion is about putting high-quality primary care back at the center of the health system, so doctors can keep patients healthy rather than just treat them when they are sick. Dr. Josh Umbehr is one of the original health care rebels for this new model, called direct primary care. I was introduced to Dr. Umbehr by Sean Hannity, and the good doctor was generous with his time explaining the benefits of this new approach. He also invited my team out to Wichita, Kansas, to visit his clinic and attend a seminar hosted by the city's Chamber of Commerce on how small businesses can partner with direct primary care clinics to provide employee health benefits. Wichita has a thriving direct primary care practice. At the event, Dr. Umbehr and a half-dozen local direct primary care doctors explained to gathered small business owners how they could partner with one of their clinics to deliver better health benefits to their employees at far lower expense than relying on the traditional health insurance small-group market. They do this by marrying the self-insurance model described in rebellion number 2 with a direct primary care clinic to act as the preferred primary care practice for their plan. Employers benefit from a low fixed price that covers most routine health expenses, and employees benefit from a much better patient experience. This difference in the patient experience is evident by visiting Atlas MD, Dr. Umbehr's clinic. One of the first things you notice upon walking in is the lack of people. Go to a typical doctor's office, and there are usually a dozen or more people in the waiting room, two or three receptionists processing paperwork and making phone calls, and then a half-dozen nurses to support the one or two doctors, who are rushing among patients. Atlas MD is different. There are no receptionists, just a registered nurse and two doctors. The patients who arrived were seen almost immediately, and there was a much more relaxed atmosphere than at a typical doctor's office. Because he charges a monthly, all-inclusive membership fee, his practice doesn't have to deal with the insurance company bureaucracy that requires thousands of different billing codes and prior authorization. This eliminates the need for all sorts of administrative overhead.

Dr. Umbehr told us that about half of his patient interaction is virtual: phone calls, video conferences, and even text messaging. When patients come into the office, Dr. Umbehr has plenty of time to sit down with them and really explore their health issue to recommend a course of treatment personalized to their health and lifestyle needs. Dr. Umbehr says he sees only about four to six patients a day in office. A typical primary care doctor sees forty to fifty patients. Patients benefit in other ways. They have an ultrasound and bone density scanner in office that patients can utilize with no additional fees. He also struck deals with local imaging and lab testing facilities for an 80–95 percent discount that patients pay as an add-on to their monthly bills. Atlas MD and many other direct primary care practices also have pharmacies on site. These enable patients to save a lot of money because it completely bypasses the current convoluted drug pricing system. Patients pay the wholesale cost of the drug plus 10 percent at Atlas MD, which is pennies for generics. Here are some examples of what Dr. Umbehr's patients pay for common medications:

- A month's supply of generic Zyrtec: $1.20
- A month's supply of generic Prozac: $.72
- A month's supply of generic Prilosec: $.99

These wholesale prices prices are lower than most people's copays. Dr. Umbehr's clinic has a small pharmacy right there with the most common medications. He is also able to special-order medication from wholesalers for his patients. The membership fees that get you access to this 24/7, all-inclusive treatment package are extremely reasonable. They range from $50 to $100 per month depending on a patient's age. Children can be added for $10 per month. Given that patient copays are typically about $20, this fee can easily be less than the amount a family with young children would spend on copays for a normal fee-for-service doctor. It can also be a good deal for people with chronic conditions who need to see the doctor often, especially when you consider how little Dr. Umbehr's patients pay for drugs.

There are now more than 1,200 health practices operating "direct primary care" practices throughout the country and that number is growing. In fact, many specialists such as cardiologists are switching to this model. This is because direct medical care is not just a better patient experience, it is also a better experience for doctors. Direct medical care ends the conflicting allegiances and financial pressures that doctors face in the health industry and allows them to focus solely on delivering the best care for their patients. It is the patient who is their real customer, not an insurance company or big health system. President Trump recognized the potential of direct primary care early in his administration. He and his team at HHS released new rules that allowed Medicare enrollees to get direct primary care services.

They also allowed the use of health savings accounts to pay the membership fees. Not only does this make enrolling with a direct primary care doctor more affordable, but it also allows employers an easy way to pay their employees' membership fees through a contribution to the HSA.

ON-SITE MEDICAL CARE FOR EMPLOYEES

Some companies have taken a similar approach, but instead of partnering with a direct primary care clinic to be the preferred primary care provider for their employees, these companies are opening their own clinics at or near work sites.

Harris Rosen is one of America's original health care rebels. In 1991, he decided he'd had enough. His group of hotels in Orlando was doing well, but the constant year-over-year increases in health insurance premiums were a huge threat to his businesses. Specifically, he was frustrated that his insurance premiums increased every year whether his employees filed more or fewer claims.

As did some of the other businesses I have highlighted, he chose to move from a commercially fully insured product to becoming self-insured. Instead of renting an insurance company's network like most self-insuring companies, he created his own insurance entity, ProvInsure, which directly contracted with area providers. He also created a small medical clinic on site for all his employees and covered dependents. This combination of cutting out the middlemen paired with an intense focus on good primary care and preventative medicine is the secret sauce behind RosenCare—an extraordinary employee health package that has better health outcomes and happier employees, and one that spends about half as much per covered life as comparative patient populations. When we learned about the now 12,000 square feet Rosen Medical Center at Gingrich 360, we got in touch with the Rosen team and Mr. Rosen was gracious and invited us down to Orlando to tour his medical center. There we learned that his thinking behind creating his own medical center was not just about saving money on primary care doctors. It was also about seeing if an intense focus on preventative medicine to improve overall health could increase productivity and reduce expensive hospitalizations. Rosen and his team decided that if they were going to emphasize the importance of primary care, they had to make visiting the medical center as easy as possible. That's why Rosen's employees can visit the medical center at any time without having to request time off work. They can either walk or if needed, have a company shuttle take them over for free while staying on the clock during the visit. For many years, there was no copay to visit the center. Now it is only $5 for sick visits and $0 for physicals, physical therapy, dietitian, screening and testing services.

The medical center also has a pharmacy, where patients can pick up most their prescriptions immediately upon being diagnosed. They also worked out a deal with a local Walmart so health plan members can pick up prescriptions at no cost to the member. In addition to saving patients money, this dramatically improves compliance. The Rosen team shared with us that their diabetic population and cardiovascular population maintain an approximately 95 percent medication compliance rate. Nationwide compliance is 50–60 percent.

The medical center also has many standard imaging machines, allowing Rosen to save hundreds of thousands of dollars a year on Xrays, ultrasounds and other tests while saving patients time and money. It also has exercise facilities, with free classes available for employees. And it includes a physical therapy team for injuries that emphasizes functional movement improvements and a team approach that shuns pain pills in favor of natural alternatives. As a result, Rosen's employees are much less likely to turn to surgery to deal with injuries or pain issues.

Harris Rosen's emphasis on health and well-being does not stop at the doors of the medical center. He has worked hard to build a culture of wellness at Rosen Hotels. For instance, Rosen's employees are encouraged not to smoke and are provided a variety of tools they can use to keep their weight under control. The health plan pays for treatments to stop smoking and provides free Weight Watchers for all employees, in addition to the fitness classes. Rosen himself sets an example from the top. He is eighty years old but looks about sixty. Every day you can find him spending an hour swimming in the pool at the Rosen YMCA or at one of his hotel properties.

The result of this innovative direct contracting and focus on high-quality primary care, preventative medicine, and healthy lifestyles is that Rosen Hotels spends about half the cost per covered person as its competitors in the hospitality industry with similar demographics. Rosen estimates they have saved more than $400 million compared with the national average per covered life. It is important to note that although Rosen cut its costs in half, there was not a commensurate reduction in benefits; quite the contrary. RosenCare has no deductibles, no coinsurance, and 90 percent of prescriptions are free. It is one of the most generous health plans in the country.

This is why Rosen's employees love their health plan. The employee turnover at Rosen Hotels is about one-third the normal rate in the industry. RosenCare truly is a case of better health care, happier patients, and much lower costs. It's a win-win-win. You would think that the model of the Rosen health plan would be seen as a huge competitive advantage by Rosen and his executive team, and they would try to keep it under wraps. Instead, they have been fully transparent about what they are doing for decades and have tried (mostly in vain) to get other companies—including their competitors—to adopt their model. For Harris Rosen and his health care team, better health is a higher calling, not a business strategy.

Fortunately, Team Rosen's persistence is beginning to pay off. The School District of Osceola County fired its health plan consultant and clinic operator in 2019 and hired RosenCare to build a better system. The challenge will be not only to handle all the additional new patients, but also to instill a culture of wellness and health that took decades to develop at Rosen Hotels & Resorts.

THE BREWING PRIMARY CARE REVOLUTION
IN HEALTHY AGING

There is another health care rebellion in the works that relates the importance of good primary care and keeping people healthy. This one is occurring in the lab but could soon be coming to your doctor's office and medicine cabinet.

On a recent episode of my podcast, *Newt's World*, I hosted two doctors who are at the forefront of the new science of healthy aging: Drs. David Sinclair and Nir Barzilai.[21] Their rebel approach, and that of those like them, has been to approach aging as a disease that can be treated rather than as an inevitable process of decline into poorer and poorer health.

Dr. Barzilai's approach has been to study centenarians (people who've lived past one hundred). He learned that while there were some lifestyle similarities, such as continuing to be active, busy, and social, many of these centenarians did not practice what we would consider a healthy lifestyle. Many smoked, drank too much, and were overweight, yet still had more energy and cognitive awareness than your typical seventy-year-old. Their bodies just seemed immune or extremely resilient to the damage that life inflicts on us. He began searching for the common themes among these long-lived humans and found that they all shared a common set of gene expressions.

The key concept to understand is that these are gene *expressions*. While it is generally true that our genes cannot be changed, it turns out that the way our genes express themselves is heavily dependent on our environment. This means that for the rest of us who don't naturally have these genes "switched on" like the centenarians Dr. Barzilai studied, there are things we can do to activate them.

We've always known that eating healthy and exercising made us healthier. What we are learning now is *why*. It turns out that these healthy activities can turn on the longevity genes. Dr. Barzilai also learned that there are pharmaceutical compounds, some of which are already used to treat other conditions, that can activate these longevity genes. He is leading clinical trials right now studying if they can be used to allow all of us to age healthier.

Dr. Sinclair's approach was different, but he came to the same conclusions. He began studying simple animals with short life spans to observe the process of aging at the cellular level. His conclusion was that the same fundamental mechanisms drive aging in all forms of life on earth, and that these mechanisms are heavily influenced by our environment. His lab at Harvard is doing amazing things in mice, such as taking older, sicker mice and "resetting" their genome so it behaves like that of a younger mouse. In mice that have received treatment, Dr. Sinclair and his team are literally seeing gray hairs disappear, arteries clean themselves, and nerves regrow.

Now, it is important to understand that Drs. Sinclair and Barzilai are not seeking immortality for humans. Their goal is to allow us to maximize our *healthspan*—the number of healthy years a person has. One of the consequences of this would be to increase our life span, but adding more years is not where the revolutionary impact of their science will have its main effect.

During our interview, Dr. Sinclair made a profound point about how arbitrary definitions can limit our thinking. He pointed out that we define a disease or medical condition as something that affects less than half of humans. And since aging is something that affects everyone, we don't apply the same sort of resources and intensity toward understanding the condition and treating it.

This is important, because aging is by far a greater risk factor for chronic illnesses like dementia, diabetes, heart disease, and other conditions than anything else. In fact, approaching aging as a disease that can be treated represents an upstream treatment for all these other conditions, which together drive trillions of dollars in health care spending per year as well as incalculable human suffering. The implications of the work of Drs. Sinclair and Barzilai are staggering and exciting. It should be supported and expanded upon by officially classifying aging as a disease. This would enable our public health institutions to better support clinical trials into treatments to slow down the negative health consequences from aging. Fundamentally, this type of research and the treatments that come out of it is preventative medicine that will supercharge the benefits of a greater emphasis on primary care in America. You can listen to an episode of my *Newts World* podcast that featured Drs. Sinclair and Barzilai at NewtsWorld.com.

APPLE, FITBIT, AND AT HOME MEDICAL TECHNOLOGY

Right now, most people's experience with their primary care doctor is the annual checkup. This preventative medicine is critical, because it helps catch problems early before a patient even knows there is something wrong. Addressing health problems early leads to better health and lower costs.

Still, the annual checkup is not particularly effective. If a patient is healthy, it is a waste of time and money. If a patient has a medical issue, then the annual checkup is almost certainly going to identify it later than ideal. However, the growing use of wearable medical devices like the Apple Watches, Fitbits, and other options represent a coming fundamental shift in primary care.

First, they are becoming critical tools in helping patients manage their own health. A member of my staff, a bit of a fitness nut, recently started using a wearable that tracks heart rate, heart rate variability, respiratory rate, sleep quality, and calories burned. It uses that information to give him strain and recovery scores every day, which he uses to modulate his physical activity. It tells him how much sleep he needs every night, the optimal time he should go to bed based on his sleep patterns, and whether he should skip his normal workout in favor of stretching or some other recovery activity. It also asks him questions every day about what he's eating and drinking, how much time he spends looking at a screen, and many other lifestyle factors, and tracks that information against his vitals so he can see the impact that they have on his sleep quality and recovery. He claims the information is useful for avoiding sickness and injury. You can imagine how good primary care doctors could help their patients utilize these tools to improve their own health maintenance.

Second, wearables are only going to get more advanced. As they start to track more information (and as 5G technology becomes ubiquitous), these devices could completely invert the current model of annual checkups into one of continuous real-time monitoring with real-time feedback about our health and well-being. This new paradigm would catch potentially life-threatening conditions much earlier than the annual checkup—saving lives, improving quality of life, and saving money as well.

It is worth noting that not all this data needs to be collected via a wearable. Some of it could be collected via in-home devices. This will be particularly useful for patients with chronic conditions, because it would be much more convenient than having to go routinely to the doctor. It is also a powerful pairing with telehealth options, because it allows doctors to collect patients' vitals remotely.

One example of these at-home kits is TytoCare TytoHome remote exam kit. They cost around $300 and are widely available at Best Buy. It includes a thermometer, otoscope, stethoscope, and tongue depressor. A hospital system we work with at Gingrich 360 has partnered with TytoCare to provide the devices to their most at-risk patients at a discount so they can better manage their health. Making checkups more convenient increases compliance.

Finally, real-time or at-home monitoring of vital signs would be a powerful defense against pandemics like the Wuhan virus. A few years ago, a company that markets a Wi-Fi-connected thermometer started analyzing all its data and discovered it was able to predict flu outbreaks earlier than the CDC. During the 2020 coronavirus pandemic, the company was able to apply its machine learning to track total fever reductions and flare-ups to determine where social distancing measures were working and where they were not.

The simple fact is that this triple revolution of primary care, patient-doctor control of health care, and a focus on staying healthy all our lives will increase our life span, increase our productive, fulfilling lives, and reduce the cost of health care. This is a revolution worth having.

12.

★ ═══════════════════════════════════════ ★

AMERICA'S HEALTH CARE REBELLIONS, PART III

I have described the first three major rebellions in health care that will bring us to a much more effective and affordable system. This chapter covers the final two: fully integrated health care and health coverage without complex provider networks.

Rebellion Number 4: Fully Integrated Health Care

At its core, doctors moving to direct medical care and employers taking control away from middlemen represents a rebellion against a fundamental misalignment of incentives in health care. This misalignment is a byproduct of the way health care is currently paid for in America.

The dominant payment model in health care today is third-party, fee-for-service. The third-party payer is the health plan instead of the person receiving the health care (a patient's out-of-pocket costs notwithstanding). Fee-for-service means that health care providers charge per incident of care.

There are two clear problems here: The problem with third-party payers is that the desire of the payer to save money can interfere with the doctor's treatment advice for patients. The problem with fee-for-service is it does not reward doctors for keeping patients healthy, because healthy patients do not generate revenue. Fee for service is the chief culprit behind America's overtreatment epidemic. Doctors surveyed in one study estimated that about 20 percent of all medical care in America is unnecessary.

This combination of third party payment and fee for service causes a tug-of-war among the health plan, the doctor, and the patient, which leads to rising administrative bloat, a focus on acute care over primary care, and massive price variation for health care services. The result is a health care system that costs too much and delivers too little in terms of the overall health and well-being of the American people.

We've learned how some doctors are bypassing the third-party, fee-for-service payment model by charging a single price for everyone. For surgeons, this is an "all-in," bundled price for their procedures. For direct-care doctors, it is a monthly membership fee for all the services they provide.

We've also learned how some employers are aligning incentives between their employees and their health plan by creating incentives for employees to choose low-cost, high-quality providers, or by creating on-site medical care.

There is another rebellion brewing against the third-party, fee-for-service system. Some innovative health systems are investing to essentially take the direct medical care model and apply it to all health care services. They are doing this by creating their own health insurance companies to end the hostile relationship between the health care provider and the payer. The result of the health systems taking so-called first dollar for health care—the insurance premium—is that they make more money if patients are healthy, and they lose money if patients need to consume a lot of their services. This fundamentally changes the broken incentive structure to fully align patient, provider, and payer incentives toward maximizing the health and well-being of patients.

Fully integrated health care is different from value-based care (a common health industry term that is often touted as an alternative to the fee-for-service model). Value-based care refers to payment models between third-party payers and medical providers that pays bundled rates for procedures and gives bonuses based on health outcomes.

Value-based care is a positive development, but it has limited potential because of the presence of the third-party payer. It is highly difficult to develop value-based contracts because of the difficulty on agreeing to quality outcomes. These contracts also almost always increase administrative overhead and lead doctors to feel like they are being micromanaged by distant health insurance bureaucrats. America experienced a little of this during the HMO and managed care disasters of the 1990s. Health care spending slowed, but patients and doctors revolted. By the early 2000s, per capita health spending was back on its steep upward trend.

In contrast to value-based care, a key component of fully integrated health care is that the third-party payer is eliminated by the provider-run health plan. This is the model behind some of the highest-performing health systems in the country in terms of cost and quality, including Kaiser Permanente in California, Intermountain Healthcare in Utah, and Geisinger Health in Pennsylvania. Many other health systems are moving toward this model as well.

One of these systems is Sanford Health, a rapidly growing hospital system with whom we work at Gingrich 360. On a recent call, Sanford Health's CEO, Kelby Krabbenhoft, explained the difference between health systems that merge to get bigger so they can extract higher payments from third-party payers, and those who achieve scale to become fully integrated.

There has been growing scrutiny of hospital mergers in recent years—and with good reason. Numerous studies have shown that the more concentrated a health marketplace is, the higher prices tend to be. This is because being the dominant provider gives them more leverage over health plans to extract higher payments. Studies have also shown that many of the efficiencies and quality improvements cited by health systems in support of mergers fail to materialize.

Krabbenhoft and his team at Sanford Health argue this is because simply getting bigger does not make a system fully integrated. First, adding the health insurance plan component to the health system is critical to aligning incentives. Second, many health systems will get bigger but fail to be managed in a cohesive way. Even though the different facilities share a common name and corporate bottom line, they still function as siloed, independent systems with little to no common best practices and governance.

Fully integrated systems are different. They achieve scale so they can provide a full continuum of care for their patients. For instance, Sanford Health provides health care services that span from maternity to long-term care—literally your entire life.

Furthermore, this continuum of care must be managed under a single umbrella with constant coordination among departments in order to maximize a patient's health outcomes. Unlike simply big health systems, in which primary care doctors are treated as loss leaders to drive patients toward more profitable parts of the system, a fully integrated health system invests heavily in primary care to catch health problems early and help patients manage problems themselves.

Scale is also necessary because of the way population centers are evolving in America. We are moving toward ten or eleven large, multicity, so-called megapolitan regions of common transportation, work, and entertainment centers. So, to be truly fully integrated, the hospital system needs to be where its patients are.

It can't expect patients to travel hours to get to its facilities. This is because fully integrated health care systems work best if they are the sole medical provider for the patient. Otherwise a fully integrated system loses the ability to coordinate care because the integrated system's doctors may not know what other care the patients have received. Furthermore, the more care the patient receives outside the integrated system, the more that the system's insurance plan becomes a third party payer. That makes it harder to align everyone's incentives toward maximizing overall health and well-being.

For this reason, choosing a fully integrated health system may not make sense for everyone. But for those in rural areas (where the number of providers is limited) or for those with chronic conditions who are high users of health care services, fully integrated health care can be a simple and effective alternative.

Fully integrated health care is particularly effective in dealing with the challenge of covering people with preexisting conditions. Forcing all health insurance companies to cover this relatively small patient population in the individual marketplace drives up premiums for everyone else. However, the economics for fully integrated health systems is different. Roughly 70 percent of a health system's costs are fixed. This means that the newly enrolled patient with preexisting conditions is a much smaller relative drain on the integrated health system's resources than a traditional insurer system. The insurer system would be assuming all the provider medical bills—charges that are driven more by the cost of operating a hospital system than the specific care that is performed. So while insurers are virtually guaranteed to lose money on a newly enrolled, sick patient, fully integrated health care systems are much more likely to be able to make up the initial investment in their care through ongoing monthly premiums.

These much more favorable economics could also help increase the number of Americans with insurance coverage. Under the integrated payer-provider model, an uninsured patient who shows up at a hospital could be immediately enrolled into that hospital's proprietary insurance plan (or, if eligible, enrolled in Medicaid). Rather than suddenly being stuck with huge hospital bills for their treatment, the patients would instead be responsible for much more manageable and predictable premium payments.

Fully integrated health systems also have a big advantage in dealing with pandemics like the Wuhan virus. Because they are located over large regions, governed under a common set of practices, and have access to both provider and payer data, they can detect and respond to pandemics faster than uncoordinated medical systems. They can be a powerful partner for governments seeking information on the types of social distancing measures to enforce.

Fully integrated health care may also prove to be an especially attractive option for federal and state government health programs. Medicare and Medicaid patient populations are sicker than the rest of America. Medicare is this way because the patients are older, Medicaid is this way because patients are poorer. Contracting directly with a fully integrated health system to manage large patient populations in a megapolitan region could deliver better health outcomes with lower overall cost through proper alignment of incentives and better care coordination.

President Trump and his team at Health and Human Services recognize this potential. They created a new direct contracting model for Medicare that would pay a single flat rate for handling all a patient's health care needs. Enrollment just began, so we won't have data on results for a while, but the system is promising.

One more note about the fully integrated health system option: we need full price transparency for it to work. Without price transparency, patients and employers will have a hard time determining if contracting with a fully integrated health system is a good value. We need real prices for health care services to compare the option of a monthly fee for access to all the possible services within a health system. So, fully integrated health care is not a replacement for fee-for-service; it is an alternative that exists in tandem with a fully price transparent fee-for-service model.

Rebellion Number 5: Affordable Health Coverage without Provider Networks

While some companies are offering great health coverage for their employees, the fact is that these plans still have one critical flaw: if employees leave their jobs, they lose their coverage. This is why having a robust individual marketplace for insurance is so important. It gives people an alternative if they leave or lose their job. Also, thanks to President Trump's recent reforms, it also allows companies the option to give people money in a health reimbursement arrangement that they can use to buy their own coverage.

Unfortunately, the Affordable Care Act fundamentally broke the individual marketplace. Obamacare plans have sky-high premiums and deductibles—and narrow provider networks. The result is that individual market plans are unaffordable for anyone not receiving subsidies and not particularly attractive to those with chronic conditions who need to see specialists (who are often not included in Obamacare plans' narrow networks).

Fully integrated health care options in the individual marketplace is one solution. These plans are generally more affordable because members agree to use only the plan sponsor's health system. They are particularly attractive to those with chronic illnesses, who utilize a lot of health care and need a high degree of care coordination.

However, most Americans do not have a fully integrated health system near them. Even those who do may want more flexible health coverage options; this is especially true for those who are relatively healthy.

This leads us to another health care rebellion, one that was accelerated by Obamacare. As costs exploded and networks shrank in the individual market, millions of Americans sought out alternative health coverage that was more affordable and customizable to their needs. President Trump recently expanded the use of short-term, limited-duration plans to give Americans more affordable health insurance options. But for many years after Obamacare took effect, the only alternative for many Americans was to enroll in a type of health coverage that was previously used only in strongly religious communities: a sharing ministry.

Sharing ministries are not technically insurance, so they are exempt from many of Obamacare's and other government rules that drive up costs. This has allowed sharing ministries to present a much more affordable option for Americans looking for health coverage. Monthly payments for sharing ministries are about half of the premiums you would pay for coverage in the individual marketplace.

Collectively, more than one million Americans are enrolled in a health care sharing program and share more than $670 million in health care bills each year. Three of the largest are Medi-Share, Samaritan Ministries, and Christian Healthcare Ministries. Participants agree to help one another pay their medical bills and to live by a Christian code of ethics that should result in lower medical bills. This code of conduct is reinforced by notifying members when their monthly contribution is used to pay another member's bills and whose contributions helped pay their bills. The specifics of the medical expenditure are not shared, but members can contact one another to say thank you and ask for prayers, or to let members know they are praying for them.

While sharing ministries are technically not insurance, the experience for participants is similar. Participants agree to contribute a set amount every month to a pool used to pay members' health care expenses—much like a premium. Participants also have different levels of copays for routine in-person doctor visits and emergency rooms. Many of the programs also have no-copay telehealth options. The plans also have an annual household portion (AHP) of medical expenses that functions like a deductible.

Sharing ministries are more affordable than traditional insurance. They also feature nationwide provider networks. In addition to the telemedicine option, which members can use anywhere, members can find a doctor in the ministry's provider network anywhere in the country. This is because the sharing ministries are not state-based. Coverage does not stop at the border.

Sharing ministries also allow people to utilize out-of-network health care providers, though they will cover only the in-network rate. If the provider charges more than that amount, the remaining balance may need to be paid by the member. This is still an improvement over traditional health insurance, which will not cover any portion of an out-of-network provider's charges. This last feature is crucially important, because it could represent the future of health coverage in a price transparent system.

NO MORE "OUT OF NETWORK" PROVIDERS
Sidecar Health may be the most innovative and exciting health coverage option in America today. Like a sharing ministry, it is exempt from most of Obamacare and other government rules. The monthly fees for Sidecar Health are about 40 percent lower than premiums in the individual marketplace, and coverage can be much more personalized. Participants can choose as much or as little coverage as they want and can choose the size of their deductible—including having none. Sidecar also has no enrollment periods, you can sign up any time, and coverage starts fourteen days after enrollment.

Sidecar is not the traditional sort of managed-care or preferred provider network health insurance that we are used to. Instead, Sidecar is a program manager and administrator of indemnity insurance plans. Plan members contract and interface with Sidecar, but the claims are paid for by Sidecar's insurance partners.

Indemnity insurance is what most health insurance used to be before the rise of managed care plans in the 1980s. Instead of contracting with certain providers and excluding others, indemnity insurance's only relationship is with its plan members. This had the advantage of allowing patients to have coverage at any health care provider. However, it fell out of favor because it was cumbersome for patients. Since everything was paper-based, tracking your plan's reimbursement amount for every procedure and then calling multiple providers to check their price took a lot of time. Also, the model required the medical provider to bill patients, so patients would be responsible for getting the insurance company to reimburse them. These requirements left patients dealing with a lot of paperwork and having to front a lot of initial cost.

Sidecar has fixed this by taking advantage of modern information technology and a debit card.

Members have access to an app in which they enter the medical service they need. They are told how much Sidecar will pay for the service and then given a list of providers in the area for whom they have price information. However, Sidecar's members are not limited to that list; they can then apply that amount toward using any provider they wish. If they choose a provider that charges more, members pay the difference in next month's premium. If they choose one that charges less, the difference gets deducted. So, members are rewarded for shopping around with even more savings. Plus, there are no surprise medical bills.

The addition of the Sidecar debit card for payment is particularly ingenious and a true breakthrough. First, it makes the previous cumbersome patient experience with indemnity insurance of having to pay bills and then submit copies of the bill by mail for reimbursement almost seamless. Patients pay using the Sidecar debit card and take a picture of the itemized bill from the provider.

They then upload it to the app. Sidecar takes care of the rest and applies the difference or a credit to next month's bill.

More significantly, the debit card makes the experience seamless for doctors. It allows them to get paid immediately at the point of service instead of requiring them to submit a bill for reimbursement to an insurance company. So, for the doctor, treating a patient using Sidecar is indistinguishable from treating one paying cash. Since the doctors get paid instantly and in full, this gives Sidecar members access to the discounted cash or self-pay prices discussed in Chapter 10. This is a big reason why Sidecar costs less than normal insurance. Whereas sharing ministries are united in a code of conduct around living a healthy, biblical lifestyle, Sidecar members are united in a code of conduct about shopping for the best price. This keeps premiums low.

PUTTING IT ALL TOGETHER

Right now, indemnity insurance options like Sidecar are being used by people who are particularly comfortable shopping around for cash or self-pay prices. For all the reasons we have discussed, this is not particularly easy to do. Most health care providers don't publicize these rates, if they even have them set in stone.

However, the Trump administration's rules on transparency will change this. Providers will be required to make all their charges public—including the self-pay price—and information technology companies will arise to allow people to easily compare prices. These services would sync with Sidecar-like health coverage services to instantaneously display a provider's self-pay price minus its reimbursement to give people an instant list of what they would owe with all providers. Quality ratings will also be incorporated, so Americans will be better informed.

And meanwhile, the administration's interoperability rules for electronic health records will make it even easier to shop for health care services online, since people will be able to send their health records to doctors to get price quotes in the case of services that have a lot of variables.

Companies will have more and better options for providing health coverage for employees. Price and quality transparency will give them the visibility they need to create steering incentives for their employees to go to the highest-value health care providers. This will save companies billions, which can be reinvested into salaries and workforce development. Companies will also have the simpler option of helping employees pay for coverage they choose in the individual marketplace. Thanks to President Trump's reforms, these options will be affordable and customizable to what the employees need.

Finally, properly aligning incentives among doctors, patients, and payers will restore primary care back to the center of American health care—an investment that will keep Americans healthier and happier.

This is a vision for a truly free market in health care that provides the best possible combination of competition among health care providers to lower prices and improve quality. It will create health coverage for financial certainty, and properly align incentives among patients, doctors, and payers to keep Americans healthy. It is the health system of the future that America's health care rebels are building, and President Trump and Republicans are helping to make it a reality. It is a fundamentally better and more attractive vision than the government-run health care future of Vice President Biden and the radical Democratic Left. It may seem hard to believe, but these past four chapters have barely scratched the surface on the issue of health care. There are many more challenges to be solved. Fortunately, there are also many more health care rebels in America solving them. I encourage you to visit our book website at Gingrich360.com to learn more.

13.

★ ▬▬▬▬▬▬▬▬▬▬▬▬▬▬▬▬▬▬▬▬▬▬▬▬▬▬▬▬▬ ★

THE DEEP STATE IS
CRIPPLING AMERICA

We are at a critically important moment in history—one in which we can either lead to a future defined by liberty, or surrender to one defined by totalitarianism.

As I wrote in my best-selling book, *Trump vs. China: Facing America's Greatest Threat*, China is challenging us for dominance in a host of areas that will have profound impacts on the future of the world. The Chinese Communist Party has taken advantage of decades of misguided US foreign and trade policies. All along, Chinese companies have absorbed (and stolen) key American technologies and ideas. The Chinese government has subsidized these Chinese companies (which are ultimately controlled by the Chinese Communist Party) to help further develop and sell these technologies worldwide. Now—as part of its stated national strategy for dominance—China is working diligently to undercut American businesses and others worldwide.

The most immediate, glaring example of this problem is China's effort to dominate the world's fifth-generation (5G)

telecommunication infrastructure business through the remarkably successful company Huawei. In this particular contest, the
United States is currently on track to lose the race for the future. If
we fail to meet the 5G challenge, we could set our nation's relative
position in the world back for generations to come—and surrender global leadership to the Chinese Communist Party.

President Trump understands how big and important this
challenge is. At an April 2019 White House event, the president
articulated the correct goals for 5G:

> It will transform the way our citizens work, learn, commu-
> nicate, and travel. It will make American farms more pro-
> ductive, American manufacturing more competitive, and
> American health care better and more accessible. . . .
>
> 5G networks will also create astonishing and really
> thrilling new opportunities for our people—opportunities
> that we've never even thought we had a possibility of look-
> ing at.[1]

In his remarks, President Trump emphasized the importance
of a secure 5G network:

> Secure 5G networks will absolutely be a vital link to
> America's prosperity and national security in the 21st cen-
> tury. . . .
>
> 5G networks must be secure. They must be strong.
> They have to be guarded from the enemy.[2]

Furthermore, President Trump asserted that 5G coverage
needs to be extended to rural communities:

> [5G networks] must cover every community, and they must
> be deployed as soon as possible. . . .

As we are making great progress with 5G, we're also focused on rural communities that do not have access to broadband at all. . . .

We're working closely with federal agencies to get networks built in rural America faster and at much, much lower cost than it is even today. . . .

No matter where you are, you will have access to 5G.

So, over a year ago, President Trump set the right direction, outlined how vital 5G will be, and he called on America to win the contest. Ever since, he has been fighting to bring the United States back to the lead.

There is no other area in which the collective forces of the deep state have been more effective in slow-walking, ignoring, and undermining President Trump's stated goals. The president is facing legacy industries, entrenched bureaucrats, and some powerful members of Congress who are hell-bent on ensuring the status quo remains intact even if that means America loses to China and Huawei. And make no mistake: If the old guard wins, Americans will lose.

American telecommunication companies were the world leaders in developing 3G and 4G LTE mobile communication networks. So these American companies set the technical standards for these networks to be deployed worldwide. All the cell phones, operating systems, and mobile apps were developed to work with America's network. Importantly, American innovators had access to the new networks first. This early access enabled the rise of American streaming services, such as Netflix, Hulu, and Disney+. The 4G upgrade provided the infrastructure and connectivity that enabled widespread ride-sharing apps, such as Uber and Lyft. It also made possible augmented reality applications, advanced mobile games, and real-time video conferencing. So, the technological upgrade from 3G to 4G LTE totally changed the way we travel, communicate, and consume media. The economy born out of this upgrade also created an amazing amount of commerce and jobs for the United States.

5G mobile communication technology is the next major technological milestone. It provides much more than the ability to stream movies or games on your phone or tablet. Its hyper-low latency (the length of time it takes to send and receive signals) and higher capacity for data means that a host of devices will be able to communicate and share a massive amount of dynamic information almost instantly. This technology will be the foundation on which pervasive artificial intelligence systems, self-driving vehicles, long-distance surgery, and a host of other amazing capabilities are built. It will be the enabling technology that brings many of the works of science fiction into reality.

As of now, the Chinese company Huawei is clearly dominating the world of 5G development. According to the *Financial Times*, as of October 2019, Huawei had more than sixty contracts to build 5G infrastructure for carriers all over the world (not including current 4G contracts it already had).[3] At the time of this writing, no US company is building a single genuine 5G national network. Instead, companies such as AT&T are focusing solely on the American urban market. They are building shoestring networks in a few major cities and branding them 5G—when they are nowhere near having true next-generation capability. In fact, their network is severely lacking. One study in early 2019 found that in some areas AT&T's so-called 5G Evolution networks were slower than the established 4G networks.[4]

The urban-focused plan of American legacy carriers is wrong in many ways, but mainly because it offers a lesser version of 5G that will in no way compete with Huawei anywhere but in the United States—where Huawei is currently barred from operating. If the legacy companies have their way, American 5G networks will really exist only in dense urban markets. Once again, rural

Americans will be left in the cold. This would destroy some of the most exciting possibilities for 5G. What's the benefit of remote surgery if a patient in a rural town still must drive several hours to get to an area where such a thing would be possible? How can logistics companies benefit from long-distance autonomous vehicles if their trucks can't safely drive themselves in sparsely populated areas? How can the most productive modern farming technologies be developed if they can't use the most advanced telecommunications available?

Moreover, we know the legacy carriers' urban focus is wrong, because it's the same model they used for 3G and 4G. If you need to understand what's wrong with this approach, simply look at your phone's reception icon when you are traveling through rural parts of our country. I lose service for the better part of an hour when I travel to visit family in rural Wisconsin. Some of my colleagues who have family in rural Georgia simply can't rely on their cell phones when they are home for the holidays. This is merely an inconvenience for us, but think about the hundreds of thousands of Americans who live in these areas who are being totally left behind as the world becomes more connected. This is a real problem that limits the lives of millions of Americans.

A National Scandal

Huawei has been able to dominate 5G internationally for several reasons. First, it began with a $75 billion head start in the form of grants, tax breaks, and pure handouts from the Chinese Communist Party.[5] The *Wall Street Journal* reported that these subsidies have allowed the company to underbid its competitors by as much as 30 percent. The newspaper reported that, among other incentives, Huawei received $25 billion in tax breaks from 2008 to 2018. It was able to buy previously state-owned land for rock-bottom prices (in some cases as low as 10 percent of the average market rate). Government-owned banks have opened enormous lines of credit for the company—one for $16 billion and another for $30 billion. While the company claims it doesn't often draw from the loans, the available credit has allowed Huawei to aggressively outbid its competition for building 5G networks abroad. The Chinese government has identified dominating the worldwide development of 5G as one of its national priorities, so its leaders are happy to hand Huawei the money needed to outcompete the international market.

And the Chinese Communist Party has been employing this pattern for decades. In fact, Huawei wouldn't be where it is today if China hadn't driven most US network equipment and mobile device manufacturers out of business. Many US companies that once made various network infrastructure equipment and components are simply gone. China has decimated them through an aggressive strategy of key purchases, pervasive intellectual property theft, and heavy subsidization of its own businesses. US manufacturers simply could not compete, so they were either dissolved or split up and absorbed by other companies. This is what happened to Alcatel-Lucent, Motorola, and a host of semiconductor and processor makers. The few US companies that still operate outsource much of their manufacturing to China.

Michele Nash-Hoff illustrated the problem well in an article in *IndustryWeek* from January 2018 titled "Should We Allow the Chinese to Buy Any US Company They Want?" Nash-Hoff was describing the 2014 sale of Motorola Mobility to the Chinese company Lenovo when she pointed out, "The nation that invented smart phones is just about entirely out of the business of producing smart phones in America. This acquisition will give one of China's most prominent technology companies a broader foothold in the U.S."[6]

As with many of China's activities, the pro-globalist powers in Washington, DC, have simply let Huawei and other Chinese-supported companies take advantage of us. This is the second reason

Huawei and China have been so successful. A host of US bureau-crats, politicians, and telecom executives have cheerfully defended the status quo—to the detriment of America's future. It is a seri-ous national scandal, and Congress should be devoting a lot of time to understanding how the United States has failed, and is still failing, so badly in competing with China in this vital area.

For starters, to achieve the low latency and coverage that will be necessary for a truly nationwide network (which fully covers rural and urban areas) US phone carriers will need more access to the radio spectrum than is currently available for 3G and 4G LTE networks. This means opening access to parts of the radio spec-trum which are currently being hoarded by the US Department of Defense (DoD) and other federal agencies. Specifically, carriers need more access to the sub-6 GHz parts of the spectrum.

I will try to avoid getting overly technical here, but bands of the sub-6 GHz spectrum are currently used for a host of activi-ties including radar, satellite communications, broadcasting, and other operations. The Federal Communications Commission (FCC) announced in November 2019 that it would auction off a block of this spectrum, called C-band, which is currently used by satellite companies that beam television broadcasts. The auction is currently scheduled for December 2020. This frequency band will be useful for providing connectivity and low-latency trans-mission for many of our urban centers—but it is only part of the equation.

There is another sub-6 GHz band known as the L-band that will be necessary for providing wide-ranging connectivity in our rural areas. This is because lower-frequency radio waves can travel through obstructions that would slow down or stop high-er-frequency waves. Because of this, L-band signals require fewer towers and infrastructure. If we were to move forward using only the C-band spectrum, we would need to have 400,000 towers to cover the entire country. Currently, the major carriers in the

United States have about 80,000 towers combined. The process of building 320,000 more towers—and acquiring the land on which to build them—could potentially take a tremendous amount of money and decades of time. We don't have this luxury.

Currently, much of the L-band is used by our Global Positioning System (GPS). The DoD is currently putting up a strong fight against opening part of the L-band for 5G because it claims doing so would interfere with GPS signals. Many in the industry—particularly new, innovative companies that are hoping to seize on the opportunity of 5G—say that the concerns about interference are unfounded and rely on bad data. The section of spectrum in question does not overlap with the frequencies used for GPS, and the companies say the DoD is simply seeking to control spectra to which it currently has no rights.

President Trump must find an answer to this impasse. I'll be blunt: If we don't figure out how to quickly develop and deploy a nationwide 5G network in the United States—and offer it to the world before Huawei completely claims the market—the free world will face devastating long-term consequences.

Beating China

Currently, the failure of the major American telecommunication companies—and the failure of the US government—leaves us with no competitive position worldwide. We keep warning countries not to use Huawei in their 5G networks, but we don't have a replacement system to offer. In fact, US companies are not even competing in this space.

Huawei has better technology for a lower price. Naturally, in country after country, Huawei is gaining contracts. In the long term, it will mean that the Chinese Communist Party (which actively uses technology to strip liberty away from its own people) will have tremendous influence over communication networks and data collection across the planet.

It poses a tangible, immediate national security threat as well. The *Wall Street Journal* reported in February 2020 that Huawei "can covertly access mobile-phone networks around the world through 'back doors' designed for use by law enforcement."[7] Further, US officials told the newspaper they've seen evidence of this illegal spying and surveillance in Huawei's products going back more than a decade, to 2009. Later that month, US officials unsealed a sixteen-count indictment against Huawei for an alleged racketeering scheme in which China was seeking to steal intellectual property and other valuable information from US companies.[8] Importantly, US officials also allege that the company has been working with countries that are currently sanctioned by the US government—including North Korea and Iran. So, to be clear: Huawei has a history of using unfair state support to decimate American industries, has been spying on Americans for more than a decade, and is happy to covertly work with nations that want to do us harm.

The danger is so clear, it has even brought Speaker Nancy Pelosi into alignment with President Trump, whom she has otherwise dedicated almost all her time to attacking. On February 14, 2020, Pelosi told the audience at the Munich Security Conference that blocking Huawei from 5G networks was essential:

> This is the most insidious form of aggression, to have that line of communication, 5G, dominated by an autocratic government that does not share our values. . . . If you want to build a collective conscience of values and respect for human rights and the rest, don't go near Huawei, and instead, let's internationalize and build something together that will be about freedom of information.[9]

Unfortunately, despite bipartisan efforts in the United States to convince our international allies to bar Huawei from 5G networks, we are losing this argument. This is particularly true for countries with whom we share vital intelligence. In January 2020, the United Kingdom announced it would allow Huawei to access some parts of its 5G networks.[10] British officials said the country would work with Huawei only on "non-core" components of its network, such as antennas or peripheral devices, and that Huawei's share of the market would be capped at 35 percent. It also claimed that Huawei components wouldn't be used near military or nuclear sites. Similarly, German leaders have paid lip service to the dangers of using Huawei devices in Germany's network, but the country has so far declined to ban the company from its market. Following the UK and German announcements, Canadian telecommunications company Telus Corps announced it would use Huawei components for the "backbone" of its 5G network.[11] Taking a page from the British, the company claimed it would only use "non-core" components from Huawei. As I'm writing this, the Canadian government is weighing whether to allow Huawei components into its market, but it has not yet made a decision.

Even if the UK, Canada, and Germany don't allow Huawei to build vital parts of their 5G networks, it will still be tough for the United States to rationalize sharing critical intelligence with these allies.[12] We are talking about a company that has been putting back doors in its mobile devices for a decade. I have every confidence Huawei will figure out how to install back doors in the British, Canadian, and German systems in short order. It is true that Huawei's officials claim they would not cooperate if the Chinese government wanted to use its network for espionage—and officials from the United Kingdom and Germany have parroted this claim. This is baloney. China is run by a totalitarian Communist dictatorship. Huawei wouldn't have a choice but do as its government orders. If, in some act of heroism, the leadership at Huawei defied the Chinese Communist Party, I'm certain they would simply be arrested and the company swiftly nationalized.

Furthermore, having the United Kingdom, Canada, and Germany submit to the Chinese company sends a message around the world that gives cover for other nations to follow suit. Huawei has already ensnared many parts of South America and Africa. Letting the company into the heart of Europe would get Huawei (and China) one large step closer to developing and controlling the Internet of the twenty-first century. If the United Kingdom and Germany follow through with plans to allow Huawei into their 5G networks, it will be the biggest strategic defeat for the United States since the early days of World War II.

The American Answer

Even if we can ultimately convince our allies not to allow Huawei to build their 5G networks, it will not be enough. We must develop an American alternative if we are going to ensure the Internet of tomorrow is based on the ideals of free speech, privacy, and transparency. Unfortunately, we cannot count on our own legacy telecommunications companies or their allies and protectors at the FCC to do it.

In fact, the traditional leaders in this zone have already failed us. They have ignored the rise of Huawei—even when it surpassed Ericsson in 2012 as the largest telecommunications equipment maker in the world. None of the traditional government and private-sector players in the 4G world have proposed solutions large enough to beat Huawei in the world market. So far, Verizon and AT&T—our two largest carriers—have focused on small projects in specific US cities. This is partly due to the bureaucratic fight over releasing spectrum, but it is also due to these companies being deeply in debt and wanting to milk their previous investments for as long as possible.

After it bought Time Warner in 2019, AT&T was sitting on $180 billion in debt. It is not positioned to develop a truly nationwide next-generation mobile network. As of September 2019, the company still held more than $165 billion of debt.[13] Similarly, as of February 17, 2020, Verizon was carrying more than $115 billion in debt.[14] The recently announced merger of T-Mobile and Sprint shows some promise, as the companies have said they plan to create a "broad" nationwide network utilizing both midband and millimeter wave spectra.[15] However, the company's own maps show a great deal of its coverage is actually 4G coverage. That will not allow rural areas to access the kind of technological change that 5G will offer. Furthermore, shrinking the number of major carriers increases oligopolistic behavior, minimizes customer power, and guarantees Americans will continue to pay the highest wireless prices in the modern world.

As I mentioned earlier, it is currently impossible to create a wholly American system. This is because we don't have any companies that can build necessary network components. Instead, US carriers must rely on Samsung, Ericsson, or Nokia to physically build the equipment we need. To put it simply, our traditional bureaucratic and business leaders have lacked seriousness and urgency—and urgency is what we need. The Mobile World Congress in Barcelona in 2019 should have been an enormous wake-up call. There were 109,000 participants. Huawei dominated the exhibition and left the conference with many new contracts. The United States looked pathetic. We offered no alternative to the scale of Huawei's technological capabilities. As of today, nothing has changed. The 2020 exhibition was canceled due to concerns over the spread of the coronavirus. While the reason for the cancellation is terrible, it in some ways bought the United States time to get its act together. To borrow Winston Churchill's phrase from World War II, the next Mobile World Congress is a good motivation for "action this day."

As a first step, President Trump should direct the DoD to issue a request for proposals for innovative plans to develop a truly nationwide 5G system and respond to Huawei's expansion.

It's clear that the DoD can't get its own bureaucracy to work. Only a clear directive from the president will force the system to move. This should be a DoD initiative, because our national security is at stake if the Chinese Communist Party ultimately controls the next-generation Internet. We already know that the Chinese Communist Party uses data collection and control of information to impose its will on its own people. Handing China control of the worldwide database of information that will undergird large-scale artificial intelligence systems is a scary prospect.

Let me be clear: I am not suggesting that the DoD should become a telecommunications company. The DoD shouldn't own, pay for, or run the future nationwide 5G network. However, only the DoD has the institutional authority to open the door to a system this large. We are, after all, competing with Huawei, a 194,000-employee company (with state backing) that makes $122 billion in revenue and operates in more than 170 countries.[16]

Instead of asking for government solutions, the request should specifically insist on finding multiple nationwide private-sector solutions and include multiple players implementing a 5G network. Specifically, we should invite new players to the game. Considering our large infrastructure investors, entrepreneurial startups, and massive technology firms, America is home to a lot of knowledge, entrepreneurial risk-taking, and capital. Combined, our tech and investment firms dwarf the legacy telecommunications players and bureaucracies. Some of our technology firms have more than $100 billion in cash each. There are big infrastructure investment firms that have already indicated they would put tens of billions of dollars into 5G projects. There is no need to have taxpayers bear the brunt of this burden.

Further, the request should strip power from the legacy bureaucracies that have failed us and really open up the future to new ideas. The best possible outcome would be for the United States to develop a market-based system that competes with

Huawei because it's truly better. To this end, I have long advocated a market-based wholesale system. Under this type of model, prices would be set by real market forces of supply and demand rather than rates inflated by companies with massive debts to pay. Under the current system, the FCC auctions off spectra to a handful of massive companies that are willing to take exorbitant loans. The companies then make massive bids to drive smaller competitors out of the game. These companies then sit on spectrum—leaving it unused—so that no one can challenge their business models. We should instead have a system that puts all available spectra at play all the time.

The FCC bureaucracy opposes a market-based system because it takes power out of its hands and shifts it to the consumers. The old telecommunication companies oppose a market-based system because it would dramatically lower the cost of wireless service to the consumer—possibly by 40 percent. The shift to a much more competitive, lower-cost market would be a major blow to Huawei, because its financing has been based on the inability of the big, American companies to compete on price.

A wholesale system would also help President Trump make good on a commitment he made to rural America. Outside the request for proposals, President Trump should identify a leader in the White House to develop and implement an all-of-government, many-layered campaign to overtake and ultimately replace Huawei as the leading 5G developer outside China. Importantly, this individual must be a leader, not merely a coordinator, because there are too many decisions that will have to be enforced. This effort also must be housed in the White House, so he or she will have the access, reach, and authority to move various parts of the system and bureaucracies. Part of this person's challenge will be developing a plan of incentives to help carriers in foreign countries remove their Huawei equipment and replace it with new American- or ally-made systems. Again, we have already been too late to convince people not to buy Huawei equipment. We must offer a desirable alternative for them to replace it. Part of this plan must also include an element to promote and rebuild this sector of manufacturing in America. Otherwise, we will find ourselves in this same situation in a short amount of time. China is not going to change its drive toward dominance.

And along those lines, we must begin a coordinated public-private research and development effort to leapfrog 5G advancements and create a 6G world. Between investment and intellectual property theft, the Chinese Communist Party is—and will likely remain—formidable. It also has significant momentum. We must plan to leapfrog their efforts in 5G just as we leapfrogged the Russians by going to the Moon in response to *Sputnik* and developing stealth systems after the Soviets invested heavily in antiaircraft systems.

The race to developing the preeminent 5G communications network has already started, and we are far behind. If we want to ensure that the future is defined by liberty over authoritarianism, then we need to get in the race and win. Helping President Trump overcome the communications deep state is a key step toward American survival and a genuine national security imperative.

14.

★ ▬▬▬▬▬▬▬▬▬▬▬▬▬▬▬▬▬▬▬▬ ★

COMMUNIST-RULED CHINA
AND COVID-19

The scale of Chinese dishonesty in hiding the coronavirus until its spread became overwhelming. Watching China blame the United States for the virus that clearly originated in Wuhan, China, and then using its manufacturing dominance in medicine and medical supplies to help countries deal with the virus it sent them, has been sobering.

The real Chinese dictatorship has become more apparent and more threatening in the process of dealing with the pandemic. This crystallizes a change in our view of China, which has been gradually growing over the last decade.

For decades, the United States believed that China would transition from a country ruled by a Communist totalitarian dictatorship to one that is governed by the rule of law that protects individual freedoms and human rights. We thought that by China becoming a stakeholder in the international community, the Chinese Communist Party (CCP) would stop the systematic oppression of its people and would open itself up to partnerships and cooperation with other countries and economies. We have now seen, particularly under the leadership of Chinese Communist Party General Secretary Xi Jinping, that we were wrong.

Our misdiagnosis of the Chinese Communist Party and its totalitarian system has now created serious challenges for the United States. These challenges threaten our national security, interests, and values. China's theft of US intellectual property remains a serious problem, as the Communist Party's use of predatory economic practices that prop up domestic businesses and severely disadvantage foreign entities has continued. Amid the COVID-19 outbreak, American businesses and manufacturers have discovered how overly dependent they are on Chinese supply chains. The Chinese Communist Party has outlined ten major industries that it aims to dominate under its "Made in China 2025" plan, including biopharmaceuticals and high-performance medical devices, next-generation information technology, aerospace and aviation equipment, maritime engineering equipment, and high-tech maritime vessel manufacturing.[1]

The party has expanded its global propaganda efforts by setting up Confucius Institutes at academic institutions, leveraging its vast market to incentivize Hollywood producers to alter movies to align with party positions, and forcing journalists and academics to self-censor their reporting to avoid access restriction. China is increasing its control of the digital space through apps such as TikTok, which is facing allegations that it abides by Communist Party censorship requirements. It is also gaining digital power through the global rollout of Huawei's 5G technology that threatens the security of shared information and communication.[2] The Chinese Communist Party also has been expanding its global footprint through the Belt and Road Initiative and strengthening its regional control in the South China Sea through its aggressive military buildup and illegal construction of artificial islands.

These efforts result in a clear competition between two systems that is being waged in the United States and across the world. One system is based on freedom, individual liberty, and the rule of law. The other is controlled by the Chinese Communist Party. President Trump and members of Congress have warned about the existential threats that are now presented by the Chinese Communist Party and have taken action to counter them. I explain these challenges and actions that the United States has taken in greater detail in my recent best-selling book, *Trump vs. China: Facing America's Greatest Threat.*

Overcoming the challenges and mitigating the threats that we face with the Communist Party will require a long-term US effort that will involve all levels of society and necessitate collaboration with our allies and partners. However, Americans are becoming increasingly frustrated with the party's malign activities domestically and globally. For example, in a January 2020 poll conducted by McLaughlin & Associates for the Committee on Present Danger: China, 50 percent of respondents said they consider China to be an economic competitor and 18 percent consider China to be an adversary.[3] Additionally, a Gallup poll in February 2020 reported that 67 percent of respondents have an unfavorable opinion of China. Gallup has data on this particular question regarding Americans' opinion on China dating back to 1979, and this is the highest percentage of survey respondent negativity that has been reported.[4]

Additionally, Americans are concerned with the Chinese Communist Party's ambitions. The McLaughlin & Associates poll found that 81 percent of respondents would be worried if China controlled space, 70 percent were concerned about the United States relying on China's wireless technology, 77 percent were against China exporting its totalitarian social credit score system to other countries, and 75 percent were worried about China's increasingly dominant global position resulting from the Belt and Road Initiative.[5]

The more we learn about the Chinese Communist Party's system, its oppression of the Chinese people, its blatant disregard for the rule of law, and the goals that its leaders have set, the more apparent the challenges we face become. By examining the recently revealed facts about the Chinese Communist Party's handling of the Hong Kong protests in 2019, the widespread oppression of minorities in the region of Xinjiang, and the initial cover-up of the coronavirus outbreak, the fundamentally deceitful and manipulative nature of the party has become clearer. It affirms the concerns reflected by Americans in the aforementioned polls, and it becomes increasingly evident that these realities will affect the US relationship with China going forward.

Unveiling Unrest: The Hong Kong Protests

In 2019, residents of Hong Kong erupted into protests against the Chinese Communist Party's encroachment on their legally protected freedoms and liberties. As a result of these mass demonstrations, the party's oppression of the people of Hong Kong and the extent of the peoples' frustration and anger toward the government became undeniable.

On June 9, 2019, demonstrators took to the streets in opposition to a government-proposed extradition bill. This bill would have subjected the people of Hong Kong to mainland China's totalitarian judicial system and further diminished the autonomy of Hong Kong. According to organizers, more than one million people participated in the demonstration, which is equivalent to nearly one in seven Hong Kong residents.[6] Just one week later, on June 16, an estimated two million people marched again in defiance of the government.[7]

Though the extradition bill was eventually withdrawn, the protests persisted and evolved into additional demands for the government. These included an independent inquiry into police brutality, more democratic freedoms, reprieve for arrested demonstrators, and a demand for the party to cease referring to the peaceful pro-tests as "riots." Over the course of the following months however, the situation escalated from peaceful marches to more violent clashes.

The world watched in horror as more and more reports emerged of increasing violence and police crackdowns. At the height of the protests, thousands of arrests were made, thousands of tear gas cannisters were used, and thousands of rubber bullets were fired.[8] Government buildings and businesses were vandalized, and dem-onstrators occupying airports and shopping malls shut down the city's operations.[9] According to Reuters, the total number of Chi-nese military personnel in Hong Kong doubled since the start of the protests. There were as many as 12,000 Chinese troops in Hong Kong by the end of September, an increase from 3,000 to 5,000 that were present in the previous months.[10] Protesters were beaten, drenched in blue-dyed water, and attacked by criminal gangs. In early October 2019, on the day that China celebrated seventy years since the Chinese Communist Party came to power, the first pro-tester was shot with a live round by police. The Hong Kong gov-ernment used its emergency powers to declare that wearing face masks to a public assembly could be punished with up to a year in prison and a fine. A student who was twenty-two years old fell from a parking garage structure (close to where police and protest-ers were engaged in clashes) and died days later. In November, pro-testers occupied university campuses, where the police fired tear gas and water cannons at them. The protesters took shelter and launched gasoline bombs, bricks, and arrows.[11]

The seriousness of the situation in Hong Kong and the determi-nation of the protesters who have been involved in the demonstra-tions led many observers to question how Hong Kong got to this breaking point. Decades ago—when Hong Kong was handed over to China by the British in 1997—the people of Hong Kong were legally promised that they would have a high degree of autonomy and retain the same freedoms they had under British control. However, since China regained control of Hong Kong, the ruling Chinese Communist Party has deliberately broken these promises.

In 1984, the British and Chinese governments signed an agreement known as the Sino-British Joint Declaration. This agreement outlined the terms of governance when Britain ceded control of Hong Kong to mainland China. The Chinese Communist Party promised in the agreement that Hong Kong would have largely independent jurisdiction over its affairs. The Sino-British Joint Declaration stated, "The Hong Kong Special Administrative region will enjoy a high degree of autonomy, except in foreign and defence affairs which are the responsibilities of the Central People's Government."[12]

The Chinese Communist Party also agreed that the freedoms people in Hong Kong possessed would be protected—even though Hong Kong was joining a country ruled by communism. The concept that defines mainland China's relationship with Hong Kong is known as "one country, two systems" and is a cornerstone of the Chinese Communist Party's system of governance. "One country, two systems" is the idea that reconciles the differences in the amount of freedoms and liberties granted to the people of Hong Kong versus those living in mainland China. (It is also the reason that the United States has historically granted Hong Kong special privileges.) The joint declaration stated that "the current social and economic systems in Hong Kong will remain unchanged, and so will the life-style. Rights and freedoms, including those of the person, speech, the press, assembly, association, travel, movement, correspondence, strike, choice of occupation, academic research and religious belief will be ensured by law in the Hong Kong Special Administrative Region."[13]

All these promises made to the people of Hong Kong by the Chinese Communist Party were later enshrined in the 1997 Basic Law. The Basic Law also states that the "ultimate aim" for electing

Hong Kong's chief executive (Hong Kong's leader) is through universal suffrage using democratic procedures. The laws protecting Hong Kong's autonomy and freedoms were stipulated to remain unchanged until 2047—but this hasn't stopped the Communist Party from violating them.

The freedoms of the people of Hong Kong have been increasingly repressed. Freedom House issues rankings on countries' and territories' rights and civil liberties on a scale of 0 to 100 (0 is the least free and 100 is the freest). Hong Kong's score dropped from 68 in 2009 to 59 in 2019.[14]

Evidence of Hong Kong's freedoms being squeezed by the Chinese Communist Party are apparent in the election process. Despite being 26 points behind in a Hong Kong University poll the day before the election, Beijing's favored candidate, Carrie Lam, won the election to become chief executive of Hong Kong in 2017. Lam was elected by a committee made up of loyalist elites heavily influenced by Beijing's interests in what critics called a "selection, not an election." A pro-democracy legislator, Nathan Law, said at the time, "Lam's victory despite her lack of representation and popular support reflects the Chinese Communist Party's complete control over Hong Kong's electoral process and its serious intrusion of Hong Kong's autonomy." [15]

Additionally, according to Human Rights Watch, political participation is limited in Hong Kong. For years, Hong Kong lawmakers and candidates who advocate for democracy or independence have been kicked out of office or disqualified.[16] Law is one such example: shortly after Carrie Lam's election, he was unseated for having earlier stated his oath of office and then adding "Power returns to the people. Absolute and autocratic powers will not live forever. There should be democratic self-determination, and there will be continuous struggle." Since Law's pledge wasn't allegedly taken in a "sincere" or "solemn" manner, he was treated as though he had declined to take the oath.[17]

Law wasn't declining to take the oath that his new office required. He was exercising his freedom of speech. In doing so, he was threatening the Chinese Communist Party's grip on Hong Kong. It was one of many examples of Beijing infringing on the promised personal freedoms guaranteed by law to the people of Hong Kong.

The result of the Chinese Communist Party's assault on the legally codified autonomy and freedoms of Hong Kong is what ultimately led to the widespread protests and unrest. Allowing Hong Kong to exercise the liberties it was promised poses an existential threat to the party's maintenance and expansion of its power.

In a clear act of defiance against the Chinese government, in November 2019, pro-democracy candidates won a sweeping victory in local elections, as record numbers of voters cast their ballots in staunch opposition to the pro-Beijing government. (Keep in mind, these elections were for district council seats, which are some of the lowest positions in the government; they focus on community issues such as bus stops and traffic signals. Just over half of Hong Kong's legislature is democratically elected, and the chief executive is selected by a committee that is heavily tilted in favor of Beijing. The district councils choose approximately one-tenth of the 1,200-member selection committee.)

Nonetheless, this election was significant because it showed how widespread support for the protests had become and was a clear vote against the status quo. Seven of ten eligible voters cast their ballot, and pro-democracy candidates won 389 of 452 elected seats. For context, typical turnout is just over 40 percent in district council elections, and the total number of registered voters hit a record high. More than one half of the seats flipped in favor of pro-democracy candidates, which is a higher number than these candidates had ever won. As the *New York Times* noted, the election signified a critical turning point for pro-democracy advocates.[18]

The Old Gray Lady wrote, "The vote was the first test of whether the protests could transform public anger that has led millions to take to the streets into actual votes, or whether the populace had grown weary of acts of civil disobedience that have snarled transportation and forced the closing of schools and businesses."[19]

Clearly, the people have spoken, and though Lam has said that her administration "respects the election results" and promised to "listen to the opinions of members of the public humbly and seriously reflect," the demonstrators are not likely to halt their efforts until all of their four remaining demands are met and substantial change is realized.

In recent months, the mass demonstrations have significantly tapered off, due in part to the outbreak of COVID-19, but they have not stopped. Smaller-scale, local protests have continued, and these have been driven in part by the already prevalent mistrust and frustration with the government and exacerbated by missteps in handling the virus. Allegations of police brutality and widespread arrests have continued to circulate, and one activist, Kong Tsung-gan, told *The Guardian* in March 2020 that the "policing of protests during the outbreak has been 'more oppressive than ever.'"

According to the pro-democracy Hong Kong politician Albert Ho, there have certainly been fewer clashes since the onset of the virus; however, he observes that the authorities seem to be using this period to round up individuals and organizers central to the movement.[20]

The United States has come out in support of the demonstrators, most notably through the signing of the Hong Kong Human Rights and Democracy Act into law; it gives the United States tools to take diplomatic action and impose economic sanctions against a repressive Hong Kong government. As part of this law's implementation, which allows the United States to sanction individuals accused of participating in human rights abuses affiliated with the protests, opposition lawmakers in Hong Kong drafted a list of recommended senior officials and police chiefs in March to sanction.[21] Last year, President Trump also signed into law a bill that made illegal the sale of US-made munitions, such as tear gas and rubber bullets, to Hong Kong authorities.[22]

The passage of these laws was a strong statement made by President Trump and Congress in support of the Hong Kong protesters. But the question remains: What will happen to the movement after the threat from the coronavirus winds down? Over the course of the past year, we've learned that the people of Hong Kong are determined to live in freedom as legally promised. However, we've also learned through the government's reactions that it is determined to keep the status quo in place. Only time will tell if, and to what extent, the demonstrations and the inevitable party resistance will resume. But one thing remains certain: The United States must continue to stand in favor of freedom and democracy and in support of the Hong Kong protesters.

Leaking and Learning the Truth about Xinjiang

Despite the Chinese Communist Party's best efforts to conceal and downplay the mass imprisonment of Uyghurs and other Muslim and ethnic minorities in China's western region of Xinjiang, the party's campaign of systematic human rights abuses has been widely reported. Under the guise of combating terrorism, the Chinese Communist Party has created so-called vocational training centers where an estimated 800,000 to more than two million detainees have been forcibly detained in "reeducation" internment camps since April 2017.

A testimony by Deputy Assistant Secretary Scott Busby to the Senate Foreign Relations Committee in December 2018 described the conditions inside the camps. Busby noted:

Former detainees who have reached safety have spoken of relentless indoctrination and harsh conditions. They report mandatory classes where detainees are required to recite Communist slogans and sing songs praising the Chinese Communist Party. Failure to quickly learn these lessons leads to beatings and food deprivation. There are reports of the use of stress positions, cold cells, and sleep deprivation in the camps. We have also seen reports of other forms of torture or cruel, inhumane or degrading treatment, including sexual abuse. One common goal in reports from former detainees seems to be to forcing detainees to renounce Islam and embrace the Chinese Communist Party. For example, praying and using common Muslim greetings are forbidden in the camps. There are reports that authorities constantly surveil detainees to ensure that they do not pray, even in their own beds in the middle of the night. Detainees are reportedly forced to eat pork and drink alcohol. Some have reported being forcibly medicated with unknown substances.[23]

Additionally, outside these facilities, the Chinese Communist Party created an "open-air prison," where people have been closely monitored. Checkpoints staffed by police have been set up to monitor movements, and families have been forced to open up their homes for "home stays" by Communist Party officials. Thousands of mosques have been shut down or destroyed, with some being transformed into propaganda centers for the party.[24] According to a 2018 Human Rights Watch report, people living outside the camps must attend mandatory Chinese flag-raising ceremonies, meetings to advance political indoctrination, and Mandarin classes. Moreover, the report noted that surveilled individuals have been monitored by neighbors, officials, and a mass tech-surveillance system.[25]

Much of Xinjiang has been sealed off or restricted to outsiders and journalists, but a series of documents were incrementally leaked in November 2019 and February 2020 that provide details into the party's mass-detention program. The *New York Times* reported on acquired documents that outlined the party's ideological framework for establishing the system of oppression in Xinjiang. The documents revealed that in 2014, Xi Jinping traveled to Xinjiang, where he gave a series of secret speeches that laid the foundation for the crackdown on Uyghurs and other Muslim and ethnic minorities. Leading up to the tour, a violent attack had taken place a few weeks prior, and a suicide bombing was carried out by militants on the last day of his visit. "We must be as harsh as them," Xi stated in one speech, "and show absolutely no mercy."[26]

In Xinjiang, Xi told officials, "People who are captured by religious extremism—male or female, old or young—have their consciences destroyed, lose their humanity and murder without blinking an eye." He likened extremism to a virus or a drug, saying that addressing it entails "a period of painful, interventionary treatment." And though he didn't directly mention internment camps, Xi told officials, "There must be effective educational remolding and transformation of criminals."

At a later conference in Beijing, Xi did admit that it was "biased, even wrong" to restrict or eradicate Islam. However, despite the fact that the large majority of Uyghurs abide by moderate traditions, and Xi's predecessors had known that previous attacks in Xinjiang were carried out by a few fanatics, Xi took the position that extremism had gained a foothold within the broader society. The alleged threat of widespread violence led Xi to declare, "The weapons of the people's democratic dictatorship must be wielded without any hesitation or wavering."

The first indoctrination sites were open in Xinjiang months after Xi's visit, but the effort was dramatically expanded when Chen Quanguo, a Communist Party official, was transferred from Tibet to Xinjiang in 2016. According to the documents, Chen told police officers and troops in February 2017 to get ready for a "smashing, obliterating offensive." In the ensuing weeks, plans were finalized to detain Uyghurs on a mass scale, and Chen issued the order, "Round up everyone who should be rounded up" (meaning those who had "symptoms" of religious extremism or those who held views contradictory to those of the government).

According to the *New York Times*, a document was also obtained that advised local officials on how to handle students who had returned home to Xinjiang for a school break to find that their families were locked in the internment camps. It was a sample question-and-answer script in which officials were advised to tell the students their relatives were "in a training school set up by the government," and though they weren't criminals, they couldn't leave. There were subtle threats included in the script such as advising officials to tell students that how they behaved would affect the duration of their relatives' detention. "I'm sure that you will support them, because this is for their own good," the document advised officials to say, "and also for your own good."[27]

Also, in November 2019, documents released by the International Consortium of Investigative Journalists (ICIJ) provided a clearer picture of how the camps operated. The ICIJ released four "bulletins" describing the centralized data collection structure, known as the Integrated Joint Operation Platform. These documents show how the system of mass surveillance and the camps worked in unison. Additionally, the ICIJ reported on a "telegram" titled "Opinions on Further Strengthening and Standardizing Vocational Skills Education and Training Centers Work."[28] This secret document was a manual that outlined guidelines for the internment camps. The document dictated that in order to "prevent escapes" the camps must:

> strictly manage door locks and keys—dormitory doors, corridor doors and floor doors must be double locked, and must be locked immediately after being opened and

closed. Strictly manage and control student activities to prevent escapes during class, eating periods, toilet breaks, bath time, medical treatment, family visits, etc.[29]

Another document, a 137-page spreadsheet, was later leaked in February 2020. It provided insight into the type of information authorities gathered to monitor and track detainees and residents. More than three hundred names, government identification numbers, daily religious activities, and occupations of detainees were listed in the document, as well as the names of hundreds more of their relatives and neighbors. Entries dated back to 2017, and the last listed entry was recorded in March 2019. As the document confirmed, authorities used the "Three Circles"—family, social, and religious associations—to evaluate each detainee and record the official judgment on whether the prisoner could leave the camp. People were flagged for not drinking alcohol, having a beard, and for having a passport. Travel plans, movements, and religious practices, such as prayer habits and participation in ceremonies, weddings, and funerals, were tracked. People were detained for reasons such as having too many children, being an ex-prisoner or having a family member who was a former prisoner, participating in an unauthorized pilgrimage or visiting a "sensitive country," engaging in illegal preaching, or being prone to radicalization due to familial religious practices. For some exiled Uyghurs who haven't been able to contact their families in Xinjiang, this document's release was the first time they learned the fate of their loved ones.[30] [31]

According to Adrian Zenz, a German scholar who studied the spreadsheet, approximately 75 percent of those listed as detainees are no longer held in the internment camps.[32] Amid widespread global condemnation, Chinese officials have also claimed that a majority of detainees have been released. In July 2019, the chairman of the Xinjiang Uyghur Autonomous Region, Shohrat Zakir, said that most of those held in camps had been released; however, he did not say how many detainees remained and did not provide any evidence to support his claims. In line with the party's claims that the internment camps were used for job-training purposes, Zakir said as part of his presentation, "Ninety percent of them have found suitable and enjoyable jobs that bring them considerable income."[33] Later, in December 2019, Zakir said that all of those in the so-called reeducation centers had "completed their studies." Chinese state media broadcast pictures of dismantled facilities to reinforce this message.

But this wouldn't be the first time outsiders had been deceived about the situation in Xinjiang. Initially, China denied the existence of the camps and later even claimed they were voluntary. It's difficult to know for certain what's happening on the ground, because officials block reporters from freely moving around in the region and locals don't want to openly speak about their circumstances.

However, the *Wall Street Journal* reported in February 2020 that many of the blatantly overt security measures previously in place had been scaled back, while other, subtler control tactics still remained, thereby signaling a new phase in the party's Xinjiang strategy. Technology for facial recognition and ID checks are still active, and many overseas Uyghurs still have no information about their family members.

So then, what has happened to all the former detainees? Activists and Uyghurs living overseas have heard concerning reports of those in the camps being charged with criminal offenses and jailed. The *Wall Street Journal*'s reporters did see another building that was formerly referred to as a reeducation facility that clearly was still in use. "It's a jail," a uniformed guard said. "It's never been a school." But others have said those released are forced to work in factories.[34]

A 2020 Australian Strategic Policy Institute (ASPI) report titled *Uyghurs for Sale* described in depth forced labor practices that are taking place across China as the party has entered the strategic phase following the "graduation" of camp detainees. The ASPI looked at twenty-seven factories in nine Chinese provinces that are using Uyghur workers who have been transferred from Xinjiang. The report concerningly found that these factories allege to be integrated into the supply chains of eighty-three global brands that are a part of the automotive, clothing, and technology sectors. The ASPI report listed companies such as Apple, Amazon, Gap, General Motors, Google, Microsoft, Nike, and Polo Ralph Lauren that are directly or indirectly benefitting from the factories and potentially capitalizing on the CCP's abusive labor transfer practices.

At least eighty thousand Uyghur laborers from 2017 to 2019 are estimated to have been transferred out of Xinjiang—some directly from the internment camps—and placed in factories throughout China. The ASPI noted that the actual number, however, is likely to be much higher. Although the ASPI was not able to confirm that all such work transfers had been forced, the report did find "highly disturbing coercive labor practices consistent with [the International Labor Organization's] definitions of forced labor." Local governments and private brokers are paid per laborer by the provincial government in Xinjiang for facilitating such work assignments. The ASPI wrote that it is "extremely difficult" to resist or escape from these assignments, as the threat of continuous surveillance and arbitrary detention is prevalent.

This forced labor effort aligns with the government's "Xinjiang Aid" policy. Under this policy, labor transfer programs move and assign workers to factories as a key part of the "reeducation" and "vocational training" process. A 2019 work report from a local government stated, "For every batch [of workers] that is trained, a batch of employment will be arranged and a batch will be transferred. Those employed need to receive thorough ideological education and remain in their jobs."

Evidence and testimonies uncovered within the report suggest that these factory assignments and use of Uyghur labor are not voluntary as Chinese officials and state media claim. Uyghur laborers are typically put on segregated trains for transportation to their work assignments. When their contracts are finished after a year or more, they are most often returned home in the same way. In the factories, many Uyghur workers are subjected to a segregated "military-style management" lifestyle. At times outside work hours, laborers go to Mandarin-language classes organized by the factory and undergo "patriotic education." Freedom of movement is limited, and workers are constantly surveilled. One government minder is assigned to every fifty Uyghur workers. Laborers are watched by security personnel in addition to being physically and digitally tracked by the authorities and factory managers. Uyghur workers are forbidden from freely practicing their religion and live in guarded, segregated dormitories in isolation from their families back in Xinjiang. In some cases, the party will send a cadre to monitor a Uyghur worker's family back in Xinjiang to deter against any misbehavior at the factory. Moreover, in some cases, Uyghur workers are paid less than their Han counterparts, and they cannot return home for holidays.[35]

Forced minority labor has also been taking place specifically in Xinjiang, as the Congressional-Executive Commission on China found in its 2019 report. Citing numerous reports, the commission found that there were cases where forced labor was performed by detainees within the internment camps. In other cases, forced laborers were released from a camp, then assigned to a factory or were directly assigned to forced labor without first being a prisoner in the camps. The report quoted Adrian Zenz, who warned that "[soon], many or most products made in China that rely at least in part on low-skilled, labor-intensive manufacturing, could contain elements of involuntary ethnic minority labor from Xinjiang."[36] This affects a variety of industries, notably the textile and garment industry, since 84 percent of China's cotton is produced in Xinjiang.[37]

So, what's the bottom line? Companies in the United States and across the world are unknowingly or willingly turning a blind eye to the possibility that their profits are made by oppressed populations that are being forced into labor throughout China. Now is the time for Americans to take action here. This is one more reason why we should end our supply chain dependence on China. The ASPI said that some brands have demanded that their vendors end relationships with compromised suppliers this year—although only a small number have issued instructions to do so. Companies such as Nike, Polo Ralph Lauren, Gap, and Microsoft have issued statements saying they were reviewing the claims and evaluating the sourcing of their suppliers' labor.[38][39][40]

As more and more information emerges, we have been able to get a clearer picture of the widespread abuses targeting minority groups in China. The campaign targeting these groups has escalated to the point where the Congressional-Executive Commission on China wrote in the 2019 report that they believe "Chinese authorities may be committing crimes against humanity."[41]

The Trump administration and Congress have taken steps to condemn and stop the continued oppression of Uyghur and other ethnic and religious minorities in Xinjiang. In October 2019, President Trump put twenty-eight Chinese organizations on the US Entity List for being implicated in the Chinese Communist Party's campaign against minorities in the region. This designation in effect prohibits designated bad-acting entities from purchasing US products.[42]

Additionally, in December 2019, by a vote of 407 to 1, the US House of Representatives passed an amended version of Senator Marco Rubio's Uyghur Human Rights Policy Act. The bill would require the president to put into place sanctions and export controls on individuals and items that are facilitating the human rights abuses in Xinjiang.[43] In March 2020, Senator Rubio introduced the bipartisan and bicameral Uyghur Forced Labor Prevention Act, which will make sure that goods that are imported from Xinjiang to the United States have not been made using forced labor. This bill will cover supply chains in Xinjiang and any throughout the rest of China that use the labor-transfer programs to manufacture goods.[44]

The United States has an ethical and moral responsibility to advocate for and support the protection of human rights. These recent measures are decisive, necessary moves to counter the Chinese Communist Party's systemic oppression of minority groups and prevent its exploitation of vulnerable populations.

Exposing the COVID-19 Cover-Up

As I am writing this, the entire world has been shaken by the COVID-19 pandemic. Right now, I don't know when we will overcome this epidemic, but I remain confident that through bold, large-scale measures, which we have been seeing rolled out under President Trump's leadership, we will be victorious in the global war on the coronavirus. What matters now is the decisive action that we take as a nation in order to protect public health, prevent the spread of the virus, ensure we have enough medical resources and supplies, and provide aid to individuals, families, and businesses that have been economically affected.

In order for these decisions to be implemented and for people to be able to protect themselves and their families from infection, accurate information and updates must be shared among governments (domestically and internationally), organizations, and citizens.

The Chinese Communist Party has sought to control the narrative of the coronavirus outbreak by silencing doctors and critics, circulating rumors about the virus's origin, and rolling out a worldwide propaganda campaign praising the way the party has handled the pandemic. Such deceptive actions have contributed to inhibiting the world's capability of effectively containing the virus. But this isn't the first time the party has instituted an information-control strategy to keep a lid on the true extent and seriousness of a crisis. Similar information-control practices were used almost twenty years ago during the severe acute respiratory syndrome (SARS) outbreak.

The Chinese Communist Party's mishandling of the SARS epidemic in the early 2000s is widely known globally. International health experts condemned China's slow response to the outbreak and its efforts to mislead the public about the spread of the virus. In April 2003, at the height of the outbreak, Hu Jintao, then the Chinese Communist Party's General Secretary, admitted during a Politburo meeting that the government had lied about SARS and declared the party had decided to wage a war against the epidemic.[45] The Chinese government fired the mayor of Beijing and the minister of health as a result of their early mismanagement of the SARS outbreak, and the vice minister of health, Gao Qiang, said that the Health Ministry was "not well prepared" and "didn't give clear instructions or effective guidance."[46]

According to critics, if the Chinese Communist Party had been more aggressive in its response to SARS when cases first started emerging, the rapid spread of the disease throughout China and around the world would have been reduced. Wu Guoguang, at the time a professor at the Chinese University of Hong Kong who is now with the University of Victoria, said, "I think . . . their first priority was to make up something to improve their public relations image." Wu remarked that "now they have to deal with the real crisis, not only the PR crisis."[47]

A former *Washington Post* bureau chief in Beijing, John Pomfret, described in a January 2020 article his experience in Guangdong during the SARS outbreak (the province in China where the first cases of SARS were discovered) and how desperately the Chinese Communist Party tried to suppress information about the outbreak from circulating. Pomfret noted the clear parallels between the SARS outbreak and the COVID-19 pandemic. He described that in both cases, local authorities were slow to address the emergence of the viruses. Those who contradicted the government's claims that the situation was under control were persecuted and labeled "rumor-mongers." The Chinese Communist Party moved to respond only after more and more brave people challenged its narrative and called for action. Pomfret reflected:

> I remember when optimists, including some of my Western colleagues, claimed the SARS epidemic had taught the party a lesson that openness was the wave of the future. In reality, China has made a firm commitment in the past decade to controlling information all the more tightly.[48]

Being open and transparent about the discovery and outbreak of an unknown virus is critical to stopping its spread. Putting in place a combination of interventions—namely, early case detection and isolation—heavily affects the speed of the spread and size of the outbreak. A study conducted by researchers at the University of Southampton found that by the end of February, when China had 114,325 cases of the coronavirus, if interventions had not been implemented when they were, the figure would have been sixty-seven times higher. Moreover, if interventions had been introduced a week earlier than they were, the total number of people infected would have been reduced by 66 percent. If implemented three weeks earlier, the number of people infected would have been 95 percent lower.[49]

Cover-ups prevent early measures from being instituted to stop the spread of a virus. As Pomfret noted, this was a lesson many thought the Chinese Communist Party had learned from the international embarrassment of the SARS crisis. But as time goes on, we learn more about how the Chinese Communist Party did the same thing in the handling of the coronavirus, and now the world finds itself confronting a global pandemic. What's more, the outbreak of the coronavirus shouldn't have come as a surprise to the Chinese Communist Party. According to a 2007 report by scientists at the State Key Laboratory of Emerging Infectious Diseases at the University of Hong Kong, which was created by the Chinese government's Ministry of Science and Technology:

> Coronaviruses are well known to undergo genetic recombination, which may lead to new genotypes and outbreaks. The presence of a large reservoir of SARS-CoV-like viruses in horseshoe bats, together with the culture of eating exotic mammals in southern China, is a time bomb. The possibility of the reemergence of SARS and other novel viruses from animals or laboratories and therefore the need for preparedness should not be ignored.[50] [51]

At the time of this writing, we still don't know for sure the origin of the coronavirus, but as Ian Jones, a virology professor from the University of Reading, England, has noted, according to initial research, the virus resembles a coronavirus carried by horseshoe bats.[52] What we do know, however, is that the Chinese Communist Party mishandled the outbreak, which ultimately led to a global pandemic beginning in Wuhan, in China's Hubei Province.

In order to better understand how the Chinese Communist Party failed to address the coronavirus outbreak and cover up the seriousness of the threat, we need to go back to the early days of the epidemic.

Citing details provided by the independent publication Caixin Global, *The Times* of London reported that by late December 2019, laboratories in China had discovered an unknown, highly infectious virus, but "were ordered to stop tests, destroy samples and suppress the news."[53] One anonymous lab technician's account, which was published in numerous Chinese news sites, claimed that as early as December 26, 2019, his company had determined that the samples they had received from Wuhan were of a new coronavirus with an 87 percent resemblance to SARS. Health officials in Wuhan were briefed the next day.[54] By December 29, there were increasing signs that the virus, which had been infecting numerous people, many tied to the Hua'nan market, was contagious among humans.

After observing numerous patients with unexplained pneumonia symptoms, Dr. Ai Fen, the head of the emergency department at Wuhan Central hospital, notified her hospital's leadership, which informed the Chinese Center for Disease Control and Prevention district office. The China CDC responded that it had been learning of similar reports across Wuhan. Dr. Ai ordered a laboratory test for one of her infected patients, and on December 30, the results concluded it was a case of "SARS coronavirus." She informed her superiors and sent a picture of the results and a video of lung scans from another patient to a medical-school classmate. The image and video were the two first publicly-leaked pieces of evidence regarding the outbreak of the coronavirus after being sent to Dr. Li Wenliang at Wuhan Central.

The afternoon of December 30, Dr. Li told more than one hundred of his medical-school classmates in a WeChat group (despite knowing that the chat group could be censored) that there were "seven SARS cases confirmed at Hua'nan Seafood Market" and later updated the posting with "coronavirus confirmed, and type being determined." That night, information about the virus was disseminated across social media, until government censors shut it down.

Following warnings from local hospitals, a retrospective search was conducted by the Wuhan office of the China CDC that on December 30 found several cases of pneumonia infections tied to the Hua'nan market. The World Health Organization's

COMMUNIST-RULED CHINA AND COVID-19   249

China office was notified the following day, and health officials in Wuhan made their first official public statement, confirming that more than two dozen cases of suspected viral pneumonia had been discovered while claiming that "the investigation so far has not found any obvious human-to-human transmission or infection of medical staff." The officials also asserted that "the disease is preventable and controllable."[55]

By January 2, 2020, the Wuhan Institute of Virology identified and mapped the genetic sequence of a new coronavirus. This is an essential step to creating a vaccine to stop an epidemic. On January 5, a Shanghai medical research center informed the National Commission that it had also identified a SARS-like coronavirus from a sample exported from Wuhan and had mapped its genome. This critical information was all kept from the public at the time. It wasn't until January 9—two days after the *Wall Street Journal* exposed it—that the Chinese authorities publicly stated that there was an outbreak of a new coronavirus and had mapped the genetic sequence. While some have applauded China for sharing the genetic sequence of the virus with the world and claimed it constitutes evidence of a change in the way the party has been handling this pandemic compared with SARS, the Chinese officials didn't do so until January 12. They should have acted at least a week earlier.

For the first half of January, despite evidence pointing to the contrary, Chinese officials downplayed the threat of human-to-human transmission. "We knew then that the government was lying," according to a local doctor. "But we don't know why they needed to lie. Maybe they thought it could be controlled."[56]

It wasn't until January 20 that China acknowledged there was human-to-human transmission of the virus. Also, on January 20, Xi made his first public statement on the coronavirus, despite knowing about and being in charge of the response to the outbreak since at least January 7. Xi was clearly in charge and aware

of the situation as tens of thousands of families participated in
Wuhan's Lunar New Year banquet on January 18 and as approximately five million people were able to leave Wuhan without
screening. Wuhan and three other cities were eventually locked
down in what was the largest quarantine in history at the time
on January 23 (this record has since been eclipsed). But the lock-
down in China happened after the virus had been given the freedom to spread throughout the country—and the world—due to
the blatant mismanagement and suppression of the facts.[57] By January 21, Thailand, Japan, South Korea, and the United States had
already reported their first cases.[58]

China not only refused to be transparent about the outbreak
despite the evident warning signs that the coronavirus could
become a serious worldwide problem, but also refused help from
international organizations and teams of experts that could have
lessened the devastating impact of the virus. The secretary of the
US Department of Health and Human Services (HHS), Alex Azar,
stated in an interview with CNN on February 14 that more than a
month prior, he and Dr. Robert Redfield, director of the US Centers for Disease Control, which is overseen by HHS, offered to
send a team to China to assist their Chinese colleagues. However,
China had not given permission for the team's entry into the country. Secretary Azar told CNN in mid-February, "Dr. Redfield
and I made the offer on January 6—36 days ago, 60,000 cases and
1,300 deaths ago."[59] Typically, teams from the CDC's Epidemic
Intelligence Service can be on their way to help within twenty-four
hours.[60] Similarly, the World Health Organization made offers to
send a team of international experts in January, but they didn't
arrive until February 16.[61] Some public health officials and dip-
lomats speculate that this delay came at the behest of top-level
officials who wanted the world to believe that China didn't need
outside help, or to conceal the true devastation of the virus on the
ground.[62] Whichever the case, the bottom line is that the lack of

transparency and willingness to collaborate with global partners in the early days of the outbreak exacerbated its drastic effects.

The signs and evidence of the seriousness of the unknown coronavirus and the capabilities of its being transmitted among humans was clearly denied and downplayed throughout the end of December and January. Critical time needed to stop its spread and ensure the safety of populations was lost. Ultimately, it was the bravery of doctors such as the aforementioned Ai and Li that helped reveal the threat and seriousness of the coronavirus. In an article for China's *People* magazine, which was described by the China Media Project as "one of the strongest to appear to date in Chinese media,"[63] Dr. Ai described her December 30 decision to share the diagnostic information image and video with her colleague. Dr. Ai was scolded by her hospital's discipline department and received a "harsh and unprecedented reprimand." The official chided her, saying:

> When we go out to take part in meetings we can't even raise our heads. This or that director criticizes us and talks about how our hospital has that Ai Fen. As the head of the emergency unit at Wuhan Central Hospital you are a professional. How can you go and stir up a rumor like this without reason, without any organizational discipline?"

Some have called Dr. Ai a whistleblower, and she now says that she regrets not blowing the whistle louder on this issue. She doesn't see herself as being a whistleblower but as being the "one who handed out the whistles."[64]

As a result of aiding in the spread of information and warnings about the virus, Dr. Li and seven other whistleblowers were reprimanded by the police. In a demonstration to keep others quiet, the Wuhan Public Security Bureau issued a summons to these individuals for perpetrating rumors and reported on the detentions in a newscast watched by tens of millions of viewers, *Xinwen Lianbo*. The state-run Xinhua News Agency quoted the Wuhan authorities, who said, "The police call on all netizens to not fabricate rumors, not spread rumors, not believe rumors," and that Web users should "jointly build a harmonious, clear and bright cyberspace." On January 3, Dr. Li was released after admitting he committed "illegal acts" in a signed document (a typical tactic that is used by Chinese Communist Party authorities).[65] But most important, the case of Dr. Li and others scared many into silence during some of the most critical days for controlling the outbreak.

Dr. Li returned to work after his release. A week later, he got a cough. He was hospitalized on January 12 and died from the coronavirus on the morning of February 7.[66][67] Within one and a half hours after his death, a hashtag translated as "I want freedom of speech" was trending on the widely used Chinese micoblogging site Weibo. According to NPR, it had almost two million posts, but they were removed by the time the sun rose the next day.[68] Dr. Li was a symbol of bravery for his supporters. Due to public opinion, the official position targeting these eight whistleblowers was reversed. The state's chief epidemiologist later said these eight individuals were deemed worthy of "utmost respect."[69]

But other critics have not been met with the same reluctant praise—and aren't likely to be—as the Chinese Communist Party has shifted to spreading the narrative worldwide that Xi Jinping is a hero who is waging the "people's war" against the coronavirus. The Chinese government has even published a book in English—with translations into French, Spanish, Russian, and Arabic in process— titled *A Battle against Epidemic: China Combatting COVID-19 in 2020*. The book is a collection of state media reports praising General Secretary Xi, the Chinese Communist Party, and the superiority of the Chinese system in overcoming the virus outbreak.

The party is also working to sow doubt about the origin of the virus. The Chinese ambassador to South Africa tweeted on March

7: "Although the epidemic first broke out in China, it did not necessarily mean that the virus is originated from China, let alone 'made in China.'"[70] On March 12, Hua Chunying, who leads the Chinese Foreign Ministry's Department of Information, tweeted that it was "absolutely wrong and inappropriate to call this the Chinese coronavirus." Twitter is banned in China, so clearly these statements are targeted toward international users.

Shortly after, a Foreign Ministry spokesman, Zhao Lijian, tweeted: "It might be the US army who brought the epidemic to Wuhan. Be transparent! Make public your data! US owe us an explanation!"[71] This claim stems from the fact that hundreds of military athletes were in Wuhan in October 2019 for the Military World Games. This conspiracy theory, among others, is also permeating inside China. Such stories have been posted and read by millions of Chinese on social media. As Steve Tsang, a professor with the China Institute at the SOAS University of London, noted, it's likely because such conspiracy theories are in line with the party's agenda. "We know the Chinese government censor both the traditional media and the social media very, very tightly," said Tsang. "And practically nothing that the Chinese government terms unacceptable will be allowed to stay for any period of time. So if something stays, it's because it has been allowed to stay."[72]

American officials, namely Secretary of State Mike Pompeo, have been fighting this disinformation campaign by calling out the Chinese Communist Party for mishandling the outbreak. In a March 2020 press briefing, Secretary Pompeo argued:

We know this much: We know that the first government to be aware of the Wuhan virus was the Chinese government. . . . That imposes a special responsibility to raise the flag, to say: "We have a problem. This is different and unique and presents risk." And it took an awful long time for the world to become aware of this risk that was sitting there, residing inside of China. . . . The Chinese Communist Party had a responsibility to do this—not only for Americans and Italians and South Koreans and Iranians who are now suffering, but for their own people as well.[73]

As more and more information has been revealed about the Chinese Communist Party's COVID-19 cover-up, we are getting a clearer picture about how their blatant missteps in the early days of the epidemic led to a worldwide pandemic. Before he disappeared without warning in March, party member and business tycoon Ren Zhiqiang wrote a scathing essay that called Xi a "clown" and criticized the party's rampant lies surrounding the outbreak. Ren wrote:

Those who live in a democratic country with freedom of speech perhaps don't know the pain of the lack of a free press and free expression. But Chinese people know that this epidemic and all the unnecessary suffering it brought came directly from a system that strictly prohibits the freedom of press and speech.

The Chinese Communist Party announced in April that he is being investigated for "serious violations of discipline and law."[74] The lies told by the party to its people and the world regarding the virus, the oppression of freedoms in Hong Kong, and the persecution of minority groups in Xinjiang have led to widespread suffering. As we wake up to the realities of China's totalitarian dictatorship and continue to learn more about the party's willingness to strategically deceive and systematically attack human rights and freedoms to further secure its own power, China's bad behavior will inevitably affect and reshape the US-China relationship.

15.

★ ▬▬▬▬▬▬▬▬▬▬▬▬▬▬▬▬▬▬▬▬▬▬▬ ★

NEW LANGUAGE FOR
AMERICAN SURVIVAL

America's safety and survival are at stake. Securing them will require bold and dramatic change. The resistance to this change will be deep, angry, and highly protective of old bureaucracies, doctrines, and habits.

I have been studying national security for more than sixty years (since August 1958), and I have consistently asked three questions:

1. What does America need to do to survive?
2. How could you explain it to the American people so they would give you permission to do it?
3. How would you implement it if you had permission?

I am more worried today about American survival than at any previous time in my six decades of study. The world is changing incredibly rapidly. The challenges to American survival are growing in scale and complexity. We live in a world where our national security requires real-time, almost certainly automated, responses to cyberattacks on a global basis. At the same time, we must also sustain traditional military power for conventional, large-scale combat, and people who can specialize in the slow, patient development of antiterrorism campaigns in dangerous places.

Furthermore, protecting national security now includes the US Treasury Department implementing sanctions against targeted opponents, the Centers for Disease Control and Prevention monitoring potential pandemics as a threat to the safety of Americans, the continuing struggle against Chinese efforts to steal our intellectual property, and constant screening for potential terrorists as people enter the country or fly on airplanes. This scale of complexity requires new thinking, new systems, and new policies.

However, our bureaucracies and many of the professionals who advise and lead them are still operating on the assumptions of an earlier era. President Trump has begun the process of challenging our existing bureaucracies, policies, and assumptions. As a businessman, he brings a much different set of attitudes and a pragmatic focus on results. It is no accident that a large number of Republican Never-Trumpers are in the professional national security community. President Trump has had the courage to ask basic questions that have challenged the entire intellectual construct of more than a half century of professionalism. Their sense of competence—and indeed, their identities as experts—are being challenged by President Trump, who is willing to ask the unmentionable and think the unthinkable.

Fighting a war for eighteen years with no strategy for victory can be explained by a generation of supposed national security experts. But it struck Trump the candidate as a bad policy, and he campaigned to end it. It took three national security advisors to finally get one who understood what the president had been consistently saying since 2015.

Both Presidents George W. Bush and Barack Obama had complained that our European allies were failing to invest in their own defense. However, the experts had cautioned that you could not push the Europeans too hard or NATO might collapse. As a businessman, President Trump looked at German prosperity, and German refusal to pay for their own defense, and decided to aggressively rattle their self-confidence and challenge them to live up to the alliance's requirements. Initially the Europeans were horrified and shocked that an American president could tell the truth so publicly and directly. Then, an amazing thing happened. Country after country began to increase spending on North Atlantic Treaty Organization forces and national defense. The Trump pressure campaign increased European spending by more than $400 billion through 2024.

The Chinese Communist Party has begun to develop better capabilities in space. President Trump's response was to call for a US Space Force that would develop an unchallengeable American superiority in space. For the first time since 1947, a new military service was created. This was vital, because the US Air Force is dominated by a fighter pilot culture (twelve of the last fourteen Air Force chiefs of staff were fighter pilots). They are focused on air power, not space power. The resistance to thinking about and preparing for conflict in space was enormous. President Trump took it on and won.

For over twenty years, the United States had a law in place calling for the US embassy in Israel to be moved to Jerusalem. Every year, past presidents waived the law on the advice of the professionals. They said that doing so would lead to an eruption of anti-American feeling throughout the Middle East. President Trump met with leaders from fifty-eight Muslim countries in his first foreign trip in Riyadh, Saudi Arabia. He then kept talking with leaders in the region. When he moved the US embassy, against the advice of the professionals, there was virtually no reaction after it opened on May 14, 2018. This was vitally important for Israel and our relationship.

Again and again, President Trump has looked at the emerging challenges and realities and applied new thinking and new proposals. Yet despite the president's intense efforts, the United States still has an incredibly long way to go in understanding the emerging new world of threats and realities. In fact, the language and structures we have developed to deal with World War II, the Cold War, and the post–Cold War eras are themselves blocking us from understanding the new realities—and from thinking through the needed new approaches and structures.

The United States' national security system is remarkably like the leading companies Clayton Christensen described in his landmark book *The Innovator's Dilemma*. Christensen argued that "disruptive innovation" was hard for successful companies to adapt to precisely because they were so successful using earlier systems. Consider the fact of the Pentagon. Opened in 1943 to enable 31,000 people to manage a global war with manual typewriters and carbon paper, it still has roughly 26,000 people—even when smartphones, tablets, and laptop computers have revolutionized communication.

Large bureaucracies are remarkably good at protecting themselves. When a large bureaucracy has more people than it has projects, the answer is to get half the people to inspect what the other half is doing. The result is a huge, cumbersome bureaucracy that slows down innovation and increases its cost. One effect of having a Pentagon full of people in the information age is that the bureaucracy develops processes that make innovation much more expensive—and take much more time to achieve. The result is that it is increasingly difficult to keep pace with the rate of new developments and the rise of new competitors.

Furthermore, the built-in knowledge and professionalism of the system guarantees it will promote people based on their ability to use the old processes, language, and intellectual constructs. It is almost impossible for people with new, different ideas to excel in the Department of Defense structure—or any large bureaucracy.

Finally, because the United States is both involved around the world and overrun with lawyers, who keep adding regulations and reporting requirements to virtually every activity, it is so exhausting to keep the machine running that few people have the time to think creatively or to pursue genuinely disruptive innovations. All this is compounded by Congress inventing even more reporting requirements and adding more non-security-focused requirements to running these large systems.

I once asked a highly respected national security advisor what his strategic plan was, and he laughed at me, saying: "My plans come from the front pages of the *Washington Post* and the *New York Times*. I don't have the time for strategic planning, and I am not sure it would help get my job done."

In a time of disruptive change, it is wildly dangerous to assume that spending more resources on old systems, plans, and activities will lead to American security. We need new thinking more than we need new money. In fact, pouring more money into obsolete systems with outdated approaches may simply lead to more expensive defeats.

Consider the challenges that require new thinking, doctrine, culture, and structures of implementation when dealing with China. Competing with China will require profound changes in how we think, how we are structured for survival, and how we develop and implement winning strategies. China is vastly different from the challenges we faced in the past. As Claire Christensen and I outlined in our best-selling book, *Trump vs. China*, this is a competitor totally different from Wilhelmine Germany, Nazi Germany, Imperial Japan, or the Soviet Union. China is a five-thousand-year-old civilization. It has an education system of enormous momentum based on professional examinations that have been almost continuously offered for 2,200 years. The Chinese way of war grew out of the Warring States period (475–221 BC), which ended when the Emperor Qin unified China for the first time (and gave it his name). The greatest Chinese study of principles for success in warfare is Sun Tzu's *The Art of War* (written around 500 BC). Its recommendations are remarkably different from those of the Western way of war.

The American military has the finest tactical and operational system in the world. However, it is weak in strategic thinking and planning. It's also extraordinarily resistant to learning lessons from its shortcomings. Colonel Harry Summers described a conversation he had with a North Vietnamese officer in his superb book *On Strategy: A Critical Analysis of the Vietnam War*. Summers pointed out that the United States had won virtually every tactical fight, and the North Vietnamese officer replied (correctly) that was true, but irrelevant.

That comment jarred Summers so much that he went on to rethink the war, to study Prussian general and military scholar Carl von Clausewitz, and in 1982 to publish his book. The national security system essentially ignored Summers's pioneering work. Twenty years later, Army major John Nagl published *Learning to Eat Soup with a Knife: Counterinsurgency Lessons from Malaya and Vietnam*. The knife and soup reference a quote from T. E. Lawrence, or "Lawrence of Arabia," who was trying to explain how different and how hard fighting a guerrilla war is.

Nagl's book was so tough on the US Army's refusal to learn the lessons of the Malayan campaign (wherein the British had successfully defeated a Communist guerrilla insurgency) that I asked him if it had hurt his career. His response was that it would have been a problem if anyone in the army had read it. Since it was not on a required reading list, he was safe.

This unwillingness to think strategically and to learn the lessons of defeat is one of the two greatest threats to American survival (the other is the collapse of our educational system). Consider, strategically, some of the following principles of Sun Tzu and how hard they are for Americans to learn:

"All warfare is based on deception": The United States has no program to constantly monitor Chinese writing, speeches, and behavior looking for models of deception. We keep negotiating with them as if they are telling the truth.

"What is essential in war is victory, not prolonged operations": Compare this with the eighteen years in Afghanistan.

"For to win one hundred victories in one hundred battles is not the acme of skill. To subdue the enemy without fighting is the acme of skill." Every American leader should learn the principles of go, the Chinese equivalent of chess. It is wildly different from chess. The strategies inherent in China's takeover of the South China Sea, the Belt and Road initiative, the growth of Huawei and the domination of 5G, the steady rise of Chinese influence in international rule-setting organizations—all of these should be analyzed in the context of Sun Tzu and the principles of winning at go. Even as we watch the coronavirus pandemic spread across the globe, news media are praising China for supposedly helping underdeveloped countries. In truth, China is growing its influence as part of its Belt and Road Initiative.

Another version of this principle is translated, "Hence to fight and conquer in all your battles is not supreme excellence; supreme excellence consists in breaking the enemy's resistance without fighting." The Chinese Communist Party may not want to outright defeat us. They may just want us to collapse when we realize we have lost.

Furthermore, the Chinese are working to implement strategies at the all-of-society level. These are often dual-use strategies. Belt and Road is both an economic strategy making money for China and a geopolitical strategy growing Chinese presence and influence around the world. Huawei is both a competent, aggressive corporation and the vehicle for China to dominate the next-generation Internet worldwide—and obtain massive intelligence-gathering advantages over the West.

None of our national security systems think or operate at this level. Understanding and defeating China will require a series of major changes. Here are some examples:

There should be a website with weekly unclassified reporting from every embassy on Chinese economic, propaganda, and military activities in their countries. Such a website would dramatically increase the American people's understanding of how widespread and massive the Chinese effort is. This proposal is listed first because understanding the scale and speed of the Chinese effort is essential if the American people, the news media, and the Congress are going to support the kind of changes we need.

A "Red Team" that is immersed in Chinese strategic writing, speeches, and plans should be established, possibly at the National Defense University. This Red Team should perform at the national level the kind of aggressive, realistic training that the opposing force (OPFOR) provides at a tactical level at Fort Irwin. The national Red Team should have ties to the senior educational institutions in the defense, diplomatic, and intelligence communities.

The State Department must organize a worldwide campaign to knit together a coalition of freedom and the rule of law to win back control of various international organizations from the recent successful efforts by the Chinese Communist Party to gain dominance in the international rules-setting systems.

Strategies need to be developed and implemented for rolling back Chinese gains in 5G (Huawei), the South China Sea territorial claim, the effort to exploit Africa's resources, intellectual property theft, and efforts to develop military overmatches against American forces. (There is stability in being clearly able to win, and there's dangerous instability if the Chinese come to believe they could defeat us—or could fight to a tie, forcing us to negotiate on their terms.)

We have to develop strategies for our research-and-development base (including stopping Chinese theft), for our manufacturing base (including insourcing a lot of activities that had been outsourced to China and elsewhere) and to rebuilding our STEM (science, technology, education, and mathematics) education capability. If we do not rebuild our competitiveness in these three areas, we will eventually lose to China no matter how strong our military investment is.

Further, we need to create a system for an all-of-America and all-of-allies capacity to win economic, diplomatic, and military contests that upend competition and blur war and peace. Vice President Pence has now had two successful experiences developing an all-of-America and, to a lesser extent, an all-of-allies system of planning and implementation. First, he leads the National Space Council, whose advisory groups include the private sector (now the most dynamic part of the space effort). NASA is bringing in more than a score of foreign countries that want to be part of a freedom-in-space initiative. Second, Pence is leading the White House Coronavirus Task Force, which in his words is "an all-of-America" effort. He has brought together federal, state, and local governments along with the private sector, and, through the Centers for Disease Control and Prevention, virtually every country in the world.

Beyond Traditional Defense

National security in the twenty-first century extends far beyond the military. After more than a year of watching the disjointed and conflict-ridden effort to respond to the rise of Huawei and China's 5G bid to define the future Internet with Chinese rules, we clearly do not have a doctrine or a structure capable of all-of-America or all-of-allies planning and implementation.

Many massive, powerful bureaucracies will fight against effective leadership and decision making at this kind of level. We have used this approach in the Civil War and both world wars, but we have never tried to sustain it in peacetime. The reality we now face is that there will be a series of competitions—with the Chinese dictatorship, the Russian dictatorship, radical Islamists, and an assortment of smaller, semi-allied dictatorial regimes (Iran, Venezuela, Syria, North Korea, Cuba, etc.).

We have a system for war and peace. We do not have a system for endless competition. Yet the lesson of Sun Tzu's *Art of War* is that the goal of permanent competition is to make war unnecessary, because your opponents simply collapse through psychological defeat, loss of nerve, and the establishment of a correlation of forces that makes their situation hopeless.

The recent realization about America's vulnerability to having 80 percent of its prescription drugs cut off, since most of their basic components are manufactured in China, is an example of the kind of pre-violence behavior that could be designed to weaken, demoralize, and undermine an opponent.[1] Developing a system of planning, coordination, and implementation for this range of permanent challenges will require dramatic and deep changes in the American system. This may take a generation to complete, but each defeat and failure will drive home the need for a much more effective system than we currently have.

The emergence of cyberwar and artificial intelligence will lead to the development of a real-time global command post. This should be a separate command located outside Washington. It should be focused on the combination of technological development and responding to the Chinese emphasis on asymmetric warfare. It is conceivable that a confrontation over Taiwan or the

South China Sea could lead to a nonviolent response such as a cyberattack closing down all American ATMs. How many hours or days would it take for Americans to really feel crippled by a lack of access to the money in their bank accounts?

A cyberwar enhanced with artificial intelligence will inherently have the potential to be global instantaneously. It will also move at such a speed that only preprogrammed, automated responses could possibly cope with it. The real-time global command post will inherently be layered above the combatant commanders—and designed to fight a unique kind of war. The combatant commanders would continue to have regional responsibilities and regional capacity for action. Some steps have already been taken in this direction by the past chairman of the Joint Chiefs of Staff, General Joe Dunford, but a lot more needs to be done to have a robust, effective capability in the world that is emerging.

Planning back from success is one of the two biggest failures of the current national security system (the lack of a serious introspection discussed earlier is the other). Today the United States does not plan for success. The United States plans for process.

Consider the following campaigns in which the US is involved:

Against Cuba (for 60 years),
in Vietnam (for 19 years),
in Afghanistan (for 18 years),
against Maduro in Venezuela,
against the Iranian dictatorship (it has been at war with us for 41 years and still has both a nuclear weapons program and a ballistic missile program),
the Syrian Civil War (which has gone on for 9 years and created openings for Iran and Russia),
the global war against Al Qaeda and ISIS (which, although resulting in the deaths of many terrorists, has also resulted

in lost ground in Europe, Canada, and the United States to radical Islamist militants—and the production of fanatics continues worldwide),

the response to the driving of Christians from the Middle East since 9/11 in unprecedented numbers,

the effort to combat organized crime and corruption in Mexico (both of which are stronger than ever, resulting in a virtual civil war underway in our most populous neighbor), and against the North Korean dictatorship (which, despite a lot of maneuvering, remains committed to a nuclear program with rockets).

One of the reasons we don't plan for victory is the potential cost. A process-focused plan allows the politicians and bureaucrats to allow enough short-term effort to be doing something, but it doesn't force the bureaucracies, policies, and budgets to change to the degree that a victory plan would require.

The keys to planning for victory are:

Define victory as an end state. As a senior general once said to me: "Tell me about the day after the war. What are you trying to accomplish?"

Assume your opponent also has a capacity to evolve and will be both determined and adaptive. Always ask of a plan "and then what?"—because after we have acted, the other team gets to react. Their reaction may not be what we expected.

Be clear to yourself about the price in time, lives, and money you are prepared to pay. If that will not produce victory, redefine your goals to fit your resources and accept that your ability to change the world may be less than you would like.

An American government that insisted on realistic plans for victory would be a much more cautious country—and a much more formidable opponent to its enemies.

Lessons Learned as a Major Driver of Policy and Doctrine Evolution

The American bureaucracies work hard at implementation but not nearly as hard at analyzing what is working and what is failing.

The fact is, after thirty-seven years' combined experience in Vietnam and Afghanistan, we are no closer to an effective doctrine for achieving our goals in those kinds of circumstances than we were in 1955. Our language of war and peace, and the distinction we draw between combat and nation building, make it almost impossible for us to think through affordable strategies (in terms of lives and money) for beating nontraditional enemies. This includes enemies present in such places as Yemen, Somalia, Nigeria (where Boko Haram continues to wage a guerrilla war), and the Sahel (where Islamist extremists threaten every government). For that matter, it also includes helping the Mexican people defeat the violent criminals who threaten the fabric of their country.

The stovepipes our professionals operate within cripple our ability to develop coherent, synergistic efforts for victory. In Iraq, it was clear in the 2005 period that stability required electricity and jobs. However, the State Department did not have the operating systems to effectively develop those two projects. At the same time, the American military—which had a lot of operational capacity—saw its job as military security and refused to focus on electricity or jobs.

Often, this unwillingness to create an all-of-society and all-of-government lessons-learned process makes it virtually impossible for us to officially understand what is happening and to develop a realistic strategy and implementation system to achieve victory. Consider five examples of real foreign policy challenges: (1) Venezuela, (2) a potential China-Russia alliance against the United States, (3) corruption throughout much of the third world, (4) the scale and wealth of what George Tenet called "the Grey World," and finally (5) a decisive antiterrorist campaign.

The Venezuela Anti-Maduro Campaign

The United States has helped organize a fifty-nine-government coalition in favor of Juan Guaidó replacing Nicolás Maduro as the president of Venezuela. Yet Maduro's dictatorship survives. The major problem with our efforts (first against then-dictator Hugo Chávez and now against Maduro) is that we underestimate the size and power of the international coalition propping up the dictatorship.

Vladimir Putin and the Russian government have a major investment in Venezuela. Russia currently controls 70 percent of Venezuela's oil production and is making an estimated $2 billion a year in profits from that trade.[4] Russia supplies security for Maduro. There are credible reports that at one point Maduro lost his nerve and was on the way to the airport to flee the country when Putin personally called him (Maduro was in a vehicle driven by Russians) and ordered him to calm down and go back to his office.

The Cuban dictatorship has had a long tradition of being allied first with Chávez and now with Maduro. There are an estimated twenty-five thousand Cubans working in Venezuela to prop up the dictatorship. They include members of security forces scattered throughout the bureaucracy. People assert that the toughest and most dangerous Cuban security forces have been sent to Venezuela in part to get the forces out of Cuba.

China has loaned Venezuela more than US $20 billion and is the largest market for Venezuelan exports. There are also 400,000 Venezuelans of Chinese descent.[2] China, like Russia, enjoys being in America's backyard and causing headaches for Washington that might distract it from other parts of the globe.

Finally, Iran and its proxy, Hezbollah, have been present in Venezuela since the 1990s. Hezbollah plays a role both with the 100,000-plus Muslims living in Venezuela and with the drug cartels for whom it launders money—at considerable profit to the Maduro dictatorship.[3]

All of the on-the-ground anti-American factors are compounded by the fact that the United Nations sides with the Maduro dictatorship against the pro-American Guaidó. Any effective American strategy to replace Maduro has to begin with the understanding that there is a serious coalition of anti-American governments actively propping him up. All the diplomatic pressure in the world will not succeed if the Russian, Cuban, and Hezbollah security forces are willing to kill people to keep Maduro in charge. Replacing Maduro will require a strategy that first drives Russian and Cuban security forces out and then accommodates Russian and Chinese financial interests, so they can see that they will not lose billions if there is a new regime.

A Venezuela-centric strategy simply will not get Maduro out of power. It will take a coalition-centered strategy. This should be the lesson of the last decade of failed efforts.

The China-Russia Collaboration

When General Secretary Xi Jinping calls Putin his "best friend," American analysts should rethink their assumptions about the great power competition. There is increasing evidence that Xi and Putin see their future as allies fending off American pressure. The Russian decision to bring in Huawei to develop a 5G network is an example of their looking for places to cooperate and undermine American interests. Recent Chinese-Russian joint military exercises and the joint Russian-Chinese-Iranian naval exercise in the Persian Gulf are examples of gradual coordination.

A more robust and dangerous Russia-China collaboration could come in three forms:

First, the Russians and Chinese could plan their international diplomatic activities more closely to build an anti-American coalition at the United Nations, and in virtually every other international body. This is already beginning to happen, as the various dictatorships and authoritarian regimes realize their future is better served with an anti-American coalition dominating international rules and activities.

Second, a loosely coordinated process in which a crisis involving the United States with one of them would increase the potential for the other to take some independent aggressive actions. For example, if the United States got drawn into a confrontation with Russia in Syria or Ukraine, China might decide to become more aggressive in the South China Sea or with Taiwan or Hong Kong.

Third, China and Russia could pool their scientific and technological developments to build an advanced military capability in a variety of areas. Both countries have substantial advanced weapons capabilities. If they work together, they might be able to field a new generation of systems that would simply make the American equipment obsolete and vulnerable to catastrophic defeat. American strategic planning must include the threats a Russia-China coalition would represent, and this will require a far more agile system than the one we currently have.

Corruption Abroad

Corruption is endemic in much of the world, and it makes it much more difficult to develop an effective American strategy for creating stable, free, rule-of-law governments. Corruption was a major factor undermining the Republic of Vietnam and both draining American resources and weakening popular support for the government. The Vietnamese Communists had a significant advantage over their Saigon-based competitors, because the communists were positioned as the anticorruption, morally strict system.

Corruption has been a major factor in both Iraq and Afghanistan. It results in a great deal of American money being wasted. But more important, the American model of professional, honest effort within the rule of law is simply undermined and discredited when our allies line their own pockets and their supporters' pockets instead of focusing on serving their countries.

Over the next generation, America will be operating in countries with deep traditions and systems of bribery and corruption. We still have no model for how to deal with this. The failure to think through operating honestly within a corrupt culture makes it much harder for us to compete with the Chinese and Russians (neither of whom have any inhibitions about bribery and favoritism) or create a believable, trustworthy alternative to authoritarian regimes or terrorist networks.

Figuring out how to enforce honesty within a corrupt culture is a good example of how we need new thinking across the totality of government and even all of society. This is not something with a diplomatic, military, or intelligence answer. It is one of the hardest problems we face.

Navigating the Grey World

The "Grey World," as George Tenet, the former director of the Central Intelligence Agency, called it, is the underside of global economic, information, and transportation developments. Whether it is trafficking in human beings (about 71 percent of whom are women), in drugs, in weapons, or in moving goods across borders illegally, the totality of illegal systems on the planet is enormous. There is a steadily growing mismatch between the forces of law and order and the forces of violence and illegality. In many countries (and certainly in many of the cities even in relatively stable countries) the forces of illegality can coerce the forces of law and safety. The Grey World challenge needs to be thoroughly rethought at the highest levels.

Defeating Radical Terrorism

The United States has been under attack by Islamist radical terrorists at least since Ayatollah Ruhollah Khomeini took control of Iran in 1979. For the next half century, both Shia and Sunni Islamists have tried to find ways to drive the West out of the Middle East and to impose their violent, radical, extremist views on people around the world.

We have been engaging in a long series of border skirmishes in which we have been very careful to avoid describing the nature of the enemy, forcing the Saudis to stop funding the spread of extremism, or responding forcefully to the Iranian efforts to attack us. After a half century of experience, it should be possible to develop a decisive campaign to shatter and suppress the extremists and make the world safer for freedom and the rule of law. There is no sign that that demanding a strategic planning project is under way.

Understanding the Existential Threat

As I wrote at the beginning of this chapter, the entire American enterprise of freedom, the rule of law, individual opportunity, liberty, and prosperity is facing an existential threat. Our enemies are evolving and gathering at a faster rate than our bureaucracies can cope with. The threats are increasingly beyond the narrowly defined bureaucracies and the incremental pace of deeply resisted change. If America is to survive in safety, we are going to have to take up the tough questions President Trump has been asking and turn them into a national discussion about our survival.

This isn't a partisan issue. This is a patriotic issue, and the survival of America as a free country depends on its outcome.

16.

★ ▬▬▬▬▬▬▬▬▬▬▬▬▬▬▬▬▬▬▬▬▬▬ ★

EFFECTIVE COMPASSION

Which American political party is more compassionate? Merriam-Webster defines compassion as "sympathetic consciousness of others' distress together with a desire to alleviate it."[1]

Despite what you hear from media reports and the Left, statistically, people who identify as either a Democrat or a Republican are equally compassionate.[2] Those who make up our parties are equally sympathetic toward alleviating the distress of others. The difference comes in how we act on that desire.

As Republicans, we favor more private-sector solutions. Republicans place higher confidence in religious institutions, civic associations, strong families, and voluntary social networks in which people choose to help their families and neighbors. The more local the investment or the program, the more likely it is to get to the people who need it and the more customized and quicker the solutions can be. With a private-sector program, it is easier to be flexible, to make exceptions, to cut through red tape, and to direct time and resources to the most productive and efficient activities. Government programs don't have this luxury. They are blunt instruments, with specific applications designed to follow rules—and not make exceptions. The rigidity prevents government programs from looking at peoples' needs in their entirety. They certainly have their place, but they will always have these hindrances.

When America is faced with a crisis—as we currently are with the coronavirus pandemic—we have always been able to put partisanship and government bureaucracy aside. Public and private enterprises work together. But it takes a leader with faith in America and its private institutions to help bring together a proportional response to public health crises. And make no mistake, we are in a public health crisis that demands leadership, dogged focus, and unconventional approaches. I'm not talking about the coronavirus pandemic. I'm talking about a public health crisis that has been going on for years now.

Deaths of Despair

Callista and I have two close family friends whose children died by suicide in the last year. Another lost a child to an opioid overdose. Like their families, we were stunned and saddened to learn of their tragic losses—news that unfortunately is much too common.

Deaths of despair, including suicides, overdoses, and other fatalities related to mental illness or substance use, are near all-time highs—so much so that overall US life expectancy peaked in 2014. Suicide remains the tenth-leading cause of death in America. In 2018, the latest year the Centers for Disease Control and Prevention released statistics, 48,344 people died by suicide, a 35 percent increase since 1999.[3] Suicide rates among farmers, veterans, and teenagers are rising especially quickly.[4] Suicide is now the second-leading cause of death for young people in America.[5] Tragically, one out of every six students nationwide (grades 9–12) has seriously considered suicide in the past year.[6] This statistic alone would signal a failure of our systems, both public and private. But while more people are dying by suicide, we are also seeing even more people die of drug overdose.

We lost 67,367 American lives to overdose in 2018, a fourfold increase since 1999 that now outpaces deaths from motor vehicle accidents. New research suggests that these numbers could actually be more than 25 percent higher due to reporting errors.[7] Alcohol-related liver disease increased 40 percent in the same time period.[8] And we're not over the hump—deaths from fentanyl, cocaine, and methamphetamine are still rising.

For too long, our society has seen suicide and addiction as moral failings of the individuals or their families. In reality, the moral failing is all of ours—that we as a society do not have a sense of urgency to repair the public and private failures leading to these statistics. In the case of opioids, most people who become addicted start with a prescription from a doctor after a surgery or injury. They are doing what the doctor told them to do, and their brain is triggered for addiction. As my Advocates for Opioid Recovery co-advisor and former Congressman Patrick J. Kennedy reminds me, no one chooses to be addicted.[9] No one chooses to willfully destroy his family and lose everything he has worked to achieve.

These deaths of despair are stark signals of the total failure of our health system and our social infrastructure. The moral and ethical responsibility is enough to warrant a crisis-level response. Continuing this trajectory could have a catastrophic impact on the longevity of American civilization, our economic leadership, and our national security as a force in the world. The causes and solutions are unclear and complex. But to address these dual crises, we must look deeply at how we can improve our medical system, our criminal justice system, and our general social infrastructure.

Diseases of the Brain

I have always been a proponent of brain science—and an early supporter of eliminating any disparity between mental health and other types of health care. Mental health *is* health. When I was Speaker of the House, we took the first step toward mental health equality in passing the Mental Health Parity Act of 1996, which was improved in 2008. This bill was supposed to ensure that insurance companies cover treatments for mental health the same as they would for treatments of other illness. Unfortunately, the law is not fully enforced. A recent GAO report surveyed states' efforts to enforce the parity law, which found:

> From 2017 to 2018, only twelve states conducted targeted parity reviews.
>
> Some states said they have *never* conducted targeted parity reviews.
>
> Twelve other states don't even track mental health or substance use disorder parity complaints.[10]

The report also found that the Department of Labor, which is charged with enforcing parity, has fewer than one investigator for every 12,500 employer benefit plans the agency oversees.

Another recent report from the actuarial firm Milliman shows the results of this failure to enforce parity. The Milliman data, which covers thirty-seven million people, shows that:

> People are being *forced* to go out-of-network for treatment, because their insurers don't have care available in-network.
>
> Across the country, patients must go out-of-network more than *five times more often* for mental health and addiction outpatient care compared with medical and surgical care.
>
> For the same services, mental health and addiction providers are paid *21 percent less* than primary care providers.

The insurers spend a paltry 1 percent of reimbursement on addiction treatment, and only about 4 percent on mental health treatment—numbers that have barely moved during the largest public health crisis of our time.[11]

It is impossible to know the true number, but given the levels of deaths of despair from suicide, drug overdoses, and the number of people living with mental illness who are incarcerated or homeless, it is safe to say we are not proactively managing America's mental health.

When the largest mental health institutions are prisons, we've got a medical system failure. When half of the four million Americans living with serious mental illness are not receiving any treatment, we've got a problem. When people with untreated serious mental illness compose an estimated one-third of the total homeless population in the United States, we've got a problem. When nearly two-thirds of the people living with addiction are not receiving medical treatment—or are not being offered medication-assisted treatment (the standard of care for beating opioid addiction)—we've got a problem.

President Trump is taking action. In 2019, the president convened a White House Summit on Mental Health.[12] He signed a bill that increased funding for mental health programs by $328 million to invest in evidence-based programs. He is a strong supporter of both community-based programs and improving access to inpatient treatment when it is necessary.

For example, President Trump has advanced assisted outpatient treatment in which, under court order, adults with severe mental illness who meet specific criteria—such as a prior history of repeated hospitalizations or arrest—are provided treatment for their illness in their communities. These programs are available in forty-seven states and the District of Columbia. They have been proved to reduce hospitalization, arrests, long-term incarceration, homelessness, and victimization. They also help prevent violent acts associated with mental illness, including suicide and violence against others. When patients are in assisted outpatient treatment programs, they work with their health care providers to create highly individualized plans. These typically involve case management, personal therapy, medication, and other tools known to promote recovery. Assisted outpatient treatment programs monitor the treatments to ensure participants commit to adhere to their treatment plans.

President Trump also supports ending the shortage of inpatient mental health treatment facilities by modifying an outdated Medicaid policy. The old policy is known as the Institutions for Mental Disease payment exclusion. It prohibits the federal government from spending money on certain inpatient facilities for people on Medicaid (the government insurance for the poor and disabled).[13] This limitation was put in place back in 1965 to prevent the appalling warehousing of people in large inpatient federal treatment facilities. No one wants to see this history repeated, but arbitrarily limiting the number of people inpatient facilities could treat meant those facilities will not be built. The result: We have ten times more individuals with serious mental illnesses in prison beds than in state psychiatric hospital beds.

These important changes will provide more than $5 billion in new federal funding to states that ensure a full continuum of care is in place to help people with serious mental illness and, in many cases, get them off the streets and out of prisons. While pursuing a permanent policy change, President Trump has already solicited and approved states' efforts to use Medicaid dollars to offer these services as the first-of-their-kind demonstration project.[14 15]

Governors must also do their part. They must improve their civil and financial commitment to care for their residents with mental illness. States in 2015 were spending less on mental health than they did in 1981, according to a 2019 study by the National Association of State Mental Health Program Directors Research Institute.[16] State and local leaders will be the ones who build mental health systems with the needed crisis intervention services, to ensure that people get treated in medical facilities, rather than in prisons.

According to analysis done by the *Washington Post*, through October 2019, Republican state legislators proposed a combined 5,372 bills that mention "mental health." This is twice as many as they sponsored five years ago—and many Republican governors in several states have made mental health reform key components of their legislative agendas. However, this is half the number of bills Democratic state lawmakers put forward. Quantity is not always quality—but this is an area in which Republicans should not lose focus.

The opioid epidemic surged while President Barack Obama was in the White House. Obama's big move was asking the US Surgeon General to write a report. This is not exactly meeting urgency with urgency.

Within one hundred days of taking office, President Trump did what he does best—he took action. He created the White House Commission on Combating Drug Addiction and the Opioid Crisis. In his first year:

> The Department of Health and Human Services announced and began active implementation of its five-point plan to combat the epidemic. The plan included efforts at prevention, expanding access to treatment and recovery support (with an emphasis on medications for the treatment of opioid use disorder), improving pain management, targeting overdose-reversal drugs, and conducting research.[17]
>
> The president declared the epidemic a nationwide public health emergency.

He held a White House press event pledging to expand treatment to evidence-based medicine, break down outdated barriers to treatment, and initiate a massive public awareness campaign.

First Lady Melania Trump has crossed the country many times to visit counties hardest hit by the crisis.

Meanwhile, the White House worked with Congress to get much-needed legislation. In 2018, the president signed HR 6, the SUPPORT for Patients and Communities Act, which significantly delivered on the promises he made.

For example, the law improves access to evidence-based treatment by authorizing coverage of 1,600 structured opioid-treatment programs around the country. It allows providers to treat and prescribe medication-assisted treatment via telemedicine. It provides a Medicaid waiver for states that seek to lift the Institutions for Mental Disease exclusion and expand inpatient treatment options in their states. It also allows doctors, nurse practitioners, and physicians assistants to provide medication-assisted treatment to more patients, and it continues to provide grants to mobilize recovery resources in communities around the country.

Let me be clear: There is absolutely more to be done to curb this epidemic, but President Trump is doing his part by providing leadership and using his constitutional authority to make the necessary improvements.

I recently joined the bipartisan advisory board of Mental Health for US, a coalition of more than ninety mental health and addiction organizations that want to see more policy makers at all levels proactively address mental health and addiction.[18] The coalition has a bipartisan policy platform filled with ideas on improving prevention, access and intervention, and supporting long-term recovery. These policies are generally noncontroversial and widely supported in the medical and mental health community.[19] Many of the policies go beyond immediate health care support and urge support for law enforcement, educators, and community services.

Criminal Justice Reform

Many of the reforms proposed in the Mental Health for US platform build on innovation that is already happening.

One-third of individuals with severe mental illness have their first contact with mental health treatment through a law enforcement encounter.[20] Our jails and prisons have become our de facto treatment systems—but they don't have the expertise or resources to care for people with mental illness and addiction. My good friend Nathan Deal, the former Georgia governor, passed sweeping criminal justice reform in his state that decreased prison admissions of African Americans to historic lows and saved taxpayers millions of dollars.[21] Central to his plan was expanding accountability court programs that divert nonviolent offenders who suffer from substance abuse or mental illness into mandated treatment and social support programs rather than prison.

Other states have also had success with drug and mental health courts. My friend the political science historian Norm Ornstein lost his son to mental illness–related circumstances. The Matthew Harris Ornstein Memorial Foundation, named in memory of Norm's son, commissioned a must-watch film—*The Definition of Insanity*—which highlights Miami-Dade County's efforts to stop the cycle of needless incarceration and divert people living with mental illness and addiction to treatment instead of prison.

People need evidence-based care, and they need to be treated in their communities. In a county like Miami-Dade, where nearly 10 percent of the adult population lives with serious mental illness, it is critical. That's where Judge Steven Leifman's jail diversion program steps in. *The Definition of Insanity* follows Judge Leifman's team as they help community members through their mental health court program. After screening and assessment, people are recommended to various mental health treatment programs instead of jail. If they complete the twelve-month program, their charges are dismissed. Since 2000, when the program was implemented, thousands of people have been treated and diverted away from jail, and recidivism rates are down.

These types of accountability courts—mental health, drug, and veteran courts—should be commonplace in all states. They are the type of programs we should elevate—programs that are addressing people's mental health and addiction in meaningful and helpful ways. Treating people like patients rather than prisoners is key.

Social Infrastructure

Government certainly has a role to play in helping curb these epidemics. But part of the solutions to some of the mental health issues—and other diseases as well—lie in bolstering our social support systems such as family networks, civic groups, and religious institutions to help people feel less lonely and isolated.

Research shows that people who are socially isolated are at higher risk for suicide.[22] Research also shows that we are lonelier than ever. In the last thirty years, the percentage of American adults who report being lonely has doubled from 20 percent to 40 percent. This is despite being more connected electronically than ever before. Additionally, membership in formal groups such as professional local community organizations has declined by between 10 percent and 20 percent over the last five decades.[23] Participation in social groups has been on a downward slope for years, and it appears to continue today. This is alarming for people personally and for our society.

This issue of loneliness is not only for those who are socially isolated. Age is a factor, too. Research shows that loneliness actually peaks in adolescents and young adults, and then rises again for the elderly.[24] The correlation between social connection and health is so strong that the American Psychological Association (APA) has dubbed loneliness as important a risk factor in premature death as obesity and smoking.[25] Both APA and the World Health Organization are urging that improving social support networks is a public health priority.[26] The former US Surgeon General Vivek Murthy has been on a mission to educate the public health community about loneliness as a high risk factor for premature death and explain its association with diseases such as heart disease, dementia, depression, and anxiety. He goes as far as saying, "We will not solve the addiction problem in America if we don't address social connection. And so, if we recognize that, then it becomes part of the solution that we have to invest in, not an alternative to working on addiction."[27]

Social isolation is clearly a public health problem. Some of the systemic interventions that can be advanced by government and medical leaders, according to the APA, include putting a greater emphasis on social skills training for children in schools, urging community planners to include shared social spaces that encourage gathering and interaction, and assimilating the idea of doctors writing social-connectiveness prescriptions just as they would drug prescriptions. Dr. Murthy also suggests additional research to understand more who is affected, how loneliness is manifesting, and how to address and prevent it.

In addition to public health and government intervention, the private sector has a significant role to play as well. Families, schools, religious institutions, and civic associations are all part of the important social infrastructure that keeps us connected.

One important correlation that often gets missed in our current society is the rise in deaths of despair and the rise of the percentage of people who consider themselves religiously unaffiliated. In the last thirty years, this figure has tripled in size to over 26 percent, according to Pew Research Center.[28] Additionally, Pew reports there is a growing generational gap in American religion:

More than eight-in-ten members of the Silent Generation (those born between 1928 and 1945) describe themselves as Christians (84%), as do three-quarters of Baby
Boomers (76%). In stark contrast, only half of Millennials (49%) describe themselves as Christians; four-in-ten are
religious "nones," and one-in-ten Millennials identify with
non-Christian faiths.

Only about one-in-three Millennials say they attend
religious services at least once or twice a month. Roughly
two-thirds of Millennials (64%) attend worship services
a few times a year or less often, including about four-in-
ten who say they seldom or never go. Indeed, there are as
many Millennials who say they "never" attend religious
services (22%) as there are who say they go at least once a
week (22%).[29]

Research shows that the more connected people are to a
greater good and a higher purpose, the less likely they are to die
by suicide. Further, there is strong evidence to suggest that religious involvement may help prevent suicide.[30] Unfortunately, mental health and addiction stigma does not stop when people enter
the synagogue, mosque, or church. Many people in religious institutions suffer in silence. They fear others will see their feeling of
discontentment and malaise as a weakness of faith. Perhaps they,
themselves, see it as a test of their faith and believe they should be
able to pray their way out of it.

Religious institutions and organizations should be leading the
way in communicating that mental illness is always a medical and
often a spiritual issue. Central to mental illness are the physiologi-
cal changes in the brain, and ones that can inflict tremendous suffering if left untreated. But just as there is a link between spiritual
belief and better physical health in cancer patients, there is also a

strong role for faith in mental health healing and addiction recovery.[31]

One successful program for which faith is central to the healing process is Alcoholics Anonymous's twelve-step program. More than 115,000 AA peer support groups meet regularly to discuss issues and concerns related to their alcohol addiction—and to support members through triumphs and relapses. Central to the steps is a surrendering to and belief in God.[32] Clinical studies have shown this program to be more effective than standard medical alcohol addiction treatment, and relapse rates improve when AA is combined with medical treatment.[33] AA is a tremendous program, and one that I hold in high regard for how it has helped save the lives of many of my friends who have lived in active recovery for decades.

However, it's important to remember that not all addictions are created equal. We must not be too dogmatic in our approaches. In my work with Advocates for Opioid Recovery, I was disturbed to learn that many people living with opioid addiction who attended their local Narcotics Anonymous meetings—an organization similar to AA but for addiction to medication or illegal drugs—were discouraged from entering into medication-assisted treatment. As I said before, medication-assisted treatment is the standard of care endorsed by every major medical society, the National Institutes of Health, and the World Health Organization. In fact, people in one NA group I'm aware of were told by some members if they were to take one of the FDA-approved medications to help control their cravings and withdrawal symptoms, they were not welcomed back to NA. Not only is this morally disturbing, but ethically, this advice contributes to the dangerous "cold turkey" detox, which leads directly to many overdose deaths. My hope is this anecdote was an isolated case and not reflective of the larger program.

It is incredibly dangerous for someone living with opioid use disorder to go through detox-only programs. Because opioids, unlike many other drugs, cause significant changes in brain chemistry, a person is extremely likely to overdose if he uses again after abruptly detoxing. That's why medication-assisted treatment is the gold standard of care: medications help stabilize the brain, while behavioral counseling and social supports address a person's whole health needs. In some cases, the medication makes it nearly impossible to overdose on an opioid.

Religious institutions and other recovery groups should not ignore the real medical issues that some in their networks are facing. It is important for these same societal groups to learn to recognize the signs of crisis and know how to respond to help people get the medical treatment they need. Civic groups and churches cannot take the place of medical professionals, but giving people a higher purpose and connection to others is an important part of the solution.

When my family friend Missy Owen lost her son Davis, a star student and athlete, to opioid addiction, she took action. Davis's stress as an active student caused him to turn to the opioids he found in his family's medicine cabinet. He used them to address his painful and sleep-deprived existence. The Owens family tried everything to help their son, including inpatient treatment at some of the most expensive facilities in the nation. But within forty-eight hours of his last inpatient treatment stint, Davis overdosed and died. After his passing, Missy realized that, outside his family, Davis did not have the social and community support he needed to succeed in his recovery. This inspired her to launch the Davis Direction Foundation and create what has become a model community center for people in recovery: the Zone.

Based in my old congressional district in Marietta, Georgia, the Zone is a recovery community organization that mobilizes resources within and without its walls. This includes peer support, trade skills education, and recreation, all of which make it possible for survivors to find the path to long-term recovery that works best for them. Missy has partnered with local schools and law enforcement and other community organizations to build out the necessary programs for which survivors are looking. Recently, they launched Zoned 4 Re-Entry, a partnership between the foundation and the Cobb County District Attorney's office to help people involved with the accountability courts get the job training and personal life skills they need to succeed. Response to the Zone has been so positive, Missy now hosts a conference called Building Communities of Recovery for people to learn from its model. The conference also brings together other community leaders from around the country to share ideas and best practices.

Effective Compassion

America is a great country. We are leading innovation in so many areas of health care—from lifesaving drug innovation to new discoveries that help blind people see. We have effectively transformed many cancers into chronic illnesses instead of death sentences. Even now, as I write this, our country is appropriately rallying together to help keep the new coronavirus at bay. Yet when it comes to mental health and addiction trends, our response has been slow, and we have a long way to go. We need to approach the solutions in a bipartisan manner and elect leaders who will follow the science and the evidence to promote and accelerate programs that work.

We will not solve homelessness by allowing people with mental health and drug addiction issues to live in tents on the street. In fact, we would not even solve homelessness by giving every homeless person in America a roof over their heads. The issues with which they grapple will simply drive them out of any shelter or home. We won't slow the tragic tide of suicide by attempting to crack down on bullying alone. Further, we will not stem the opioid crisis by giving people free needles—or free opioids. These solutions might seem like compassion—but they are not effective compassion.

We must work together to solve the underlying issues that push people toward homelessness, suicide, and addiction. We must achieve and implement effective compassion.

17.

★ ▬▬▬▬▬▬▬▬▬▬▬▬▬▬▬▬▬▬▬▬▬▬ ★

MAKING EARTH GREAT AGAIN

As a child growing up in Pennsylvania, I had constant exposure to the importance of conservation and managing our
natural resources wisely. The Pennsylvania Game Commission
was founded in 1895 to help manage the state's wildlife resources.
Its monthly magazine was a beautiful introduction to the values
and importance of conservation.

Pennsylvania had a long tradition of intelligent conservation.
Gifford Pinchot, one of President Theodore Roosevelt's closest
allies in conservation, became the first head of the US Forest Service and was elected governor of Pennsylvania. He personified the
wise conservation of natural resources.

I grew up believing in the Pinchot dictum that "conservation means the wise use of the earth and its resources for the last-
ing good of men." In fact, I was so enamored with nature that I
wanted to be either a vertebrate paleontologist studying dinosaurs
or a zoo director. Any aspect of the natural world intrigued me
(and still does). My first encounter with politics came when I was
ten years old and tried to get Harrisburg, Pennsylvania to create
a zoo.

When I became a teacher at West Georgia College, I taught on the second Earth Day, then created a course on environmental studies. I ultimately ended up as the coordinator of environmental studies—an interdisciplinary program that involved faculty from a half-dozen departments.

In those thrilling early days of the environmental movement, we used a book, *The Limits to Growth*. At the time, *The Limits to Growth* was an exciting warning about the dangers of human expansion in a limited ecosystem. Gradually, over several years, I began to mistrust its message and its usefulness. First of all, it exemplified the principle of garbage in, garbage out. It was an obvious mathematical certainty that if you created an equation of unlimited growth within a system of limited resources, you would ultimately produce a disaster. The two key questions were (1) were the resources really that constrained, and (2) were the growth pressures that inevitably destructive?

The more I studied the rationale of the more radical advocates of environmentalism, the more I realized they were intellectually just plain wrong. In fact, if you go back and look at the most shocking predictions from the early 1970s, you will realize that none of their catastrophist projections have occurred.

The phony shock effect of radical environmentalism returned me to the roots of a sound, practical conservation. From that perspective, I got to know Terry Maple and the brilliance of his work at Zoo Atlanta. Terry and I believed there was a better, more effective, and more sustainable approach to saving the natural world. We wrote a book called *Contract with the Earth* to outline how a pragmatic environmentalism could be more effective than a demagogic alarmist approach to saving the environment.

The environment and the health of our planet are vitally important. A Gallup poll conducted in March 2019 found that 74 percent of people surveyed were personally worried about the quality of the environment. Additionally, 76 percent of those surveyed in a summer 2019 *Washington Post*-Kaiser Family Foundation poll said that climate change should be considered a crisis or a major problem.[1]

We should take reasonable steps to help create a cleaner planet. Responsible environmental stewardship is an important mission for us as Americans—and as human beings. We should all want to preserve and protect the planet for future generations. This goes for Republicans especially. Conservation is a conservative principle, after all. The environmental challenges we face are serious and worth addressing. However, many extremists on the radical Democratic Left have chosen to use hysterical rhetoric and emotional approaches rather than facts in dealing with environmental issues. This creates a one-sided argument founded on exaggerated catastrophism—not realism—and prohibits effective, pragmatic solutions from being adopted.

Consider the comments of Congresswoman Alexandria Ocasio-Cortez (AOC) on climate change in January 2019. She said, "Millennials and people, you know, Gen Z and all these folks that will come after us are looking up and we're like: 'The world is going to end in 12 years if we don't address climate change' and your biggest issue is how are we gonna pay for it?" She even went as far as to claim that the fight against climate change will be the "World War II" of the younger generation.[2] She later backtracked on her comments, saying that her twelve-year prediction can't be taken literally.[3] I tend to agree. It shouldn't be taken literally—or seriously at all.

AOC's use of hysteria to advance irrational environmental agendas, arguments, and claims is not a new phenomenon. Such statements date back at least a half century. Then, Professor Paul R. Ehrlich (now the president of the Center for Conservation Biology at Stanford) forecast global plague, thermonuclear war, drastic pollution, and ecological catastrophe. During a 1969 speech hosted by the Institute of Biology in London, Ehrlich made a prediction about the future if the trends at that time remained unchanged: "By the year 2000 the United Kingdom will simply be a small group of impoverished islands, inhabited by some seventy million hungry people. . . . If I were a gambler, I would take even money that England will not exist in the year 2000."[4]

Clearly, Ehrlich was just plain wrong. Despite the dooms-day-style emotional rhetoric, the United Kingdom still exists today. But in January 1990, Ehrlich continued to predict future massive flooding caused by rising global temperatures. He said on the *Today* show that "The Supreme Court would be flooded. You could tie your boat to the Washington Monument. Storm surges would make the Capitol unusable."

Yet, five days later, the reporter Mark Phillips on the *CBS Evening News* anticipated a different consequence of rising temperatures. Phillips said that if no action was taken to stop global warming, it "would turn much of the planet into a desert."[5] Such "expert" contradictions beg the question: How will the earth be turned into a desert and be underwater at the same time?

Similar unfounded mass-destruction predictions were made by former Vice President Al Gore (who was called a "prophet" by former *Time* reporter Margaret Carlson in a 2007 *Bloomberg* TV interview). Then coanchor Katie Couric asked Gore during a *Today* show interview in 2006, "What do you see happening in 15 to 20 years or even 50 years if nothing changes? . . . Even Manhattan would be in deep water?" He replied, "Yes, in fact the World Trade Center Memorial site would be underwater."[6]

The media has long been empowering this kind of hysteria, which promotes unsubstantiated panic. The line between reporting and advocacy seems nonexistent when it comes to environmental issues. This is particularly true with comments from media influencers, such as CNN's founder, Ted Turner, who said in an interview in 2008, "Not doing it [fighting global warming] will be catastrophic. We'll be eight degrees hotter in . . . thirty or forty years, and basically none of the crops will grow. Most of the people will have died and the rest of us will be cannibals. Civilization will have broken down."

This decades-old echo chamber of supposed experts, politicians, media influencers, and activists capitalizes on alarmism to push forward their own left-wing agenda. The sense of extremist urgency that the radical Democratic Left attaches to environmental policy results in proposals that create more government and more regulations. The story of the earth's inevitable catastrophe is just a technique they use to justify socialist, extreme government action and involvement.

In 1990, as communism was collapsing in the Soviet Union, the economist Robert Heilbroner wrote an essay that argued that though communism failed, socialism will eventually have to emerge as a result of capitalist economic practices. In Heilbroner's essay, published in *The New Yorker*, he wrote:

> Socialism may not continue as an important force now that Communism is finished. But another way of looking at socialism is as the society that must emerge if humanity is to cope with the ecological burden that economic growth is placing on the environment.[7]

In other words, he says capitalism destroys the environment, and socialism will save us. We've already seen examples of socialism as the supposed solution to environmental problems emerge. Consider the failed Green New Deal (GND), led by AOC and Senator Edward Markey (it was also supported by numerous Democratic presidential candidates). The Green New Deal was introduced in 2019 as a nonbinding resolution. It called for the federal government to set and achieve a series of goals, one of them being net-zero greenhouse gas emissions in ten years.

But the heart of the Green New Deal wasn't about protecting the natural environment. In order to achieve the resolution's goals, it outlined a series of supposedly necessary projects and objectives—many of which had nothing to do with helping the earth. One concerned the "commercial environment" that aimed to ensure "every businessperson is free from unfair competition and domination by domestic and international monopolies."[8]

Another required universal guaranteed jobs, family and medical leave, and paid vacation time for Americans. Also according to the resolution, achieving the GND's goals required "providing all people of the United States with high-quality health care; affordable, safe, and adequate housing; economic security; and clean water, clean air, healthy and affordable food, and access to nature."

So, the failed GND proposal was a radical expansion of socialism and government control over Americans' lives wrapped in a veil of environmentalism. As a headline for a *Washington Examiner* article put it: "The Green New Deal is about power, not the planet."[9]

Additionally, Democratic presidential candidates, including Joe Biden, Michael Bloomberg, Pete Buttigieg, Amy Klobuchar, and Tom Steyer support carbon pricing through a tax, or cap-and-trade programs.[10] Cap-and-trade, in this case, is a system in which companies would have a "cap" on the amount of carbon dioxide they would be allowed to emit. The government determines the cap, and it be can be applied to an industry or across the economy in its entirety. The cap is divided into permits, which can be bought through an auction or allocated for free. Companies are taxed if they surpass their carbon dioxide cap but can buy and sell permits from one another (increasing or decreasing the amount of carbon dioxide emissions they are allocated). Typically, the total cap amount decreases with time, which drives up the cost of purchasing allowances.[11]

The burden of such carbon pricing proposals is going to ultimately be felt by consumers. Though "Mayor Pete" Buttigieg proposed rebating this revenue to lower- and middle-income Americans, who would most heavily feel the economic effects of carbon pricing, he even admitted, "I know you're not supposed to use the T word when you're in politics, but we might as well call this what it is. There is a harm being done, and in the same way that we have taxed cigarettes, we're going to have to tax carbon."[12]

So, are more taxes on carbon emissions really the answer? Other countries, such as Canada and France have thought so. But the outcomes were not what they expected. In the case of Canada, the parliamentary budget officer (PBO), an independent government watchdog, determined that its carbon tax was insufficient and would not result in the country meeting its targeted climate goals. The watchdog's report concluded that in order to create any dent in emission levels, the tax would have to significantly increase. Specifically, the PBO report said: "To close Canada's emissions gap of 79 [metric tons] by 2030 and achieve the Paris target, we estimate that additional carbon pricing (broadly applied) rising from $6 per [ton] in 2023 to $52 per [ton] in 2030 would be required. . . . Adjusted for inflation, the additional carbon price in 2030 would be $42 per [ton] expressed in 2019 dollars."[13]

Moreover, according to the *Washington Post*, researchers in the United States have said that vehicle carbon emissions would decrease by just 1.5 percent if the tax on gasoline were raised by 10 cents a gallon (the current average is 52.4 cents per gallon). However, prices can't be drastically hiked without resistance. Recall the onset of the "yellow vest" protests in France after President Emmanuel Macron announced the curbing of emissions through an increase in gas taxes.[14]

These types of policies are overreaching and ineffective. Yet the radical Democratic Left dominates this issue area in the media and academia. They claim Republican policy makers don't care about the environment and don't have alternative solutions. This is simply a lie. As Texas Congressman Dan Crenshaw has said,

"The Democrats have trained everybody to think that the only people who care about climate change are the ones who engage in hysterical alarmism or engage in real high-minded but ultimately false aspirations of 'We're going to decrease this much . . .' but they forget about the actual solutions."[15]

As members of the party of Theodore Roosevelt ("the conservationist president"), the Trump administration and Republican members of Congress are already taking practical steps and promoting initiatives that benefit the environment. Rather than being rooted in hyperbole and focused on unattainable goals, these commonsense solutions present opportunities for bipartisan cooperation. They will produce real results that will have a significant impact on the environment today—and on the world we leave future generations.

Prioritizing Innovation

Despite the Left's attempt to monopolize environmental policy, Republicans are making their voices heard. As reported by Reuters in August 2019, a survey by the Amsterdam polling agency Glocalities discovered an uptick in conservatives' concern for the environment, particularly among young Americans. US Republican survey respondents who "agreed" or "strongly agreed" with the statement "I worry about the damage humans cause the planet" increased by 11 points—to 58 percent—from 2014 to 2019. The concern among Republican voters between the ages of eighteen and thirty-four rose to 67 percent—an increase of 18 percentage points.[16]

Republican lawmakers are also proposing solutions to protect the environment. Policy makers recognize the needs for a conservative response to the radical Democratic Left's proposals. The Trump administration and Republicans in Congress have taken action to promote innovation, support conservation, and create real results that benefit Americans and the environment. For example, in February 2020, House Republicans, led by House Republican leader Kevin McCarthy, unveiled the first of three planks in their conservative environmental plan. The first plank focuses on carbon capture (catching emissions before they enter the atmosphere) and sequestration (capturing and storing carbon dioxide already in the atmosphere). I am told the second plank will be focused on clean energy and the third will focus on conservation.

As a part of this package, House Republicans included four bills; some are new, and some have been previously introduced. Unlike the Left's approach, the Republican agenda will not include a carbon tax or a clean energy mandate.[17] "Fossil fuels aren't the enemy," said Louisiana Congressman Garret Graves, who worked on the plan and is the top-ranking Republican on the Select Climate Committee. "It's emissions. So, let's devise strategies that are based on emissions strategies, not based on eliminating fossil fuels."[18]

Historically, when the United States is confronted with a really big problem, prioritizing investments in innovation has helped our country overcome whatever challenges we faced. Consider the start of the space race after the Russians launched the *Sputnik* satellite in 1957. President John F. Kennedy asked Congress to increase funding to the US space program, which he argued in a 1961 speech was an essential part of winning the political and economic conflict between communism and democracy. This investment, combined with American expertise, eventually led to the successful landing of the first man on the moon on July 20, 1969.[19]

In this case, it was the American spirit of innovation that allowed us to rise up to win the space race and confront the challenges of the Communist Soviet Union. As we now fight environmental challenges, we must apply the same innovative approach to creating solutions. Prioritizing the development of carbon-capture technology is one way to do this, but so is investing in other alternative forms of energy, such as nuclear power.

Despite negative assumptions, nuclear energy is among the most efficient, cost competitive, and safest forms of energy available. Importantly, nuclear reactors *that are operating* do not produce air pollution or carbon dioxide. The only gas emission is steam. Nuclear energy also has an immensely higher output compared with other energy sources.[20] According to the Department of Energy, the capacity factor for nuclear energy in 2018 was 92.6 percent. This means that out of 365 days of the year, nuclear power plants produced maximum power for 336 days.[21] A *YaleEnvironment360* article by the Pulitzer Prize winner Richard Rhodes notes that maintenance accounted for the remaining 29 days.[22]

Comparatively, natural gas–powered plants had a capacity factor of 57.6 percent in 2018 and provided power for the equivalent of 210 days. Coal-powered plants were slightly lower, with a capacity factor of 54 percent (197 days). Hydroelectric systems operated with a 42.8 percent capacity factor, which is equivalent to 156 days, wind turbines with a 37.4 capacity factor, equivalent to 136 days, and solar electricity arrays at 26.1 percent, or 94 days.[23]

In sum, for 2018, nuclear power plants were far more efficient sources of energy than others. Particularly compared with their wind and solar counterparts, nuclear power plants were 2.5 to 3.5 times more reliable. This makes sense, as weather patterns, which fuel wind and solar renewable-energy sources, are unpredictable: the sun doesn't always shine, and the wind doesn't always blow.

So, nuclear power plants require less maintenance than all other sources, and they can generate much more energy per plant. The US Office of Nuclear Energy states that one nuclear reactor produces power equivalent to 3.125 million PV [solar] panels and 431 utility-scale wind turbines.[24] Despite nuclear power's clear efficiency capabilities, there were only 98 nuclear power plants in the US that in 2018 produced 19.4 percent of total US electricity.[25] Fossil fuels by and large account for the majority of US electricity production, making up 63.6 percent of total electricity generated.[26]

There are several reasons why nuclear energy doesn't account for a higher percentage of US energy production. They are expensive to build, and it is challenging to obtain appropriate licenses. Additionally, Americans are divided on support for using nuclear energy. According to a 2019 Gallup poll, 49 percent of Americans oppose nuclear energy, and 49 percent favor it.[27] Part of the resistance is driven by fear of radioactivity—although nuclear energy is historically safe.

Incidents that raise questions about the safety of nuclear energy stem from the 1979 Three Mile Island incident in Pennsylvania, in which part of the core melted in a reactor; the 1986 Chernobyl accident in Ukraine, which destroyed a reactor; and the 2011 Fukushima Daiichi incident in Japan, which melted three cores following a tsunami triggered by a major earthquake.[28] Tragically, the Soviet-controlled Chernobyl plant disaster killed thirty people within three months and later caused multiple deaths.[29] However, no injuries or negative health effects were caused by the Three Mile Island accident, and Fukushima did not cause any fatalities or cases of radiation sickness.[30] There are certainly concerns about exposure to harmful levels of radiation, but these are not as widespread as one might assume.

In the case of the Three Mile Island incident, the US Nuclear Regulatory Commission concluded:

The approximately two million people around TMI-2 during the accident are estimated to have received an average radiation dose of only about 1 millirem above the usual background dose. To put this into context, exposure from a chest Xray is about 6 millirem and the area's natural radioactive background dose is about 100-125 millirem per year.[31]

As the US Nuclear Regulatory Commission found, the radiation doses received by those in the surrounding area of the Three
Mile Island accident was remarkably low. Similarly, in terms of
the effects of radiation exposure from Chernobyl, the United
Nations Scientific Committee on the Effects of Atomic Radiation
(UNSCEAR) found that over the course of thirty years after the
accident, there were no long-term health consequences present in
populations exposed to the fallout.

The exception was the onset of thyroid cancers in approximately 6,500 people in the Chernobyl region. These individuals,
however, were children or young adults at the time of the incident, were not evacuated, and consumed milk that contained 131
iodine. UNSCEAR also found that "the average effective dose [of
radiation] due to both external and internal exposures, received by
members of the general public during 1986–2005 [were] about 30
mSv for the evacuees, 1 mSv for the residents of the former Soviet
Union, and 0.3 mSv for the populations of the rest of Europe." For
context, a sievert is the measurement for radiation exposure, and a
full-body CT scan carries 10 to 30 mSv of radiation to patients.[32]

In regard to the Fukushima fallout, a report to the International Atomic Energy Agency following the catastrophe found
that "no harmful health effects were found in 195,345 residents
living in the vicinity of the plant who were screened by the end
of May 2011. . . . [There] was no major public exposure, let alone
deaths from radiation."[33]

In fact, a report by NASA actually found that nuclear energy can
save lives by avoiding health issues related to carbon emissions and
fossil fuel mining. Despite the aforementioned three major nuclear
accidents, NASA wrote, "Nuclear power prevented an average of
over 1.8 million net deaths worldwide between 1971–2009."[34]

Now, though these nuclear accidents have not had high human
casualties, the fallout from the catastrophes have had negative
effects on the surrounding environment. Damage to ecosystems

that support all life should be of concern—even if human lives are saved. To limit the risk of future accidents, we can improve on the nuclear energy technologies we currently use to heighten safety, increase reliability, and improve efficiency. Fortunately, efforts by US companies such as X-energy are well underway.

The Maryland-based X-energy is developing a pebble bed, high-temperature gas cooled reactor called the Xe-100, which has already received significant funding from the US Department of Energy. Currently, nuclear electricity is most commonly generated using two types of reactors (which were initially developed in the 1950s but have since been improved). These common reactors contain uranium fuel rods that become hot by splitting atoms through nuclear fission.[35] This heats up water, which turns into steam that rotates a turbine and powers an electric generator.

The Xe-100 reactor core contains fuel pebbles instead of rods that are each the approximate size of a billiard ball. Each so-called pebble has thousands of coated Tristructural Isotropic (TRISO) uranium fuel particles that make them essentially indestructible, capable of operating at high temperatures, and more efficient. Also, according to X-energy, the pebbles can't melt down. Plants containing this advanced technology can be built within five hundred meters of urban areas and factories—and spent fuel can be stored on location. Pebble bed modular reactors can also incorporate passive cooling, which means the reactors don't have to rely on pumps, big local sources for water, or safety systems to mitigate damage to the fuel.[36]

Additionally, X-energy's technology has significant implications for space travel and for clean-energy-powered vehicles. The pebble bed modular reactor will provide rockets with the capability to increase the speed of space travel. It could reduce the time it would take to get to Mars from eighteen months down to three. Moreover, the modular reactor produces hydrogen as a byproduct. This can be used to fuel hydrogen cell vehicles, which have

greater range than most current battery electric vehicles and operate with greater environmental integrity.

Finally, some other opposition to nuclear power stems from
uncertainty about what we should do to dispose of nuclear waste.
However, Richard Rhodes argues in his article "Why Nuclear
Power Must Be Part of the Energy Solution" that this is more of
a political problem than a technological one. The majority of US
spent fuel is currently being safely stored as its radiation declines.
Rhodes noted:

> The U.S. Waste Isolation Pilot Plant (WIPP) near Carls-
> bad, New Mexico, currently stores low-level and trans-
> uranic military waste and could store commercial nuclear
> waste in a 2-kilometer thick bed of crystalline salt, the
> remains of an ancient sea. The salt formation extends
> from southern New Mexico all the way northeast to south-
> western Kansas. It could easily accommodate the entire
> world's nuclear waste for the next thousand years.[37]

Innovation in efficient and environmentally conscious energy
sources provides significant opportunities for the United States to
be the leader in new and emerging energy technologies. When we
look at having a significant impact on the state of the environment
and protecting the world as a whole, new energy technology that is
better for the environment will be important for other countries to
deploy as well. Environmental challenges are not solely a US issue,
they are a global issue.

The Pledge to Plant

Republicans recognize that the effort to improve and protect the
environment requires a multifaceted approach. House Republicans
also outlined initiatives in the legislative agenda to reduce plastic
waste, export natural gas, and promote further "resilience," or

adaptation to rising sea levels and other consequences of climate change. Furthermore, Republicans have included legislation in the environment package that will aim to work toward the global mission to plant, conserve, restore, and grow one trillion trees.

The tree-planting effort has been strongly supported by President Trump. He first announced the United States' pledge to this reforestation effort, the One Trillion Trees initiative, in January 2020, when it was launched at the World Economic Forum in Davos, Switzerland.[38] He reaffirmed the US commitment to the goal again during the February 2020 State of the Union address, when he said, "To protect the environment, days ago I announced that the United States will join the One Trillion Trees Initiative, an ambitious effort to bring together government and private sector to plant new trees in America and all around the world."[39]

Shortly after the State of the Union, Arkansas Congressman Bruce Westerman introduced the Trillion Trees Act, which aims to plant one trillion trees across the globe by 2050. The bill has three key objectives. The first is to plant more trees to maximize forest growth that will increase the amount of carbon captured by trees. The second is to grow more wood by increasing the resilience of our existing forests against destruction from diseases, insects, and wildfires (which release large amounts of carbon into the atmosphere). Finally, the bill aims to use a tax credit to incentivize the sustainable construction of buildings. Manufacturing wood to use for building structures is less energy intensive compared with alternative materials, and since wood is 40 to 50 percent carbon by weight, the wood that is used in building construction is in effect a structural carbon reservoir. Moreover, wood is an efficient insulator, so when buildings utilize new mass timber technology in their construction, it can reduce the amount of energy needed for heating and cooling.

Congressman Westerman emphasized the importance and potential impact of this proposed legislation:

Every day, countless billions of plant cells are pulling carbon from the atmosphere and permanently storing it in wood. That's why this legislation is so important. We're taking proven science and turning it into practical solutions. Not only are we setting an ambitious goal of planting one trillion new trees by 2050, but we're also reinvesting resources into managing forests and using wood products. Since wood continues storing carbon long after the tree is cut down and turned into furniture or building materials, there is no limit to how much carbon we can sequester. We have an obligation to conserve our resources and make them available to future generations.[40]

The impact of this reforestation goal was reinforced by a previous scientific study conducted by Dr. Tom Crowther, an ecologist, and colleagues at the Swiss university ETH Zurich. Their research concluded that global reforestation, with 1.2 trillion trees would provide CO_2 storage capacity that is capable of canceling out approximately ten years of carbon dioxide emissions—or about 25 percent of atmospheric carbon.[41] The scientists estimated that there are three trillion trees on Earth, which now store 400 gigatons of carbon dioxide, and there is room to plant millions of acres more. According to Dr. Crowther, "If you were to scale that up by another trillion trees, that's in the order of hundreds of gigatons captured from the atmosphere—at least ten years of anthropogenic emissions completely wiped out."[42]

In addition to sequestering carbon dioxide, forests also trap other pollutants, including sulfur dioxide, ozone, nitrogen oxides, and particulate matter. Strong, prosperous forests provide numerous benefits, such as helping to clean water and soil, and providing habitats for wildlife. Forests also support local jobs and economies by keeping ecosystems healthy and providing materials for shelter, food, and fiber. For example, millions of people engage in fishing activities on US National Forests and Grasslands. This amounts to more than $2.2 billion.

Part of this mass-scale tree planting, conserving, and restoring initiative includes the objective of unifying and supporting the reforestation efforts of governments, nongovernmental organizations, businesses, and individuals—many of which have been long underway and have seen success. For example, the national conservation organization American Forests has planted more than sixty million trees in the past thirty years.[43] Another example is Trillion Trees, which is a partnership of BirdLife International, the Wildlife Conservation Society (WCS), and the World Wide Fund for Nature (WWF) who have teamed up and set the goal of protecting and restoring one trillion trees by connecting funders with forest conservation projects.[44]

Another successful campaign that shows that reforestation on a massive scale is possible was initiated in 2006 by the United Nations Environment Program (UNEP). Originally, the goal was to plant one billion trees—a goal that was met with the planting of its first billionth tree in November 2007. Shortly after, in May 2008, its second billionth tree was planted, and in 2011, the campaign was handed over to a German youth-led environmental organization called Plant-for-the-Planet.[45] Today, Plant-for-the-Planet has expanded the goal to plant one trillion trees, and at the time of this writing, has planted 13.64 billion trees.[46] This tree-planting initiative directly supports the UN Decade on Ecosystem Restoration, which lasts from 2021 to 2030 and was announced by the General Assembly in 2019. Ecosystem restoration is the process by which ecosystem degradation is reversed, and one way to restore ecosystems is, of course, by planting trees.[47]

Additionally, the viral campaign #TeamTrees shows the impact that social media can have on the worldwide tree planting movement by getting the right voices behind it to raise support, awareness, and funding. The founders of #TeamTrees,

Jimmy Donaldson, better known as "MrBeast" and Mark Rober, are YouTube influencers, with 30.3 million and 10.5 million subscribers respectively. The campaign began with MrBeast's audience challenging him in May 2019 to plant twenty million trees to mark reaching twenty million YouTube subscribers. This led to a partnership with Rober, and resulted in the official launch of #TeamTrees in October 2019 with the goal of planting twenty million trees by 2020. In less than two months—and a wave of videos later—they raised enough money to plant twenty million trees. One dollar equals one tree planted, and donations are given directly to the Arbor Day Foundation to fund tree planting. At the time of this writing, #TeamTrees has raised enough funds to plant more than 21.8 million trees.[48]

Evidently, planting and taking care of our trees is an effort that many people can get behind *and* support. Many already have. Engaging in reforestation efforts has clear support from a variety of different organizations, corporations, governments, international institutions, influencers, activists, and scientists. Though the idea of planting one trillion trees has been met with criticism—with skeptics asserting that it could have negative effects or not yield the results calculated by Dr. Crowther and his team—we must keep in mind that this is just one part of a multifaceted approach to protecting and restoring our environment. We still need to continue to develop and deploy alternative sources of energy and engage in active measures to limit waste and clean up debris. Planting trees is not a catchall solution (which Dr. Crowther himself admitted), but if done properly, it can be a significant step in the right direction.[49]

Managing the Land

While planting trees will have a positive impact on the environment and carbon emissions, so will proper forest management practices. Primarily, this can reduce the risks of rampant wildfires such as those that have been recently devastating California. According to studies by the Nature Conservancy and the US Forest Service, the size and intensity of wildfires can be decreased by 70 percent and resulting carbon emissions can be lowered by as much as 85 percent through engaging in active forest management.[50]

In December 2018, President Trump signed an executive order on "Promoting Active Management of America's Forests, Rangelands, and other Federal Lands to Improve Conditions and Reduce Wildfire Risk."[51] In part, this executive order requires the US Department of Agriculture (USDA) and the US Department of the Interior (DOI) to prioritize actions that reduce fuels and promote forest-restoration projects that protect local communities and grow rural economies through the usage of the products of forest restoration.

This is a perfect example of taking rational action to help our environment and make our communities safer without making doomsday predictions about the end of the world—or a future of never-ending wildfires.

Any forest ranger will tell you that reducing hazardous fuels by removing excess vegetation such as dense trees or undergrowth (which provide optimal conditions and fuel for wildfires) mitigates the risks of wildfires and keeps local communities safe. The executive order also mandates that the secretary of agriculture and the secretary of the interior to work with federal, state, tribal, and local partners to create a wildfire strategy by the end of 2020 that will better protect habitats and communities and preserve physical infrastructure.

President Trump's executive order also sets forth certain forest and rangeland management goals for federal agencies to reach. Following President Trump's executive order, the US Secretary of the Interior, David Bernhardt, issued Secretary's Order 3372, which provided a framework to safeguard people, communities, and natural resources; mitigate wildfire risks; and support the recovery of damaged lands. As a result of the president's executive order and the department's efforts, the DOI exceeded its required objectives in fiscal year 2019. In January 2020, the DOI announced that its initiatives had produced results that "had doubled and nearly tripled targets" set by the president's executive order for vegetative treatments that would reduce the risk from wildfires. This marked "the largest fuel load reduction in a decade."[52]

The DOI also decreased fuel loads and protected water quality on more than 1.4 million acres of administered lands. This is almost double the requirement for fuel load reduction and three times the requirement for water-quality protection. Additionally, by using forest-health treatments to decrease vegetation that creates conditions for wildfires, the DOI made plans to harvest and sell 750 million board feet of timber. This exceeded the original goal by 25 percent.[53] These efforts have created stronger and healthier forests and rangelands, while providing economic benefits for rural communities.

Reducing the risk from wildfires through active forest and rangeland management is also critical for the safety and livelihood of Americans and communities. According to the DOI, there was substantially lower wildfire activity in 2019 compared with previous years and the ten-year average. In 2019, 4.57 million acres were burned in 48,484 wildfires. Compare this figure with the ten-year average, which saw 6.7 million acres burned from approximately 60,000 wildfires, and the more than 52,000 wildfires in 2018 that burned 8.5 million acres of federal, state, tribal, and private lands.[54] Clearly, progress is being made, but we must continue to work with a vengeance on reducing the risks of rampant wildfires by practicing active and responsible land management.

The Economy or the Environment? A False Choice

Americans have long been fed the narrative that the environment and the economy are mutually exclusive—one must be prioritized over the other. In reality, this is not the case, as the two are closely correlated.

As President Trump stated in July 2019 during remarks given at the White House:

> For years, politicians told Americans that a strong economy and a vibrant energy sector were incompatible with a healthy environment. In other words, one thing doesn't go with the other. And that's wrong, because we're proving the exact opposite.
>
> A strong economy is vital to maintaining a healthy environment. When we innovate, produce, and grow, we're able to unleash technologies and processes that make the environment better while reshoring and, so importantly— you look at reshoring production all the way—taking it away from foreign polluters, and back to American soil.[55]

There is historical precedent for the simultaneous improvement of both the environment and the economy, as the administrator of the Environmental Protection Agency (EPA), Andrew Wheeler, noted at the same event. According to Wheeler, between 1970 and 2018, air pollution in the US dropped by 74 percent as the economy grew by 275 percent.[56]

President Trump has taken action to protect the environment *and* grow the economy. For example, President Trump signed the US-Mexico-Canada Agreement (USMCA), which ended the "NAFTA nightmare" and further protects American jobs, industry, and intellectual property. While the economic implications of the agreement dominated headlines, what people may not know is that the agreement contained unprecedented, first-ever provisions for reducing marine litter and debris, improving air quality, and supporting forest management.[57]

Moreover, in 2018, President Trump signed into law a bill to improve and reauthorize the EPA's Brownfields Program. This program assists American communities by identifying abandoned, shut down, or underused commercial facilities, cleaning them up, and making them usable again.[58] (Minute Maid Park, the home of the 2017 World Series champion Houston Astros, was built on a former Brownfield site.)[59] The 2018 law also increased the list of properties that are eligible for Brownfield grants and raised the cap on individual cleanup grants to $500,000.

The EPA estimates that there are more than 450,000 Brownfield sites across the United States; they are defined as "a property for which the expansion, redevelopment, or reuse may be complicated by the presence or potential presence of a hazardous substance, pollutant or contaminant."

In June 2019, EPA administrator Wheeler and the White House executive director for the Opportunity and Revitalization Council, Scott Turner, announced the dissemination of 151 grant awards amounting to $64,623,553 in Brownfield funding to 149 communities.[60] Not only does the Brownfields Program alleviate environmental hazards, protect the environment, clean up contaminated property, and beautify the community, but it also provides significant opportunities for economic development in disadvantaged communities. Almost three-quarters of the localities selected to receive grants have Opportunity Zones, which are "economically distressed communit[ies] where new investment, under certain conditions, may be eligible for preferential tax treatment."[61]

This is a really transformative initiative that reaches out to underserved communities. According to Wheeler, "We are targeting these funds to areas that need them the most. Approximately 40 percent of the selected recipients are receiving Brownfields grants for the first time, which means we are reaching areas that may [have] previously been neglected, and 108 of the selected communities have identified sites or targeted areas that fall within Opportunity Zones."[62]

Studies have shown that the Brownfields Program has significant economic impact by raising local tax revenue and increasing property values. Approximately $29 million to $97 million in local tax revenue was raised in one year following cleanup according to a study that looked at forty-eight Brownfields sites. The EPA supplied $12.4 million to clean these sites, meaning that two to seven times this amount of investment was generated through tax revenue. Another study concluded that homes close to restored Brownfields sites increased in value between 5 and 15 percent.[63]

The Brownfields Program leverages jobs and private investment as well, according to the House Energy and Commerce Committee. More than $16 in private investment is leveraged for every federal dollar spent, and 8.5 jobs are leveraged for every $100,000 in Brownfields environmental assessment and cleanup funding.[64] This program has a significant impact and provides the opportunity for communities to turn contaminated property into assets that have both environmental and economic benefits.

Protecting Wildlife

Effective conservation starts with the protection of ecosystem health for all organisms. Infectious disease can be prevented from jumping to humans if we protect the animals that normally serve as hosts. When ecosystems decline, it puts us in danger. As with Brownfields, degraded natural habitats can be restored and revitalized, and this should become a priority. We should therefore also be concerned about the loss of megafauna that play an important role in the health of both terrestrial and aquatic environments.

Not only do these losses threaten ecosystems, but as Dan Coats, the director of national intelligence, asserted in the 2018

Worldwide Threat Assessment of the US intelligence community, "Criminal wildlife poaching, illegal fishing, illicit mining, and drug-crop production will continue to threaten economies, biodiversity, food supply security, and human health."[65]

Indeed, many reports indicate that the coronavirus pandemic that is currently sweeping the globe started because people in China were eating illegally traded wild animals. [66][67][68] To counteract these threats, President Trump has taken action to curb illegal wildlife trafficking. Within the first month following President Trump's inauguration, he signed an executive order calling for decisive action against transnational criminal organizations that engage in illicit activities such as the "illegal smuggling and trafficking of humans, drugs or other substances, wildlife, and weapons."[69] Moreover, in the Trump administration's 2017 National Security Strategy, using military and security capabilities to counter the illegal trade of natural resources in Africa was listed as a priority.[70]

Additionally, in November 2019, President Trump signed into law the historic Preventing Animal Cruelty and Torture Act, which has been passed unanimously in both chambers of Congress. For the first time, this law made intentional acts of cruelty against animals a federal crime that can be punished with fines and up to seven years in prison. This law will help prosecute crimes of animal cruelty (with the exception of hunting, fishing, and trapping) that cross state lines. Kitty Block, president and chief executive of the Humane Society of the United States, noted that this law "makes a statement about American values." According to Block, "The approval of this measure by Congress and the president marks a new era in the codification of kindness to animals within federal law." She added, "For decades, a national anti-cruelty law was a dream for animal protectionists. Today, it is a reality."[71]

Despite these initiatives, many other species of animals still remain at risk. Populations of whales, for example, have long been jeopardized as a result of human activity. In the nineteenth and twentieth centuries, many whale populations reached extremely low numbers as a consequence of hunting. In the 1960s, the International Whaling Commission—of which the United States is a member—introduced the first protections on commercial whaling. Later, in 1986, whaling for profit was banned, but despite this moratorium, countries such as Japan, Iceland, and Norway continue to hunt whales.[72] Though the frequency of commercial whaling has decreased, some whale populations are still critically endangered and many are still at risk due to injuries inflicted by ballistics, plastic, entanglement with discarded fishing gear, and collisions with ships at sea. Whales killed by ship collisions is an increasing problem; as NBC's San Francisco affiliate reported in February 2020, whales have been hit and killed by ships at some of the highest rates in more than ten years. Citing data from the National Oceanic and Atmospheric Administration, the news outlet wrote that 239 whales were killed in "ship strikes" between 2006 and 2019. However, scientists and experts note that they believe the actual figure of whale deaths could be as much as ten to twenty times greater. These deaths are preventable, NBC discovered that at least 77 percent of shipping companies don't abide by the suggested speed limit when coming into an area near San Francisco's Golden Gate Bridge.[73] When holding other countries accountable for their commercial whaling practices, we need to be sure to also hold those within our own waters accountable for responsible practices.

In addition to helping to maintain a balanced ecosystem, whales are reservoirs for carbon sequestration. A single whale sequesters as much as thirty-three tons of carbon in its long life (some live to nearly 200), while a tree absorbs only forty-eight pounds of carbon in one year.[74] Economists have estimated that each whale is worth approximately $2 million based on its contributions to sequestration, the fishing industry, and whale-watching sector, with the entire world population generating $1 trillion of value. These economic benefits are justification for the protection of whales and should generate concern for the losses whale populations are experiencing. We can and should offer our protection to whales as we clean up the open ocean.[75]

A New Contract with the Earth

For many years I have advocated for and worked toward using a practical approach to protect and conserve the environment. In 2007, I wrote *A Contract with the Earth* with Terry Maple. The book outlines a binding contract with ten commitments that will protect and renew the earth to guarantee a bright and sustainable future for generations to come. We must revisit this contract and renew our commitments to achieving these goals if we are to ensure a healthier planet.

We must first establish the framework in which these commitments are executed. First, we must demand objectivity. The radical Democratic Left and the media politicize the debate about how to best protect the environment. In reality, there are a lot of opportunities for bipartisan cooperation. In order to influence and shape policy, we must be sure to have the support of the informed American public and present the problems that we face in a rational, factual, unbiased manner that will ensure the best chances of success.

Next, we must educate and inspire future generations of entrepreneurial environmentalists to address the complexities of environmental issues. We must think long-term and develop big, effective strategies that will create change using "outside the box" creativity and approaches. We must encourage green enterprise by supporting the discovery, implementation, and exportation of new technologies that will further environmental protection and conservation. Earth's vitality is a global issue, so through business, foreign aid, and strategic philanthropy, we must export and share new breakthroughs and ideas with others. This will benefit American industry, strengthen the economy, and position the United States as a world leader in environmental stewardship.

With this framework in mind, we ought to renew our commitments to the following goals:

As part of an updated Contract with the Earth, the United States must take the lead as the global environmental trailblazer. The United States will lead by striving to promote a world where there is minimal waste; clean air and water; healthy forests, wetlands, lakes, and oceans; and diverse biology and thriving populations of animals and plants; where fossil fuels have been modified for carbon recycling or replaced with alternatives to reduce carbon emissions; where the impact of humans on the environment is moderated; and where environmental quality is improving rather than declining. This doesn't mean destroying our energy industry—or tearing down our current infrastructure. It means focusing on innovation and improving how we use our resources.

Second, we must encourage, train, and reward the next generation of environmental entrepreneurs. Free enterprise and environmental stewardship are not at odds. We must invest in new technologies and encourage the American spirit of innovation. Further, instead of brainwashing and scaring our children, we should encourage them to think about protecting the environment—while also developing new ways for our society to thrive.

Third, outdated and inefficient technologies must be retired or adapted to meet modern environmental challenges. We must always be updating and using best practices stemming from investments in innovation to solve problems and create solutions. The United States should not just continue to use systems, approaches, methods, or tactics just because we already have them in place or because they worked in the past. New scientific discoveries are constantly emerging that evolve our thinking about environmental challenges. If what we are doing is no longer working to produce the results we need, it should be replaced, removed, or rejuvenated.

Fourth, the role of government should be transformed. Government should encourage and enable breakthroughs in solutions to resolve environmental problems—rather than restrict progress with red tape. Partnerships with organizations and businesses should be leveraged that will benefit the economy and the environment. Though regulation is necessary, it should be limited, targeted, and reasonable. President Trump has done an excellent job getting rid of unnecessary regulations while still proactively protecting the environment. His actions on improved forest management and tree planting are perfect examples.

Fifth, the United States should also be an aspirational and inspirational country. Aspirations should not be forced by the government but should rise out of collectively shared consensus and values. We must set the bar high and proceed with cheerful persistence and optimism.

Sixth, America must also be positioned to address the challenges we face. We must identify our environmental goals and enact policies that promote a healthy environment and identify and avoid future crises. We must enlist every citizen and elected government officials to best determine a course of action. We should look to states and local governments who have already enacted effective, innovative, and pragmatic policies in their own communities for guidance and ideas.

Seventh, scientific and technical literacy must be enhanced. America must encourage public learning in schools, museums, gardens, zoos, and aquariums. We must incentivize young people to enter environmental engineering and science career fields and enhance math and science programs in schools.

Eighth, the United States must emphasize the spirit of collaboration and cooperation. Politicians must take a nonpartisan approach to the environment and prioritize patriotic solutions over politics.

Ideas should be the competitors—not politicians. Politicians must also rebuild broken relationships with leaders and experts in the scientific community to best inform pragmatic decision making.

Ninth, philanthropy and investment should support environmental stewardship efforts. Strategic philanthropy will help provide the resources necessary to create real improvements in the environment and will strengthen the effectiveness and reputation of US efforts.

Tenth, we must enlist the nation to address the complex and serious environmental challenges facing our country and world. The American people and local, state, and federal governments must all participate, contribute, and work together to achieve significant progress in restoring and protecting our environment.

By adhering to these commitments, using a commonsense approach to environmental stewardship, creating pragmatic solutions rooted in objectivity rather than hysteria, and prioritizing innovation and cooperation, the United States can successfully lead in ensuring a better, healthier, and cleaner environment for future generations.

18.

★ ━━━━━━━━━━━━━━━━━━━━━━━━━━━━━━━━━━ ★

TAKING FREEDOM INTO SPACE

With President Donald Trump's leadership and Vice President Mike Pence's diligent work at the National Space Council, the United States is about to take freedom into space in a bold and remarkably broad way. In fact, there are four different strategies being developed to grow our capabilities to carry freedom throughout the solar system. These strategies include:

- Space tourism
- The Moon-Mars Development Project
- Commercial space opportunities (including mining asteroids, manufacturing in orbit, and other activities)
- Defending freedom in space through a new military service: the US Space Force

The scale of these four strategies is breathtaking. For the first time since the end of the Apollo program in 1972, the United States is being aggressive and adventurous in its approach to worlds beyond our planet.

I have followed the development of the new Trump-Pence push for a more dynamic American space program with great personal interest. I have been fascinated by space ever since *Sputnik* was launched by the Soviet Union in 1957. The American response to the Soviet challenge was overwhelming, and twelve short years later the United States landed Americans on the moon. The future seemed wide open and endlessly exciting. American prestige worldwide was extraordinarily increased by the lunar landing, and the astronauts became worldwide figures.

Then the Apollo program (which had been enormously expensive as well as remarkably successful) was ended, and the United States pulled back to focusing on low-earth orbit for manned flights built around the International Space Station and an expensive but limited shuttle program—with more distant space frontiers reserved for robotics.

There's no doubt that the American program of distance exploration by technical means, rather than humans, has produced an exquisite set of capabilities (the only eight successful landings on Mars have all been by American vehicles, seven of which were done by the NASA Jet Propulsion Laboratory). However, the average American grew less and less interested in space as the adventures of Star Trek and Star Wars remained fiction. Space exploration seemed to shrink into bureaucratic behavior, with a predictable rhythm and set of limitations. The technical space program fascinated astronomers and other scientists, but it left most Americans uninterested.

In 1984, I wrote a long chapter in my book *Window of Opportunity* outlining what America could have done if we had maintained the momentum of the Apollo program. However, other than the International Space Station and the shuttle program, nothing seemed to change. The tragic losses of two shuttles and the people on board were heartbreaking to Americans, and these tragedies have overshadowed everything our space program has done since. This is not what those of us who cared about space exploration were hoping.

Now I can report that for the first time in a generation, I am incredibly optimistic about America in space. In fact, after a series of meetings reviewing the Trump administration's plans for space, I think the wind is at our backs and we are going to have an extraordinarily fascinating and dynamic future beyond our planet.

The new dynamism in space comes from three powerful developments:

First, the Chinese Communist Party has been developing a methodical and competent space program, and the Communist totalitarian dictatorship is now challenging the American lead. In 2019, the Chinese landed on the far side of the moon and launched a rover, which traveled some 400 meters gathering data that no American had yet acquired. It is clear China is methodically developing space capabilities that will rival America's. Since space has many national security implications, the success of the Chinese program has begun to lead to an American response, especially in the Department of Defense and the intelligence community.

Second, beginning with Elon Musk's SpaceX, entrepreneurs have been developing reusable rockets that have dramatically reduced the cost of going into space. When combined with a new generation of small-entrepreneur companies with smaller rockets and dramatically newer approaches, the cost for launching smaller satellites has dropped. (For example, Relativity Space is developing simple rockets using 3-D printing. It has the goal of assembling rockets on Mars.) All this entrepreneurship has returned the commercial launch business to the United States, where it is once again a major source of foreign earnings.

Third, President Trump and Vice President Pence came into office as the most pro-space White House visionaries since President John F. Kennedy called for America to go to the moon.

President Trump set a breathtakingly daring goal of putting Americans back on the moon by 2024 and then moving on to a manned mission to Mars as rapidly as possible. Vice President Pence's March 26, 2019 speech to the National Space Council remains one of the best outlines for cutting through the bureaucracy and getting to the moon on schedule.

These three factors were synergistically reinforcing. The Chinese activities forced us to pay more attention to space as a zone of competition. The development of lower-cost, more-entrepreneurial capabilities excited the imagination of people who cared about space and got us thinking beyond the normal bureaucratic pace and cost of the big contractors.

President Trump and Vice President Pence created a government- and industry-wide awareness of new opportunities with several clear actions. First was proclaiming the 2024 moon goal. They then reconstituted the National Space Council, which had been started by President George H. W. Bush in 1989 but then disbanded by President Clinton in 1993. President Obama promised to restore the Space Council in 2008 but never did so. In June 2017, President Trump finally reestablished the council. Its momentum has been reinforced by continuing increases in the NASA budget. The Trump space initiative has been made even more dynamic by his commitment to creating a sixth military service, the US Space Force. There was more resistance to establishing the Space Force (including strong bureaucratic opposition from much of the Air Force) than to the Moon-Mars Development Project, but President Trump continued to insist and finally got the Space Force established.

With these exciting developments, the United States is now prepared to launch the spirit of freedom into the solar system at an historic scale. Let's consider each of the four paths freedom in space will take.

Space Tourism

After some slow starts, the opportunity for non-astronauts to venture into space is about to grow dramatically.

Virgin Galactic will likely begin tourist suborbital flights this year (unless their plans are halted by the spread of the coronavirus). It is close to offering the new service. It is taking orders for future trips and currently expects them to cost about $250,000. Virgin Galactic is offering only a suborbital flight at the present time, but it will be developing the ability to have quick launches and repetitive launches, which will strengthen the entire space effort. It will also be popularizing the idea that normal people can go into space.

Also, if we can stop the coronavirus, Blue Origin, with its Shepard rocket, could begin tourist suborbital flights as early as this year, but will more likely start in early 2021. SpaceX has plans to orbit the moon with tourists on a Falcon Heavy by 2023. Working with Space Adventures, Musk's company plans to use its Dragon module to take tourists to a 700-mile orbit (more than three times as far from earth as the space station) beginning in a 2021–2022 time frame.

Meanwhile, NASA has opened the International Space Station to additional tourist visits aboard the commercial crew vehicles of SpaceX and Boeing early in this decade. It has also approved a new module for the space station built by Axiom that could be a part of that new capacity.

It is helpful to remember that seven people have already been to the space station as tourists. The first tourist, an American businessman, Dennis Tito, paid $20 million to visit in 2001. While these prices may seem absurd to normal folks, it is useful to put them in context by remembering that yachts run from $8 million to $600 million. There are a surprising number of people who can afford big-ticket items, and space is just another trophy for someone with enough resources.

In a more futuristic view of space tourism, SpaceX is also talking about sending the first wave of Mars settlers on its Starship toward the end of this decade. I have a hunch that is at least a decade sooner than it will happen, but even if the first Mars settlers start arriving only by 2040, that is still an amazing development and would have seemed wildly unattainable only a decade ago. From a human-interest and an operational-experience standpoint, the growth of space tourism will be a significant first step toward taking freedom into space.

The Moon-Mars Development Project

Similarly, the Artemis project is potentially the most history-making element of the Trump-Pence space vision. It is much bigger—and in some ways more difficult—than the Apollo missions. I wrote an extensive article about this project around the fiftieth anniversary of the Apollo missions for *Newsweek* on July 23, 2019.

In short, the Artemis project is not just about getting to the Moon. It's about getting to the moon, staying on the moon, and developing it as a key element of our country's future in space. A fully developed, sustained presence on the moon will be critical for finding—and potentially harvesting—water on the moon for rocket fuel. It will be a training ground for enabling Americans to explore the surface of Mars and other celestial bodies. It will also serve as the jumping-off point to explore the rest of our solar system and mining resources from it—including Mars, asteroids, and beyond.

As Vice President Pence said at the National Space Council in Huntsville, Alabama, on March 26, 2019, "Fifty years ago, 'one small step for man' became 'one giant leap for mankind.' But now it's come the time for us to make the next giant leap and return American astronauts to the moon, establish a permanent base there, and develop the technologies to take American astronauts to Mars and beyond. That's the next giant leap."

The Moon-Mars Development Project will further inspire a new generation of young Americans to look to the stars for their careers—just as Apollo did a half century ago. It could be a huge boon for building interest and establishing more science, technology, engineering, and math programs throughout our education systems.

This project will also generate a host of other second-order economic activities—and bring many new companies into the American space sector. Entrepreneurs such as Jeff Bezos, Musk, Richard Branson, and the late Paul Allen have all shown that there are people willing and able to invest in the new space economy. As President Trump's Moon-Mars Development Project continues to grow, more entrepreneurs will follow.

We can't predict what kind of amazing things these companies could develop, because they could potentially solve problems we never knew we had—or create tremendous new opportunities that will change our society forever. No one could have predicted the technological trail that led us from Apollo to microchips, commercial satellites, global positioning systems, mobile phones with the processing power of 1980s super-computers, and artificial intelligence that we are currently walking. Consider the millions of jobs these advancements have created for America over the course of the last fifty years. This strikes at the heart of why the Moon-Mars Development Project is so important for our future—both terrestrially and in space.

Finally, the Moon-Mars Development Project will be crucial for maintaining our ability to defend ourselves. Adversaries such as Russia and China have already developed space-based weapons that could be used to cripple our communications, financial, and infrastructure systems. In fact, the United States has lost several recent wargames run by RAND Corporation wherein our opponents start out by rendering us immobile with an aggressive attack on our vital satellite constellations. As I wrote in my best-selling book *Trump vs. China*, the moon and cislunar space is the new high ground. Having a regular presence there will help give us the position and awareness to protect ourselves from such attacks.

While parts of the NASA bureaucracy have been pushing back on President Trump's 2024 deadline of reaching the moon, these elements must be overcome. We cannot afford to lose this new space race. NASA administrator Jim Bridenstine knows this and has been incredibly effective at moving the system despite resistance. He needs all the support he can get from Congress and the administration if we are going to succeed at establishing a permanent American presence on the moon—and then exploring Mars and beyond, as Vice President Pence described.

Profitable Space Opportunities

As I mentioned, in addition to space tourism, there are going to be a lot of opportunities to profitably develop assets in space. On July 19, 2015, the asteroid 2011 UW-158 came within 1.5 million miles of earth. It contains an estimated $5.4 trillion in platinum.[1]

The asteroid 16 Psyche is an enormous rock (120 miles in diameter) in the middle of the asteroid belt between Mars and Jupiter. Some analysts believe it has enough rare minerals to be worth $700 quintillion (eighteen zeroes).[2] That would be about $93 billion for every person on earth. I am told NASA plans to launch an unmanned mission to visit in 2022. It would arrive four years later to perform twenty-one months of science.

As spaceflight grows less expensive and more reliable—and with the development of nuclear engines more capable of rapid long-distance travel—asteroid mining will move from fantasy to fact. When combined with robotics, distance management, and

3-D printing, the potential for mining and manufacturing in space is going to develop much faster than people would have guessed twenty years ago.

There are already several innovative companies exploring mining in space, and within the next twenty years (when my grandson is in his thirties) economic opportunity will be beckoning us beyond earth.

Defending Freedom in Space

Beginning in the 1950s, more and more assets were launched into space.

From the beginning of the space era, intelligence gathering from space was a key interest. Then communications were added. After that, a Global Positioning System became invaluable to both the military and civilian aspects of society. Virtually everyone today uses GPS to get places.

The various aspects of space-based capabilities transformed the American military with capabilities that were, for a long time, unmatched by any other country. Precision weapons, for example, gave Americans a lethality that has been devastating to our opponents.

However, as space became more and more valuable, other countries began to develop methods of disrupting, degrading, and destroying American space-based assets. From lasers to antisatellite missiles to satellites capable of masking or destroying American satellites, our major competitors—especially Russia and China—are preparing to wage war in space.

The Chinese Communist Party's People's Liberation Army launched an antisatellite weapons test in 2007. In addition to violating international norms about space activity, this created an enormously dangerous space-borne cloud of debris that threatened billions of dollars' worth of space assets—both government and commercial.

In February 2020, US Space Force commander General John Raymond told *Time* that a Russian spacecraft was "tailing" one of our spy satellites in orbit. Raymond said, "We view this behavior as unusual and disturbing. . . . It has the potential to create a dangerous situation in space." Not only could the Russians be stealing vital intelligence, they could be jeopardizing the security of a multibillion-dollar US satellite. What would be the appropriate, proportionate response if the Russians were to destroy this piece of military equipment? This is just one more reason the Space Force is necessary.

Some visionary military thinkers believe space capability is maturing enough that assets positioned there could bring combat power to bear on earth.[3][4] One program, called Rods from God, suggests that large metal poles (the size of a telephone pole) would accelerate from space to the Earth's surface and hit with the explosiveness of a nuclear weapon, with no fallout. The space-based force projection advocates argue that weapons orbiting the earth could project American power almost instantaneously— with less expense and no vulnerable overseas footprint. President Trump recognized the importance of military developments in space when he called it, "the next war fighting domain," and he referred to it as "the ultimate high ground."

As the president explained it: "SPACECOM will ensure that America's dominance in space is never questioned and never threatened, because we know the best way to prevent conflict is to prepare for victory."[5]

The establishment of the Space Force as the sixth military service is an enormous step toward protecting freedom in space. As history has taught us again and again, it is impossible to have an arena of wealth and opportunity without also having an ability to protect it—and to dominate and defeat elements that would steal the wealth and impose dictatorship on the pioneers.

President Trump's insistence on a service dedicated to operating in space will pay dividends for as long as Americans operate beyond the earth. It will be seen by historians as a remarkably prescient decision, and its success against substantial bureaucratic opposition is a tribute to the focus of the president and the vice president. They have a serious commitment to helping freedom move into space—and then protecting that freedom once it is there.

19.

★ ▬▬▬▬▬▬▬▬▬▬▬▬▬▬▬▬▬▬▬▬▬▬▬▬ ★

ACHIEVING A BETTER AMERICA

The COVID-19 virus will recede.

The economy will recover.

There will be a lot of lessons to learn: about China; public health preparedness; getting the private sector back on track producing prosperity, jobs, and a better economic future; and getting government at every level to pull back from the enormous power it accumulated during the pandemic.

There will be a lot of ideological, partisan, and economic interests that would like to preserve the huge-government dominance. The federal machine will have taken a great deal of power to save lives from the virus and to keep people from being crushed economically during the war against the virus.

But America has already demobilized after three other wars.

Government grew unimaginably large by nineteenth-century American standards in order to win the Civil War. It was a sign of the temperament of that era that General Ulysses S. Grant was signing demobilization orders on the train back from Appomattox to Washington, DC. He reasoned that the American taxpayer should not have to pay for soldiers a single day longer than neces-sary. With General Robert E. Lee's surrender, that day had arrived.

By 1870, government retrenchment had gone so far that the US Army, the enormous force that had won a continent-wide war, had shrunk to a point where its senior leadership worried about its ability to perform even limited campaigns in the West. America had returned to its pre–Civil War model of limited federal power, stronger state governments, and a mixture of weak and strong local governments. Washington was not the center of everything, but merely one point of action among many.

World War I saw the second great mobilization of the Ameri-can system. Because President Woodrow Wilson was a liberal aca-demic with a deep belief in strong government, the war became an excuse to take over virtually the entire economy. This included the government running the railroads, the telephone system, and a host of other activities.

When President Wilson suffered a stroke while campaigning for the ratification of the Versailles Treaty, his wife, Edith Wilson, essentially took over running the government by proxy. The government's controls over the economy were rapidly replaced by a return to free enterprise. The transition from a wartime, government-defined and -financed economic buildup to a peacetime consumer- and investor-led economy happened with amazing speed.

In 1920, the economy went into a steep slide. By the end of 1921, it was in an equally steep recovery. This depression was so short that it never entered the popular memory the way the Great Depression would in the 1930s. By 1921, the federal government had largely receded to its pre–World War I size and influence. The 1920s became a booming period of deliberately minimalist federal intervention while several of the states (notably Wisconsin and New York) became real laboratories of experimentation in new government programs.

The federal government began to grow dramatically under the New Deal, starting in the 1930s, in response to the economic challenges of a long, deep depression. However, it exploded in size, importance, and reach during World War II. By September 1945, when Japan surrendered, the American government was massive in size, extraordinary in its worldwide reach, and remarkably competent, because it had attracted and mobilized many of the best and most effective people in American society.

While the federal government never receded to its pre-1930 size, there was a substantial shrinking of the federal government from 1945 to 1950.

Now we have a moment of astonishing government domination of every aspect of our lives, and of government subsidy of every element of our economy. What happens next will define a great deal of America's future.

When I began work on this book, it was a triumphal moment for America and for President Trump. The economy was setting records of continuing increases in employment. The United States had become the largest producer of oil and natural gas. The march toward conservative, constitutional judges was continuing without interruption. African American and Latino communities had the lowest unemployment rates in history.

Just a few weeks ago, as I'm writing now, the Trump system of lower taxes, fewer regulations, and tough trade negotiations seemed to be ascendant. The path of the future seemed clear, and the nation's choice for the election for this fall seemed obvious. Now, the historic impact of the coronavirus has thrown everything into a dramatic time with unknown consequences.

In a real sense, the impact of the pandemic and the economic cost of the effort to stop it are still unknown. One of my fears is that the antipandemic public health measures will be so devastating to the economy that more people will die from a bad economy than will be killed by the virus.

Historically there is a discouraging pattern to dealing with crises in Washington.

In my twenty years in Congress, four years as Speaker, and sixty-two years' involvement in public policy, I have consistently noticed three steps to disaster.

1. The news media describes a terrible situation that requires supposed "emergency" action—and defines the required action as liberal policies. Further, these must be adopted without being read, without hearings, and without improvement—because "the emergency requires *doing something now.*"

2. Liberals then introduce the destructive legislation (written mostly by elitist bureaucrats) based on values and principles that Republicans have run against for decades. The news media dutifully blesses the unseen, unread, unanalyzed liberal legislation as just what we need to end the crisis. Its members repeatedly claim the "essential emergency legislation" must be passed immediately (again without hearings, amendments, or being read).

3. The accommodationist wing of the Republican Party ignores the principled objections of conservatives—and the suggestion that someone should read the bill before a vote is held. (Accommodationist Republicans want to be liked by the liberal media, accepted as peers by the Democrats, and seen as sophisticated by the Georgetown cocktail party set.) They can consistently be counted on to dump conservative principles and accept terrible policies because, as they put it, "We have no choice in this crisis."

This process of mindless, unchallenged liberal imposition crippled President George H. W. Bush in 1990. It led to President George W. Bush signing a series of laws passed by Speaker Nancy Pelosi in 2007 and 2008, which dramatically expanded government, increased dependency, grew bureaucracies, and crippled the economy. Pelosi's bad-idea legislation continued into 2009 and 2010 and led to such an economic disaster that John Boehner recaptured the majority and the speakership with a campaign that simply asked "Where are the jobs?" that Pelosi had promised.

The radical Democratic Left and the establishment will seek to repeat this disastrous approach in response to the coronavirus threat. As I write, the Democrats have suddenly switched from bipartisan negotiation to blocking a desperately needed economic aid package in the US Senate. As Senate Majority Leader McConnell said on the floor, it is clearly blackmail by Pelosi and Schumer to force acceptance of whatever liberal-interest group demands they come up with.

When this book goes to press, we will not know if President Trump has stood firm against a wave of dramatically bad ideas. The establishment hates Trump. They will do virtually anything to defeat him for reelection. The establishment also prefers big government with big bureaucracies centralizing control in Washington.

The Trump model of smaller government, less bureaucracy, more entrepreneurs, better opportunity for businesses, and decentralization of power outside Washington is terrifying to traditional politicians on both sides of the aisle. They have spent their careers and built their alliances with unions, big business, and government bureaucracies at the federal, state, and local levels.

If President Trump allows the accommodationist Republicans to talk him into a watered-down version of Pelosi-Schumer-ism, then the recovery will be slow. The country will be frustrated, and the election will be close. This is true even with the radicalism and personal weaknesses of former vice president Joe Biden weighing down his own chances.

However, there is a path of aggressively returning to President Trump's principles, which can put big government on defense,

liberate the American people to rebuild the economy with astonishing speed, and turn America into the "medicine chest of democracy" (to borrow Arthur Herman's phrase building on the World
War II model of America as the "arsenal of democracy").

If the coronavirus disappears for the summer, one of our major
projects will be to build such momentum of treatments and technologies that we can help the entire world deal with the pandemic
should it return in the fall. Our opportunity here is to provide
leadership in health and safety—not just for the United States, but
for the entire world. This will do a lot to reestablish our position as
the leader of free people everywhere. It will also more than match
the Chinese dictatorship's effort to take credit for helping cure the
disease they unleashed on the world.

As we plan for the world after coronavirus, we must recognize
that even before the pandemic, we had only achieved about 10 percent of the dynamic world President Trump wanted to develop.
There are still huge bureaucracies that are unaccountable and
can't be managed. There are destructive policies that cripple us
in educating our young people, uplifting the poor, and competing with the world in manufacturing. There is a level of red tape in
the Pentagon that cripples our development of new weapons and
forces us to waste money so that we get far less than we should for
the scale of our investment.

Major bureaucracies, including the World Health Organization and the Centers for Disease Control and Prevention, had
major breakdowns that cost time and lives during this crisis. A
thorough reevaluation of how they performed and what needs to
be changed must occur before the virus potentially comes back in
2021.

An amazing number of regulations have been waived or suspended to accelerate responses to the pandemic crisis. How many
of those should stay waived or suspended? We should not automatically restore the rules that hindered us. This is a great moment

for modernizing and streamlining our health system. We are living through an enormous experiment in distance learning. This should be translated into new delivery systems for learning and dramatic reductions in the cost of college. It should also translate into greater parental involvement in learning for K–12 education.

Our worldwide alliance system has been badly shaken. The Chinese are waging a propaganda war against us and providing medical aid to countries to fight the virus that they made worse by refusing to be honest with the world in the early months of viral transmission. The Huawei strategy of providing medical aid in country after country has further entrenched the Chinese advantage in 5G development.

Designing a national strategy for coping with China will be a major challenge once the pandemic has died down. We have a lot of work to do, and it can't all be done by President Trump, Congress, or federal bureaucrats. Millions of Americans will have to step up and make their contribution to rebuilding America after this pandemic nightmare is over.

We have always sung that we are "the land of the free and the home of the brave." Now we must live out that bravery to retain that freedom. This is my hope for my children and grandchildren. This is the heart of my belief in Americans and the American system. As President Ronald Reagan used to say, "You ain't seen nothing yet."

Acknowledgments

★ ▬▬▬▬▬▬▬▬▬▬▬▬▬▬▬▬▬▬▬▬▬ ★

rump and the American Future was a pleasure to write, with many people contributing to the process. I believe this book will help illustrate President Trump's tremendous work on behalf of our country.

This book would not have been possible without the advice and assistance of many remarkable people.

The team at Gingrich 360 helped conceptualize this book. Additionally, their research made this book a reality. I am fortunate to work with Louie Brogdon. His influential shaping of the book was indispensable. Thank you to Claire Christensen, Aaron Kliegman, and Rachel Peterson. Their research, drafting, and editing were paramount to the successful completion of *Trump and the American Future.*

Thanks to Debbie Myers, the president of Gingrich 360, for leading our company through a time of change. Joe DeSantis, a longtime confidant and brilliant strategist, contributed greatly to the health care portion of this book. And Garnsey Sloan was extraordinary in producing episodes for my podcast, *Newt's World,* that contributed to this book. I would also like to thank our three interns, Peter Billovits, Shanna Colyar, and Emily Martin for their positive attitude and hard work.

I would like to thank my daughters, Kathy Lubbers and Jackie Cushman, for their love and support. Additionally, Kathy has been a wonderful book agent, negotiating and representing me with great success. Jackie, an avid writer, always provides necessary and helpful feedback. They both add great joy to my life.

Louie also thanks his wife, Meghan Brogdon, for enduring many nights and weekends of his editing and writing.

Stefan Passantino, an accomplished lawyer and longtime friend, continues to provide vital guidance.

I am grateful for the contributions of my colleague and partner former Congressman Bob Walker and his team at MoonWalker Associates. Their years of experience and expertise were essential as I wrote the chapter regarding space. Terry Maple, with whom I wrote *Contract with the Earth*, offered wonderful assistance with the chapter on the environment. Thanks as well to Sean Kennedy. His knowledge added greatly to the chapter on criminal justice.

Thank you to Cynthia Fisher and her team at Patient Rights Advocate. I am grateful to them for their breadth of knowledge on health care. Dave Chase and the team at Health Rosetta were incredibly helpful. Also, thanks to Dave Balat with the Texas Public Policy Foundation for his broad scope of understanding of health care. Dave Winston and Myra Miller of the Winston Group were deeply influential in the crafting and shaping of this book. Similarly, John McLaughlin, Brian Larkin, Stu Polk, and Mike Shields provided invaluable input. And Ron Peck of the Phia Group offered insightful analysis. I want to express special thanks to Bernie Marcus and Steve Hantler whose generous support was vital in making possible the research, which is at the heart of this book.

Sean Hannity's tireless work to expose the corruption of the deep state has shaped my thinking. His insights, persistence, and diligence are appreciated. His associate Lynda McLaughlin is a passionate fighter for America and a good friend.

Jim Pinkerton is a longtime colleague in thinking about politics, government, and the future.

Claire Berlinski, whose blog is endlessly thought-provoking, has had a substantial impact on my thinking.

I am grateful for all the intellectual conversations I have had with two former employees of Gingrich Productions, Vince Haley and Ross Worthington. They are now speechwriters for President Trump.

Thank you to Joe Gaylord, for his feedback regarding the words and strategies of this book. He is a remarkably intelligent advisor who understands how to effectively communicate ideas to the American people.

I also want to thank my friend Ambassador Randy Evans, who has helped shape my thinking for many years.

Kate Hartson was, again, a great partner and editor for this project. I am grateful for her encouragement and critical advice. The entire Hachette team, including Daisy Hutton, Patsy Jones, Katie Broaddus, Sean McGowan, and Dale Wilstermann provided strong support.

Thanks to Cliff May. For many years, I have looked to him for national security advice. Additionally, I am grateful to Herman Pirchner and his team at the American Foreign Policy Council. Thanks to Arthur Herman of the Hudson Institute for his insight and contributions to this project.

Stephen Moore was invaluable in this effort. I am grateful for all the work and experience that he shared with me regarding economic growth, especially with the COVID-19 pandemic. Thanks to Dr. Anthony Fauci for his service to the United States as the director of the National Institute of Allergy and Infectious Diseases. His understanding of COVID-19 was decisive in shaping this book.

Finally, without the strong support of Bess Kelly in Rome and the enthusiasm and encouragement of my wife, Callista, as she focused on her duties as ambassador to the Holy See, this book would not have become a reality.

Every one of these exceptional people contributed greatly to the successful completion of *Trump and the American Future*.

Notes

CHAPTER 1: 2020 IS VITAL

1. https://www.youtube.com/watch?v=SEPs17_AkTI
2. https://www.washingtonpost.com/news/post-politics/wp/2017/01/20/the-campaign-to-impeach-president-trump-has-begun/
3. https://www.lawweekly.org/col/2018/10/17/ikes-mistake-the-accidental-creation-of-the-warren-court

CHAPTER 2: FRENZY, CORRUPTION, AND CONFORMITY

1. https://www.nationalreview.com/2020/01/1619-project-top-historians-criticize-new-york-times-slavery-feature/
2. https://www.nydailynews.com/opinion/ny-oped-sorry-greta-youre-mostly-wrong-20190924-t7depfksqnfmhpjgcwv6iyfesm-story.html
3. https://thehill.com/homenews/campaign/302817-government-workers-shun-trump-give-big-money-to-clinton-campaign
4. https://www.goodreads.com/quotes/14365-i-am-not-a-member-of-any-organized-political-party
5. https://ballotpedia.org/Party_committee_fundraising,_2019-2020
6. https://www.washingtonexaminer.com/byron-york-harvard-study-cnn-nbc-trump-coverage-93-percent-negative
7. https://www.cfr.org/event/foreign-affairs-issue-launch-former-vice-president-joe-biden

CHAPTER 3: THE FAILED COUP ATTEMPTS

1. https://www.politico.com/magazine/story/2016/04/donald-trump-2016-impeachment-213817
2. https://www.realclearpolitics.com/epolls/other/president_trump_job_approval-6179.html
3. https://www.realclearpolitics.com/epolls/other/congressional_job_approval-903.html
4. https://www.newsbusters.org/blogs/nb/rich-noyes/2020/01/13/tvs-trump-news-three-fourths-impeachment-and-93-negative
5. https://www.newsbusters.org/blogs/nb/rich-noyes/2020/01/13/tvs-trump-news-three-fourths-impeachment-and-93-negative
6. https://www.newsbusters.org/blogs/nb/rich-noyes/2020/02/04/impeachment-gets-77x-more-tv-time-trumps-economic-successes

7. https://www.rasmussenreports.com/public_content/politics/trump_administration/november_2019/most_say_media_working_with_democrats_to_impeach_trump
8. https://www.axios.com/mueller-russia-investigation-timeline-indictments-70433acd-9ef7-424d-aa01-b962ae5c9647.html
9. https://www.cnbc.com/2019/08/02/robert-muellers-russia-probe-cost-nearly-32-million-in-total-doj.html
10. https://www.axios.com/the-democratic-leanings-of-bob-muellers-team-1513303211-1c289ad8-7276-4bb9-8fca-2bd6f3e16520.html
11. https://www.nationalreview.com/2019/06/paul-manafort-treatment-leftism-makes-people-meaner/
12. https://thehill.com/hilltv/what-americas-thinking/442520-pollster-mueller-report-shows-little-effect-on-americans
13. https://thehill.com/opinion/judiciary/473709-horowitz-report-is-damning-for-the-fbi-and-unsettling-for-the-rest-of-us
14. https://www.cfr.org/event/foreign-affairs-issue-launch-former-vice-president-joe-biden
15. https://www.npr.org/2019/11/02/775490647/impeachment-inquiry-catch-up-a-vote-by-house-democrats-makes-it-official
16. https://www.politico.com/news/2019/12/16/house-impeachment-mueller-086251

CHAPTER 4: RADICAL DEMOCRATIC BIGOTRY

1. https://onlinelibrary.wiley.com/doi/pdf/10.1002/ejsp.2263
2. https://onlinelibrary.wiley.com/doi/pdf/10.1002/ejsp.2263
3. https://psmag.com/social-justice/non-racists-are-not-free-of-bigotry
4. https://www.theatlantic.com/magazine/archive/2017/12/conservatism-without-bigotry/544128/
5. https://www.breitbart.com/tech/2019/04/04/exclusive-leak-google-heritage-foundation-meltdown/
6. https://www.washingtonpost.com/opinions/i-wanted-to-help-google-make-ai-more-responsible-instead-i-was-treated-with-hostility/2019/04/09/cafd1fb6-5b07-11e9-842d-7d3ed7eb3957_story.html
7. https://www.blog.google/technology/ai/external-advisory-council-help-advance-responsible-development-ai/
8. https://www.washingtonpost.com/opinions/i-wanted-to-help-google-make-ai-more-responsible-instead-i-was-treated-with-hostility/2019/04/09/cafd1fb6-5b07-11e9-842d-7d3ed7eb3957_story.html
9. https://www.usatoday.com/story/opinion/voices/2019/04/05/yale-law-school-masterpiece-cakeshop-religious-discrimination-column/3354031002/
10. https://www.usatoday.com/story/opinion/voices/2019/04/05/yale-law-school-masterpiece-cakeshop-religious-discrimination-column/3354031002/
11. https://law.yale.edu/student-life/career-development/employers/recruiting-policies
12. https://www.thenation.com/article/politics/anti-abortion-white-supremacy/
13. https://www.washingtonpost.com/opinions/2020/03/05/what-schumer-really-meant-when-he-told-kavanaugh-gorsuch-you-wont-know-what-hit-you/
14. https://www.nytimes.com/2018/09/26/us/politics/read-brett-kavanaughs-complete-opening-statement.html

CHAPTER 5: LOVING CRIMINALS, HATING THE LAW

1. https://cis.org/Map-Sanctuary-Cities-Counties-and-Stat
2. https://www.whitehouse.gov/briefings-statements/remarks-president-trump-state-union-address-3/
3. https://www.nytimes.com/2020/01/14/nyregion/92-year-old-woman-queens-murder.html
4. https://thehill.com/opinion/immigration/479340-how-far-will-new-york-city-mayor-bill-de-blasio-go-to-protect
5. https://tularecounty.ca.gov/sheriff/index.cfm/media/news-releases/sheriff-announces-ois-suspects-reign-of-terror-ends/
6. https://www.fresnobee.com/news/local/crime/article223318080.html
7. https://www.wsj.com/articles/homeland-security-suspends-enrollment-of-new-yorkers-in-global-entry-11580966926
8. http://harvardharrispoll.com/wp-content/uploads/2018/06/Final_HHP_Jun2018_RegisteredVoters_Crosstabs_Memo.pdf
9. https://morningconsult.com/2019/08/28/ahead-2020-democratic-voters-moving-left-immigration/
10. https://www.realclearpolitics.com/video/2019/07/02/fareed_zakaria_it_pains_me_to_say_this_but_trump_was_right_about_asylum_system.html
11. https://cis.org/Report/Cost-of-Health-Insurance-for-Illegal-Immigrants
12. https://sfist.com/2020/01/09/pics-and-video-of-chesa-boudin-inauguration/
13. https://www.wsj.com/articles/revolutionary-san-francisco-11573602909
14. https://www.lohud.com/story/news/local/rockland/2019/11/11/chesa-boudin-son-brinks-robbery-radicals-elected-san-francisco-district-attorney/2560442001/
15. https://www.sfchronicle.com/crime/article/Chesa-Boudin-son-of-imprisoned-radicals-looks-13533584.php
16. https://www.lohud.com/story/news/local/rockland/2019/11/11/chesa-boudin-son-brinks-robbery-radicals-elected-san-francisco-district-attorney/2560442001/
17. https://mediaforus.org/interviews/2019/7/14/chesaboudin
18. https://mediaforus.org/interviews/2019/7/14/chesaboudin
19. https://www.gingrich360.com/2019/11/this-is-how-radical-prosecutors-seek-to-overthrow-justice-and-the-rule-of-law/
20. https://www.sfchronicle.com/opinion/amp/San-Francisco-s-dangerous-new-DA-14986239.php
21. https://www.sfchronicle.com/crime/article/SF-District-Attorney-Chesa-Boudin-hires-new-14972069.php
22. https://www.washingtonpost.com/local/virginia-politics/a-sea-change-for-prosecutors-in-northern-virginia-as-liberal-democratic-candidates-poised-to-sweep-races/2019/11/05/a473b2e0-ff28-11e9-8501-2a7123a38c58_story.html
23. https://whyy.org/articles/soros-weighed-in-with-even-more-money-in-das-race/
24. https://www.wsj.com/articles/philadelphias-top-prosecutor-pursues-social-not-actual-justice-11578697582
25. https://www.foxnews.com/us/crowd-of-onlookers-taunt-police-during-philadelphia-standoff-reports
26. https://www.justice.gov/usao-edpa/pr/statement-united-states-attorney-william-m-mcswain-shooting-six-philadelphia-police

27. https://www.wsj.com/articles/philadelphias-top-prosecutor-pursues-social-not-actual-justice-11578697582
28. https://www.phillypolice.com/crime-maps-stats/index.html
29. https://kywnewsradio.radio.com/articles/news/krasner-reacts-to-rising-number-of-shootings-in-2019
30. https://www.inquirer.com/news/larry-krasner-philadelphia-district-attorney-staff-reform-cases-first-year-20190106.html
31. https://kywnewsradio.radio.com/articles/news/krasner-responds-to-faulkner-s-claims-he-cant-be-impartial
32. https://www.dallasnews.com/news/2019/04/18/texas-police-union-calls-for-dallas-das-removal-over-his-plan-not-to-prosecute-certain-crimes/
33. https://www.fox4news.com/news/dallas-county-da-offers-long-term-solution-to-curb-violent-crime-spike
34. https://rollins4da.com/policy/charges-to-be-declined/
35. https://ktla.com/2019/11/21/san-francisco-mayor-city-attorney-endorse-l-a-county-da-jackie-lacey-snubbing-george-gascon/
36. https://www.sfchronicle.com/bayarea/philmatier/article/SF-ranks-high-in-property-crime-while-it-ranks-14439369.php
37. https://www.laadda.com/the-attempt-to-buy-district-attorneys-continues/
38. https://patch.com/california/los-angeles/da-jackie-lacey-still-below-50-re-election-bid
39. https://nypost.com/2019/12/31/new-bail-reform-laws-set-to-start-on-new-years-day/
40. https://nypost.com/2019/12/31/new-bail-reform-laws-set-to-start-on-new-years-day/
41. https://cbs6albany.com/news/local/albany-investigating-after-woman-found-dead-in-apartment
42. https://wnyt.com/news/albany-manslaughter-suspect-paul-barbaritano-released-under-new-bail-reform-law/5596164/
43. https://www.npr.org/2016/11/01/500104506/broken-windows-policing-and-the-origins-of-stop-and-frisk-and-how-it-went-wrong

CHAPTER 6: THE RADICAL 200

1. Winston Group Discussion Points, March 6, 2020, Dave Winston and Myra Miller

CHAPTER 7: AN ECONOMY FOR ALL AMERICANS

1 . https://www.politico.com/story/2016/01/trump-economy-217496
2. https://www.politico.com/story/2016/08/joe-biden-trump-stalin-227017
3. https://www.nytimes.com/interactive/projects/cp/opinion/election-night-2016
4. https://www.forbes.com/sites/peterhans/2016/12/27/recession-in-2017/
5. https://fortune.com/2017/03/17/donald-trump-recession/
6. https://www.brookings.edu/blog/fixgov/2017/12/26/trump-in-2018-what-happens-when-the-next-recession-hits/
7. https://www.theatlantic.com/ideas/archive/2018/11/stocks-are-nosediving-recession-coming/576568/
8. https://www.wsj.com/market-data/quotes/index/US/DOW%20JONES%20GLOBAL/DJIA/advanced-chart

9. https://www.nytimes.com/2019/08/17/upshot/how-the-recession-of-2020-could-happen.html

10. https://data.bls.gov/pdq/SurveyOutputServlet

11. https://www.thebalance.com/unemployment-rate-by-year-3305506

12. https://tradingeconomics.com/united-states/unemployment-rate

13. https://data.bls.gov/pdq/SurveyOutputServlet

14. https://data.bls.gov/pdq/SurveyOutputServlet

15. https://fred.stlouisfed.org/series/LNU04032183

16. https://fred.stlouisfed.org/series/MEHOINUSA672N

17. https://www.investopedia.com/personal-finance/what-average-income-us/

18. https://fred.stlouisfed.org/series/RHORUSQ156N

19. https://www.nytimes.com/2019/04/14/business/economy/income-tax-cut.html

20. Ibid.

21. https://www.wsj.com/articles/trump-administration-to-curb-states-control-of-food-aid-11575455401

22. https://www.nytimes.com/2020/02/20/business/trump-welfare-poverty.html

23. https://www.census.gov/library/publications/2019/demo/p60-266.html

24. https://www.wsj.com/articles/president-trumps-trade-policy-is-working-11568138994

25. https://www.who.int/emergencies/diseases/novel-coronavirus-2019/situation-reports/

26. https://www.bloomberg.com/news/articles/2020-03-06/the-u-s-may-already-be-in-a-recession-thanks-to-coronavirus

CHAPTER 8: FROM EDUCATION TO LEARNING

1. https://www2.ed.gov/pubs/NatAtRisk/risk.html

2. https://www.census.gov/newsroom/press-releases/2019/school-spending.html

3. https://www.insidehighered.com/quicktakes/2017/10/11/foreign-students-and-graduate-stem-enrollment

4. https://www.nytimes.com/2019/10/31/us/chicago-cps-teachers-strike.html

5. http://laschoolreport.com/californias-graduation-rate-rises-but-theres-no-improvement-in-getting-students-eligible-for-state-universities/

6. https://www.loc.gov/resource/mtj1.048_0731_0734/?sp=4&st=text

7. https://www.gingrich360.com/2019/09/newts-world-ep-31-a-conversation-with-mike-rowe/

8. https://www.goodreads.com/work/quotes/32701-excellence-can-we-be-equal-and-excellent-too

CHAPTER 9: COVID-19 WOULD KILL SANDERS-BIDEN-CARE

1. https://www.washingtonpost.com/business/2020/04/05/americans-hit-by-economic-shocks-confusion-stumbles-undermine-trumps-stimulus-effort/

2. https://www.nytimes.com/2019/04/21/health/medicare-for-all-hospitals.html

3. https://www.cms.gov/Research-Statistics-Data-and-Systems/Statistics-Trends-and-Reports/ReportsTrustFunds/Downloads/2019TRAlternativeScenario.pdf

4. https://www.whitehouse.gov/articles/house-drug-pricing-bill-keep-100-lifesaving-drugs-american-patients/

5. https://www.lygature.org/sites/lygature/files/atoms/files/Escher-Report_12-10-08.pdf

6. https://www.washingtonexaminer.com/opinion/op-eds/the-real-prescription-for-lower-drug-prices-get-europe-to-drop-its-price-controls

7. https://www.realclearhealth.com/articles/2019/07/11/price_controls_on_drugs_would_stifle_innovation_reduce_access_110927.html

8. https://www.hfma.org/topics/news/2019/07/medicare-for-all-cost-hospitals-200-billion-annually.html

9. https://www.worldometers.info/coronavirus/

10. https://www.cms.gov/blog/thank-obamacare-rise-uninsured

11. https://www.cms.gov/blog/thank-obamacare-rise-uninsured

12. https://www.forbes.com/sites/johngoodman/2020/03/12/obamacare-at-age-ten-was-it-a-mistake/#4a2052d2f397

13. https://www.propublica.org/article/we-asked-prosecutors-if-health-insurance-companies-care-about-fraud-they-laughed-at-us

14. https://www.modernhealth care.com/insurance/medical-loss-ratios-mixed-record

15. https://www.modernhealth care.com/insurance/medical-loss-ratios-mixed-record

16. https://www.cbo.gov/system/files/2019-01/54915-New_Rules_for_AHPs_STPs.pdf

17. https://www.forbes.com/sites/theapothecary/2020/04/03/how-the-uninsured-can-gain-financial-protection-from-the-virus/

CHAPTER 10: AMERICA'S HEALTH CARE REBELLIONS, PART I

1. https://articles.mercola.com/sites/articles/archive/2015/05/02/medical-waste-overtreatment.aspx

2. https://articles.mercola.com/sites/articles/archive/2015/05/02/medical-waste-overtreatment.aspx

3. https://www.nhcaa.org/resources/health-care-anti-fraud-resources/the-challenge-of-health-care-fraud/

4. https://www.nytimes.com/2019/09/03/health/carlsbad-hospital-lawsuits-medical-debt.html

5. https://features.propublica.org/medical-debt/when-medical-debt-collectors-decide-who-gets-arrested-coffeyville-kansas/

6. https://www.washingtonpost.com/health/uva-has-ruined-us-health-system-sues-thousands-of-patients-seizing-paychecks-and-putting-liens-on-homes/2019/09/09/5eb23306-c807-11e9-be05-f76ac4ec618c_story.html

7. https://www.nytimes.com/2019/09/03/health/carlsbad-hospital-lawsuits-medical-debt.html

8. https://www.healthsystemtracker.org/chart-collection/how-have-health care-prices-grown-in-the-u-s-over-time/#item-start

9. https://hmpi.org/2019/12/09/the-transformative-potential-for-price-transparency-in-health care-benefits-for-consumers-and-providers/

10. https://www.cms.gov/Research-Statistics-Data-and-Systems/Statistics-Trends-and-Reports/NationalHealthExpendData/Downloads/highlights.pdf

11. https://www.bcbs.com/the-health-of-america/reports/study-of-cost-variations-knee-and-hip-replacement-surgeries-the-us

12. https://www.cms.gov/Research-Statistics-Data-and-Systems/Statistics-Trends-and-Reports/NationalHealthExpendData/NationalHealthAccountsHistorical

13. https://clearhealthcosts.com/in-the-press/

14. https://www.forbes.com/sites/brucejapsen/2018/03/26/poll-44-of-americans-skip-doctor-visits-due-to-cost/#1b220d226f57

15. https://higherlogicdownload.s3.amazonaws.com/ASCACONNECT/fd1693e2-e4a8-43d3-816d-17ecfc7d55c1/UploadedImages/About%20Us/ASCs%20-%20A%20Positive%20Trend%20in%20Health%20Care.pdf

CHAPTER 11: THE HEALTH CARE REBELLIONS, PART II

1. https://www.nhcaa.org/resources/health-care-anti-fraud-resources/the-challenge-of-health-care-fraud/

2. https://www.propublica.org/article/we-asked-prosecutors-if-health-insurance-companies-care-about-fraud-they-laughed-at-us

3. https://www.houstonchronicle.com/opinion/outlook/article/Texas-CEO-did-something-about-escalating-employee-14539811.php
   https://www.patientrightsadvocate.org/employee-solutions

4. https://www.patientrightsadvocate.org/stauffers

5. https://www.bostonglobe.com/business/2016/11/27/employers-rewarding-workers-who-shop-around-for-health-care/JKkmu5BI7q6fNFgbZzyZmN/story.html

6. https://www.statista.com/topics/1599/cvs-caremark/

7. https://accessiblemeds.org/2018-generic-drug-access-and-savings-report

8. https://www.modernhealth care.com/supply-chain/pbms-spread-pricing-inflates-health care-spending-commission-finds

9. https://www.beckershospitalreview.com/pharmacy/top-pbms-by-market-share.html

10. https://khn.org/news/paying-cash-for-prescriptions-could-save-you-money-23-of-the-time-analysis-shows/

11. https://www.businessinsider.com/insulin-price-increased-last-decade-chart-2019-9

12. https://www.bloomberg.com/news/articles/2020-01-09/these-big-drug-flops-show-how-health care-economics-have-changed

13. https://s3.amazonaws.com/assets.fiercemarkets.net/public/005-LifeSciences/Sanofi_Prescription_Medicine_Pricing_2020_FINAL.pdf

14. https://s3.amazonaws.com/assets.fiercemarkets.net/public/005-LifeSciences/Sanofi_Prescription_Medicine_Pricing_2020_FINAL.pdf

15. https://www.bloomberg.com/news/articles/2020-01-09/these-big-drug-flops-show-how-health care-economics-have-changed

16. https://catalyst.phrma.org/nearly-50-of-brand-medicine-spending-goes-to-the-supply-chain-and-others

17. https://www.daytondailynews.com/business/ohio-medicaid-sees-initial-success-overhauling-drug-program/ib7dlJ2uwuOcOgldrnG42O/

18. https://www.statnews.com/2018/07/26/physicians-not-burning-out-they-are-suffering-moral-injury/

19. https://www.webmd.com/mental-health/news/20180508/doctors-suicide-rate-highest-of-any-profession#1

20. https://healthpayerintelligence.com/news/addressing-the-real-implications-of-social-determinants-of-health

21. https://www.newtsworld.com/2020/01/newts-world-ep-51-antiaging/

CHAPTER 13: THE DEEP STATE IS CRIPPLING AMERICA

1. https://www.whitehouse.gov/briefings-statements/remarks-president-trump-united-states-5g-deployment/
2. https://www.whitehouse.gov/briefings-statements/remarks-president-trump-united-states-5g-deployment/.
3. https://www.ft.com/content/5f3c7f68-efdd-11e9-ad1e-4367d8281195
4. https://www.fiercewireless.com/wireless/at-t-s-5g-e-slower-than-some-4g-networks-study
5. https://www.wsj.com/articles/state-support-helped-fuel-huaweis-global-rise-11577280736
6. https://www.industryweek.com/the-economy/article/22024894/should-we-allow-the-chinese-to-buy-any-us-company-they-want
7. https://www.wsj.com/articles/u-s-officials-say-huawei-can-covertly-access-telecom-networks-11581452256
8. https://www.axios.com/justice-department-huawei-racketeering-b93ed7f1-3315-4de7-a9a1-96c9d4d5844c.html
9. https://www.cnbc.com/2020/02/14/pelosi-warns-us-allies-dont-go-near-huawei.html
10. https://www.bbc.com/news/technology-51283059
11. https://www.cbc.ca/news/business/telus-5g-huawei-1.5462994
12. https://thehill.com/policy/technology/483325-trumps-germany-envoy-warns-countries-against-using-untrustworthy-5g-vendors
13. https://investors.att.com/~/media/Files/A/ATT-IR/financial-reports/quarterly-earnings/2019/3q-2019/3Q19%20Debt%20Details/Debt_List_3Q19.pdf
14. https://www.verizon.com/about/investors/schedule-outstanding-debt
15. https://www.t-mobile.com/news/americas-first-nationwide-5g-network
16. https://www.wsj.com/articles/huaweis-revenue-hits-record-122-billion-in-2019-despite-u-s-campaign-11577754021

CHAPTER 14: COMMUNIST-RULED CHINA AND COVID-19

1. https://fas.org/sgp/crs/row/IF10964.pdf
2. https://www.cnbc.com/2019/11/26/tiktok-says-it-doesnt-censor-but-a-user-who-criticized-china-was-locked-out.html
3. http://presentdangerchina.org/wp-content/uploads/2020/02/CPDC-2020-National-Perceptions-on-China-January-2020-MA.pdf
4. https://news.gallup.com/poll/1627/china.aspx
5. http://presentdangerchina.org/wp-content/uploads/2020/02/CPDC-2020-National-Perceptions-on-China-January-2020-MA.pdf
6. https://www.nytimes.com/interactive/2019/world/asia/hong-kong-protests-arc.html
7. https://www.nytimes.com/interactive/2019/world/asia/hong-kong-protests-arc.html
8. https://www.bloomberg.com/graphics/hong-kong-protests-timeline/
9. https://www.nytimes.com/interactive/2019/world/asia/hong-kong-protests-arc.html
10. https://www.reuters.com/investigates/special-report/china-army-hongkong/
11. https://www.nytimes.com/interactive/2019/world/asia/hong-kong-protests-arc.html
12. https://www.cmab.gov.hk/en/issues/jd2.htm

13. https://www.cmab.gov.hk/en/issues/jd2.htm

14. https://freedomhouse.org/report/policy-brief/2019/democratic-crisis-hong-kong-recommendations-policymakers

15. https://www.theguardian.com/world/2017/mar/26/hong-kong-chooses-new-leader-amid-accusations-of-china-meddling

16. https://www.hrw.org/news/2018/10/25/hong-kongs-heightened-crackdown-dissent

17. https://www.wsj.com/articles/hong-kongs-millennial-dissidents-11565385401

18. https://www.nytimes.com/2019/11/24/world/asia/hong-kong-election-results.html

19. https://www.nytimes.com/2019/11/23/world/asia/hong-kong-election-protests-district-council.html

20. https://www.theguardian.com/world/2020/mar/15/hong-kong-with-coronavirus-curbed-protests-may-return

21. https://www.scmp.com/news/article/3074723/hong-kong-protests-opposition-lawmakers-draft-list-officials-and-police-us

22. https://www.congress.gov/bill/116th-congress/senate-bill/2710/text

23. https://www.foreign.senate.gov/imo/media/doc/120418_Busby_Testimony.pdf

24. https://www.foreign.senate.gov/imo/media/doc/120418_Busby_Testimony.pdf

25. https://www.hrw.org/report/2018/09/09/eradicating-ideological-viruses/chinas-campaign-repression-against-xinjiangs

26. https://www.nytimes.com/interactive/2019/11/16/world/asia/china-xinjiang-documents.html

27. https://www.nytimes.com/interactive/2019/11/16/world/asia/china-xinjiang-documents.html

28. https://www.icij.org/investigations/china-cables/exposed-chinas-operating-manuals-for-mass-internment-and-arrest-by-algorithm/

29. https://www.documentcloud.org/documents/6558510-China-Cables-Telegram-English.html

30. https://edition.cnn.com/interactive/2020/02/asia/xinjiang-china-karakax-document-intl-hnk/

31. https://www.nytimes.com/2020/02/17/world/asia/china-reeducation-camps-leaked.html

32. https://www.nytimes.com/2020/02/17/world/asia/china-reeducation-camps-leaked.html

33. https://www.cnn.com/2019/07/30/asia/xinjiang-official-beijing-camps-intl-hnk/index.html

34. https://www.wsj.com/articles/china-shifts-to-new-phase-in-campaign-to-control-xinjiangs-muslims-11580985000

35. https://www.aspi.org.au/report/uyghurs-sale

36. https://www.cecc.gov/sites/chinacommission.house.gov/files/documents/2019AR_BUSINESSANDHUMAN_0.pdf

37. https://uhrp.org/news-commentary/report-released-cotton-fabric-full-lies

38. https://purpose.nike.com/statement-on-xinjiang

39. https://www.hometextilestoday.com/industry-news/industry-groups-alarmed-by-forced-labor-in-xinjiang-mills/

40. https://mashable.com/article/apple-amazon-forced-labor-uyghur-china/

41. https://www.cecc.gov/sites/chinacommission.house.gov/files/CECC%202019%20 Annual%20Report.pdf

42. https://www.nytimes.com/2019/10/07/us/politics/us-to-blacklist-28-chinese-entities-over-abuses-in-xinjiang.html

43. https://www.congress.gov/bill/116th-congress/senate-bill/178

44. https://www.rubio.senate.gov/public/index.cfm/2020/3/rubio-mcgovern-lead-bipartisan-bicameral-group-introducing-uyghur-forced-labor-prevention-act

45. https://www.washingtonpost.com/archive/politics/2003/05/13/outbreak-gave-chinas-hu-an-opening/6e7ebf75-9689-48bb-81a9-3e28e7f25b56/

46. https://www.baltimoresun.com/bal-te.sars21apr21-story.html

47. https://www.baltimoresun.com/bal-te.sars21apr21-story.html

48. https://www.washingtonpost.com/opinions/2020/01/23/following-sars-playbook-china-keeps-dangerous-tight-leash-coronavirus-information/

49. https://www.theguardian.com/world/2020/mar/11/research-finds-huge-impact-of-interventions-on-spread-of-covid-19

50. https://www.ncbi.nlm.nih.gov/pmc/articles/PMC2176051/

51. http://www.skleid.hku.hk

52. https://www.nbcnews.com/science/science-news/where-did-new-coronavirus-come-past-outbreaks-provide-hints-n1144521

53. https://www.thetimes.co.uk/article/chinese-scientists-destroyed-proof-of-virus-in-december-rz055qjnj

54. https://www.washingtonpost.com/world/2020/02/01/early-missteps-state-secrecy-china-likely-allowed-coronavirus-spread-farther-faster/

55. https://www.wsj.com/articles/how-it-all-started-chinas-early-coronavirus-missteps-11583508932

56. https://www.wsj.com/articles/how-it-all-started-chinas-early-coronavirus-missteps-11583508932

57. https://www.wsj.com/articles/how-it-all-started-chinas-early-coronavirus-missteps-11583508932

58. https://www.who.int/docs/default-source/coronaviruse/situation-reports/20200121-sitrep-1-2019-ncov.pdf

59. https://www.reuters.com/article/us-health-coronavirus-china-cdc-exclusiv/exclusive-u-s-axed-cdc-expert-job-in-china-months-before-virus-outbreak-idUSKBN21910S

60. https://www.nytimes.com/2020/02/07/health/cdc-coronavirus-china.html

61. https://www.reuters.com/article/us-health-coronavirus-china-cdc-exclusiv/exclusive-u-s-axed-cdc-expert-job-in-china-months-before-virus-outbreak-idUSKBN21910S

62. https://www.nytimes.com/2020/02/07/health/cdc-coronavirus-china.html

63. https://chinamediaproject.org/2020/03/11/whistling-against-deception/

64. https://chinamediaproject.org/2020/03/11/whistling-against-deception/

65. https://www.washingtonpost.com/world/2020/02/04/chinese-doctor-has-coronavirus/

66. https://www.washingtonpost.com/world/2020/02/04/chinese-doctor-has-coronavirus/

67. https://www.bbc.com/news/world-asia-china-51403795

68. https://www.npr.org/sections/goatsandsoda/2020/02/08/803766743/critics-say-china-has-suppressed-and-censored-information-in-coronavirus-outbrea

69. https://www.npr.org/sections/goatsandsoda/2020/02/08/803766743/critics-say-china-has-suppressed-and-censored-information-in-coronavirus-outbrea

70. https://www.foxnews.com/us/china-smear-united-states-coronavirus-wuhan

71. https://www.cnn.com/2020/03/13/asia/china-coronavirus-us-lijian-zhao-intl-hnk/index.html

72. https://www.nbcnews.com/news/world/coronavirus-chinese-official-suggests-u-s-army-blame-outbreak-n1157826

73. https://www.nytimes.com/2020/03/18/us/politics/china-virus.html

74. https://www.nytimes.com/2020/04/07/world/asia/china-tycoon-coronavirus.html

CHAPTER 15: NEW LANGUAGE FOR AMERICAN SURVIVAL

1. https://www.cfr.org/in-brief/coronavirus-disrupt-us-drug-supply-shortages-fda

2. https://www.wsj.com/articles/china-counts-the-costs-of-its-big-bet-on-venezuela-11549038825

3. https://www.miamiherald.com/news/nation-world/world/americas/venezuela/article239407233.html

4. https://www.washingtonpost.com/world/the_americas/in-the-us-embargo-on-venezuelan-oil-russia-is-a-clear-winner/2020/02/06/c45ca39e-476e-11ea-9lab-ce439aa5c7cl_story.html

CHAPTER 16: EFFECTIVE COMPASSION

1. https://www.merriam-webster.com/dictionary/compassion

2. https://etd.library.vanderbilt.edu/available/etd-07132016-155021/unrestricted/Long.pdf

3. https://www.cdc.gov/nchs/products/databriefs/db355.htm

4. https://www.washingtonpost.com/national/as-trump-calls-for-more-institutions-gop-lawmakers-nationwide-shift-their-focus-to-mental-health/2019/10/06/df769f52-e622-11e9-a6e8-8759c5c7f608_story.html

5. https://www.thetrevorproject.org/resources/preventing-suicide/facts-about-suicide/

6. US Centers for Disease Control and Prevention, Sexual Identity, Sex of Sexual Contacts, and Health-Risk Behaviors Among Students in Grades 9-12: Youth Risk Behavior Surveillance. (Atlanta, GA: U.S. Department of Health and Human Services, 2016).

7. https://onlinelibrary.wiley.com/doi/abs/10.1111/add.14943

8. https://www.cdc.gov/nchs/products/databriefs/db355.htm

9. http://opioidrecovery.org/

10. https://www.gao.gov/assets/710/703239.pdf

11. https://www.milliman.com/insight/Addiction-and-mental-health-vs-physical-health-Widening-disparities-in-network-use-and-p

12. https://www.c-span.org/video/?467561-1/white-house-mental-health-summit-part-1

13. https://www.ajmc.com/newsroom/hhs-lifting-Institutions for Mental Disease -exclusion-for-medicaid-payment-for-inpatient-mental-health-treatment

14. https://www.cms.gov/newsroom/press-releases/cms-announces-approval-groundbreaking-demonstration-expand-access-behavioral-health-treatment

15. https://www.medicaid.gov/federal-policy-guidance/downloads/smd18011.pdf

16. https://www.nasmhpd.org/sites/default/files/latest-trends-in-state-mental-health-agencies.pdf

17. US Department of Health and Human Services, "Strategy to Combat Abuse, Misuse and Overdose: A Framework on the Five-Point Strategy."

18. http://www.mentalhealthforus.net/

19. https://www.mentalhealthforus.net/about/platform/

20. https://www.treatmentadvocacycenter.org/road-runners

21. https://www.ajc.com/news/local/deal-criminal-justice-reforms-leaves-lasting-legacy/ZMwb2vG7C4LurWoFESw46O/

22. "Handbook of Religion and Health" Harold Koenig, Dana King, Verna B. Carson, Oxford University Press, Feb 29, 2012, page 175-176

23. https://slate.com/technology/2013/08/dangers-of-loneliness-social-isolation-is-deadlier-than-obesity.html; https://www.apa.org/news/press/releases/2017/08/lonely-die

24. https://www.nytimes.com/2017/12/11/well/mind/how-loneliness-affects-our-health.html

25. https://www.apa.org/pubs/journals/releases/amp-amp0000103.pdf

26. https://www.psychologytoday.com/us/blog/nurturing-self-compassion/201901/isolation-nation

27. https://qz.com/1420602/feeling-lonely-vivek-murthy-says-to-get-out-of-your-head-and-help-someone-else/

28. https://www.pewforum.org/2019/10/17/in-u-s-decline-of-christianity-continues-at-rapid-pace/

29. https://www.pewforum.org/2019/10/17/in-u-s-decline-of-christianity-continues-at-rapid-pace/

30. "Handbook of Religion and Health" Harold Koenig, Dana King, Verna B. Carson, Oxford University Press, Feb 29, 2012, page 175-176

31. https://www.cancer.org/latest-news/study-cancer-patients-with-strong-religious-or-spiritual-beliefs-report-better-health.html

32. https://www.aa.org/assets/en_US/en_bigbook_chapt5.pdf

33. https://americanaddictioncenters.org/rehab-guide/12-step/whats-the-success-rate-of-aa

CHAPTER 17: MAKING EARTH GREAT AGAIN

1. https://news.gallup.com/poll/1615/environment.aspx; https://www.washingtonpost.com/climate-environment/americans-increasingly-see-climate-change-as-a-crisis-poll-shows/2019/09/12/74234db0-cd2a-11e9-87fa-8501a456c003_story.html

2. https://www.foxnews.com/politics/ocasio-cortez-calls-climate-change-our-world-war-ii-warns-the-world-will-end-in-12-years

3. https://twitter.com/AOC/status/1127604746066583552

4. https://books.google.com/books?id=azwQStEZq-8C&pg=PA606&dq=%22even+money+that+England+will+not+exist+in+the+year+2000%22&hl=en&ei=DCQYTa_XBI-q8AaF1ZWLDg&sa=X&oi=book result&ct=result&resnum=2&ved= 0CCgQ6AEwAQ#v=onepage&q=%22even%20money%20that%20England%20will%20not%20exist%20in%20the%20year%202000%22&f=false

5. https://www.mrc.org/media-reality-check/earth-day-special-medias-top-25-worst-environmental-quotes

6. https://www.mrc.org/media-reality-check/earth-day-special-medias-top-25-worst-environmental-quotes
7. https://www.newyorker.com/magazine/1990/09/10/after-communism
8. https://ocasio-cortez.house.gov/sites/ocasio-cortez.house.gov/files/Resolution%20on%20a%20Green%20New%20Deal.pdf
9. https://www.washingtonexaminer.com/opinion/editorials/the-green-new-deal-is-about-power-not-the-planet
10. https://www.washingtonpost.com/graphics/politics/policy-2020/climate-change/carbon-tax/
11. https://www.edf.org/climate/how-cap-and-trade-works; https://www.investopedia.com/terms/c/cap-and-trade.asp
12. https://www.washingtonpost.com/graphics/politics/policy-2020/climate-change/carbon-tax/
13. https://www.pbo-dpb.gc.ca/web/default/files/Documents/Reports/2019/Paris_Target/Paris_Target_EN.pdf
14. https://www.washingtonpost.com/politics/2019/08/08/democratic-candidates-promise-action-climate-change-heres-what-stands-way/
15. https://thehill.com/policy/energy-environment/482772-house-republicans-propose-carbon-capture-and-sequestration
16. https://www.reuters.com/article/us-environment-poll-republicans/surge-in-young-republicans-worried-about-the-environment-survey-idUSKCN1VJ17V
17. https://www.washingtonexaminer.com/policy/energy/house-republicans-unveil-realistic-climate-plan-focused-on-capturing-carbon-from-fossil-fuels
18. https://www.washingtonexaminer.com/policy/energy/how-house-republicans-won-over-conservatives-to-gain-consensus-on-a-climate-agenda
19. https://www.history.com/this-day-in-history/jfk-asks-congress-to-support-the-space-program
20. https://www.eia.gov/energyexplained/nuclear/nuclear-power-and-the-environment.php
21. https://www.energy.gov/ne/articles/nuclear-power-most-reliable-energy-source-and-its-not-even-close
22. https://e360.yale.edu/features/why-nuclear-power-must-be-part-of-the-energy-solution-environmentalists-climate
23. https://www.energy.gov/ne/articles/nuclear-power-most-reliable-energy-source-and-its-not-even-close
24. https://www.energy.gov/ne/articles/infographic-how-much-power-does-nuclear-reactor-produce
25. https://www.eia.gov/energyexplained/nuclear/data-and-statistics.php
26. https://www.eia.gov/tools/faqs/faq.php?id=427&t=3
27. https://news.gallup.com/poll/248048/years-three-mile-island-americans-split-nuclear-power.aspx
28. https://www.world-nuclear.org/information-library/safety-and-security/safety-of-plants/three-mile-island-accident.aspx; https://www.world-nuclear.org/information-library/safety-and-security/safety-of-plants/chernobyl-accident.aspx; https://www.world-nuclear.org/information-library/safety-and-security/safety-of-plants/fukushima-daiichi-accident.aspx

29. https://www.world-nuclear.org/information-library/safety-and-security/safety-of-plants/chernobyl-accident.aspx

30. https://www.world-nuclear.org/information-library/safety-and-security/safety-of-plants/three-mile-island-accident.aspx; https://www.world-nuclear.org/information-library/safety-and-security/safety-of-plants/fukushima-daiichi-accident.aspx

31. https://www.nrc.gov/reading-rm/doc-collections/fact-sheets/3mile-isle.html

32. https://e360.yale.edu/features/why-nuclear-power-must-be-part-of-the-energy-solution-environmentalists-climate

33. https://e360.yale.edu/features/why-nuclear-power-must-be-part-of-the-energy-solution-environmentalists-climate

34. https://www.giss.nasa.gov/research/briefs/kharecha_02/

35. https://www.world-nuclear.org/information-library/nuclear-fuel-cycle/nuclear-power-reactors/nuclear-power-reactors.aspx

36. https://www.energy.gov/ne/articles/x-energy-developing-pebble-bed-reactor-they-say-cant-melt-down

37. https://e360.yale.edu/features/why-nuclear-power-must-be-part-of-the-energy-solution-environmentalists-climate

38. https://thehill.com/homenews/administration/479087-trump-announces-the-us-will-join-1-trillion-tree-initiative

39. https://www.whitehouse.gov/briefings-statements/remarks-president-trump-state-union-address-3/; for the complete text of President Trump's 2020 State of the Union address.

40. https://westerman.house.gov/media-center/press-releases/westerman-introduces-trillion-trees-act

41. https://www.nytimes.com/2020/02/12/climate/trump-trees-climate-change.html; https://e360.yale.edu/digest/planting-1-2-trillion-trees-could-cancel-out-a-decade-of-co2-emissions-scientists-find

42. https://e360.yale.edu/digest/planting-1-2-trillion-trees-could-cancel-out-a-decade-of-co2-emissions-scientists-find

43. https://www.americanforests.org/what-we-do/program-project-maps/

44. http://www.trilliontrees.org/home

45. https://www.plant-for-the-planet.org/en/about-us/news/48d81c43-74fe-11e4-a0ac-902b34544d94/1/en/none

46. https://www.trilliontreecampaign.org

47. https://www.unenvironment.org/news-and-stories/press-release/new-un-decade-ecosystem-restoration-offers-unparalleled-opportunity

48. https://teamtrees.org

49. https://apnews.com/8ac33686b64a4fbc991997a72683b1c5

50. https://republicans-energycommerce.house.gov/news/blog/the-republican-record-on-climate/

51. https://www.whitehouse.gov/presidential-actions/eo-promoting-active-management-americas-forests-rangelands-federal-lands-improve-conditions-reduce-wildfire-risk/

52. https://www.doi.gov/pressreleases/interior-reduces-wildfire-risks-more-14-million-acres-federal-land-2019

53. https://www.doi.gov/pressreleases/interior-reduces-wildfire-risks-more-14-million-acres-federal-land-2019
54. https://www.doi.gov/pressreleases/interior-reduces-wildfire-risks-more-14-million-acres-federal-land-2019
55. https://www.whitehouse.gov/briefings-statements/remarks-president-trump-americas-environmental-leadership/
56. https://www.whitehouse.gov/briefings-statements/remarks-president-trump-americas-environmental-leadership/
57. https://www.nytimes.com/2020/01/29/business/economy/usmca-deal.html; https://ustr.gov/trade-agreements/free-trade-agreements/united-states-mexico-canada-agreement/fact-sheets/modernizing
58. https://republicans-energycommerce.house.gov/news/blog/the-republican-record-on-climate/
59. https://republicans-energycommerce.house.gov/news/blog/the-republican-record-on-climate/
60. https://www.epa.gov/newsreleases/epa-announces-selection-149-communities-receive-646-million-funding-brownfields
61. https://www.epa.gov/newsreleases/epa-deletes-ellenville-scrap-iron-and-metal-superfund-site-ellenville-new-york-0
62. https://www.epa.gov/newsreleases/epa-announces-33-million-brownfields-grants-seven-virginia-communities
63. https://www.epa.gov/newsreleases/epa-announces-selection-149-communities-receive-646-million-funding-brownfields
64. https://republicans-energycommerce.house.gov/news/blog/the-republican-record-on-climate/
65. https://www.dni.gov/files/documents/Newsroom/Testimonies/2018-ATA---Unclassified-SSCI.pdf
66. https://www.bbc.com/news/science-environment-52125309
67. https://www.cnn.com/2020/03/05/asia/china-coronavirus-wildlife-consumption-ban-intl-hnk/index.html
68. http://theconversation.com/coronavirus-has-finally-made-us-recognise-the-illegal-wildlife-trade-is-a-public-health-issue-133673
69. https://www.whitehouse.gov/presidential-actions/presidential-executive-order-enforcing-federal-law-respect-transnational-criminal-organizations-preventing-international-trafficking/
70. https://www.whitehouse.gov/wp-content/uploads/2017/12/NSS-Final-12-18-2017-0905.pdf
71. https://www.nytimes.com/2019/11/25/us/politics/trump-animal-cruelty-bill.html
72. https://iwc.int/lives
73. https://www.nbcbayarea.com/investigations/ship-strikes-kill-whales-at-highest-levels-in-more-than-a-decade-despite-govt-program-to-slow-down-vessels/2238072/
74. https://www.unenvironment.org/news-and-stories/story/protecting-whales-protect-planet
75. https://www.weforum.org/agenda/2019/11/whales-carbon-capture-climate-change/

CHAPTER 18: TAKING FREEDOM INTO SPACE

1. https://www.space.com/30074-trillion-dollar-asteroid-2011-uw158-earth-flyby.html

2. https://nerdist.com/article/metal-asteroid-former-planet-core/
3. https://www.csis.org/analysis/conversation-general-raymond
4. https://www.politico.com/story/2018/04/06/outer-space-war-defense-russia-china-463067
5. https://www.whitehouse.gov/briefings-statements/remarks-president-trump-event-establishing-u-s-space-command/